Advance Praise for *Break From the Pack*

"*Break From the Pack* offers a broad array of valuable and exciting insights on how to succeed in today's competitive environment. Unlike so many books that are long on generalities and short on specifics, Harari's book offers tangible examples of 'how to' and 'how not to' succeed in key strategic issues. I recommend this book to any business leader."

—Garry Betty, President and CEO, Earthlink

"Oren Harari has done it again! He has produced a fascinating book that inverts the rules and that will keep you up at night remaking your management strategy and tactics."

—Karen Ignagni, CEO, America's Health
Insurance Plans (AHIP)

"*Break From the Pack* is a refreshing look at the fundamentals of business success, written in clear, concise language with real content and practical advice."

—Gordon Bethune, retired former Chairman and CEO,
Continental Airlines, Inc.

"In *Break From the Pack*, Oren Harari has once again confronted us with challenging new realities. With clarity and humor, he has made the complex and counterintuitive feel like good old common sense. The book is both entertaining and practical. It provides a new perspective on the business challenges we are experiencing today."

—Ray McCaskey, President and CEO, HCSC (BlueCross
BlueShield of Illinois, New Mexico, Oklahoma, and Texas)

"With a style that makes business metrics almost fun, Oren Harari examines pitfalls that have felled seemingly indestructible companies and identifies how underdogs become visionary leaders."

—Michael Milken, Chairman, Milken Institute

"Executives will benefit from Harari's fresh view of market dynamics, the imperative for differentiation, and the call for executive attention to both the 'above ground' and the 'underground' of every organization. His calls for 'zero defects as the price of admission' and for a 'passion for purpose and a passion for precision' fit the health care executive's agenda perfectly. If you are one who checks out a management book by reading the final chapter first, I guarantee you'll jump back to page one of *Break From the Pack* and enjoy the full read!"

—Richard J. Umbdenstock, President-Elect, American Hospital Association

"Dr. Harari's analysis of the leadership challenges in today's global marketplace is compelling and powerful (and funky). He has developed an exceptional model to help organizations achieve top performance and competitive advantage. Business leaders in any country will find his advice clear, meaningful, challenging, and attainable."

—Kjell Nordstrom, Ph.D., Stockholm School of Economics and Coauthor of global bestsellers *Funky Business* and *Karaoke Capitalism*

Break From the Pack

In an increasingly competitive world, it is quality
of thinking that gives an edge—an idea that opens new
doors, a technique that solves a problem, or an insight
that simply helps make sense of it all.

We work with leading authors in the various arenas
of business and finance to bring cutting-edge thinking
and best-learning practices to a global market.

It is our goal to create world-class print publications
and electronic products that give readers
knowledge and understanding that can then be
applied, whether studying or at work.

To find out more about our business
products, you can visit us at www.ftpress.com.

Break From the Pack

How to Compete in a Copycat Economy

Oren Harari, Ph.D.

FT Press

FINANCIAL TIMES

An Imprint of PEARSON EDUCATION
Upper Saddle River, NJ • New York • London • San Francisco • Toronto • Sydney
Tokyo • Singapore • Hong Kong • Cape Town • Madrid
Paris • Milan • Munich • Amsterdam
www.ftpress.com

Vice President and Editor-in-Chief: Tim Moore
Acquisitions Editor: Paula Sinnott
Editorial Assistant: Susie Abraham
Development Editor: Russ Hall
Associate Editor-in-Chief and Director of Marketing: Amy Neidlinger
Cover Designer: Alan Clements
Managing Editor: Gina Kanouse
Senior Project Editor: Kristy Hart
Copy Editor: Krista Hansing
Indexer: Lisa Stumpf
Compositor: Laurel Road Publishing Services, Inc.
Manufacturing Buyer: Dan Uhrig

FT Press offers excellent discounts on this book when ordered in quantity for bulk purchases or special sales. For more information, please contact U.S. Corporate and Government Sales, 1-800-382-3419, corpsales@pearsontechgroup.com. For sales outside the U.S., please contact International Sales, 1-317-581-3793, international@pearsontechgroup.com.

Printed in the United States of America

First Printing August 2006

ISBN 0-13-188863-3

Pearson Education LTD.
Pearson Education Australia PTY, Limited.
Pearson Education Singapore, Pte. Ltd.
Pearson Education North Asia, Ltd.
Pearson Education Canada, Ltd.
Pearson Educatión de Mexico, S.A. de C.V.
Pearson Education—Japan
Pearson Education Malaysia, Pte. Ltd.

Library of Congress Catalog Number:
Harari, Oren.
    Break from the pack / Oren Harari.
        p. cm.
    ISBN 0-13-188863-3 (hardcover : alk. paper) 1. Success in business. 2. Competition. 3. Creative ability in business. 4. Originality. 5. Quality of work life. I. Title.

HF5386.H249 2006
658.4'01--dc22

2006000278

To Katy Anderson,
who broke from the pack long ago

CONTENTS

ACKNOWLEDGMENTS

This book is a result of two years of research and six months of intensive writing. During that time period, several individuals "stepped up" with support for which I am truly grateful.

At Pearson Prentice Hall, editor-in-chief Tim Moore was always available as a genuine source of support. Paula Sinnott was instrumental in shepherding the entire manuscript to fruition, even while being interrupted by the birth of her daughter! Russ Hall provided very helpful editorial input on the actual "wordsmithing" of the manuscript. Amy Neidlinger, with the assistance of Susie Abraham, was invaluable in developing and executing the vital marketing of the book. And without the expertise of Kristy Hart (and Christy Hackerd) in production, there wouldn't even be a physical book for us to read.

Andrew Dailey, Herbert Harari, and Royce Flippin read early drafts of the manuscript and gave me encouragement and valuable feedback. David Groff read multiple drafts and provided continuous insights and advice that made a huge difference.

Over the past three years, many smart, creative MBA students who I've taught at the University of San Francisco provided input and analyses that became extremely useful as I wrote this book. Two MBA students deserve special accolades: Nicole Jackson and Kyra Peyton served as outstanding research assistants. Their contributions to this book were immense. And throughout these three years, Gary Williams, the recently retired dean of the business school at USF, gave me continual support and resources to complete this project.

Throughout this process, I had numerous commitments to corporate clients. At my office outside the University, Lauren Swalberg stayed on top of these commitments, made sure that I fulfilled them, and in general maintained a remarkably calming order on the chaos that sometimes surrounds my professional life.

Lynn Johnston has been a terrific book agent. In addition to excelling at the "regular" work that an agent does, she showed great patience in reviewing, and rejecting, my early proposals and ultimately helping me shape the vision for this book.

Most important, I want to thank my wife, Leslie, and my sons, Jordan and Dylan, for once again putting up with me. The process that an author goes through is often not easy on a family. During the final six months when I actually wrote the book, I was often out of commission for them. They hung in there and deserve more praise and gratitude than I could possibly acknowledge here.

To all these individuals, and to all the others whose kind words kept me going, many thanks.

ABOUT THE AUTHOR

In 2002, Oren Harari was selected by the London *Financial Times* and Prentice Hall as one of "the world's greatest management thinkers" and was featured with 39 other prominent individuals in the book *Business Minds*. For the last 25 years, as a leading author, lecturer, and consultant, he has presented provocative new perspectives on competitive advantage, organizational change, and transformational leadership.

In his books, articles, and blogs, Harari debunks conventional approaches to management and describes the strategic decisions and leadership behaviors that actually do propel organizations into a successful position of competitive advantage. His 2002 book *The Leadership Secrets of Colin Powell* (McGraw-Hill, 2002) reached the best-seller lists of *The New York Times, BusinessWeek,* and *The Wall Street Journal.* Other books that he has authored or co-authored have achieved bestseller status and numerous accolades, including *BeepBeep! Competing in the Age of the Roadrunner* (Warner Books, 2000), *Leapfrogging the Competition: Five Giant Steps to Becoming a Market Leader* (Prima Publishing, 1999), and *Jumping the Curve: Innovation and Strategic Choice in an Age of Transition* (Jossey-Bass, 1994).

Harari has contributed to many publications, including *Harvard Business Review, Business Strategy Review, California Management Review,* and *Industrial Relations*, as well as numerous nonacademic publications. He was the senior monthly columnist for *Management Review* from 1991 to 2000, and for the following two years he was the lead weekly columnist for the online magazine *Mworld.org,* the American Management Association's informational website for the management community. Currently, he is on the editorial board of the *Journal of Managerial Issues*.

He served as a senior consultant with the Tom Peters Group from 1984 to 1996, and, in 1997 and 1998, he was the first designated "management expert" for Time Vista, *Time* magazine's direct resources interactive website for businesses around the world. Over the past decade, he has served on the board of directors of several entrepreneurial technology start-ups. He is currently a member of the U.S. State Department's Advisory Committee on Management and Leadership, as well as one of the founding members of The Integrity Institute, which is dedicated to elevating the standards of integrity for corporations and capital markets.

Oren Harari has addressed and consulted with premier corporations and senior government groups around the world. He received his Ph.D. from the University of California, Berkeley, and currently teaches in the MBA and executive MBA programs at the University of San Francisco.

For more information on Oren Harari, please visit www.harari.com.

PROLOGUE: THE NEVER-ENDING RACE TO SUCCEED

On an early Sunday morning stroll through a city I was visiting, I saw three individuals in jogging shorts running toward me in the middle of the street. They were fleet, lithe, vigorous, and impressive. I was intrigued. There were no cars on that street, which meant that traffic had been diverted. After the group passed me, I saw another small cluster of runners—six or seven people—exerting strong effort to catch up with the first group. I turned around as they huffed past me, to see that the back of their T-shirts advertised a corporate charity run.

A few minutes after the second group passed, I saw a huge pack of runners slowly approaching. It was a massive group whose members, jammed together, were plodding along in a slow, occasionally fitful way. Minutes passed. Eventually the group jogged by, jostling each other, sweating, and straining with effort, the difficulty of the race visible on their faces.

But it wasn't over yet. After a short while, I saw another group heading my way. This group was a smaller array of people who had given up any semblance of competing, or even running. They were walking; some were chatting with each other.

Apart from the good deed these people were doing, they provide us with a good metaphor for today's business reality. In every industry, a very small number of organizations are fast, fit, healthy, and clearly at the forefront. They are followed by a few pretty good wannabes nipping at their heels. These groups are clearly ahead of "the pack"— that large, undifferentiated bulk of companies of all shapes and sizes that don't stand out and don't draw the kind of positive attention from customers and investors that they'd like.

As in that charity run, the runners stuck in the corporate pack are struggling to stay in the race, but they are well behind the leaders in key metrics such as profit margins, stock value, cash flow, market "buzz," and customer loyalty. Many are falling farther behind despite their good intentions and strong exertions. Finally come the complete laggards, who, for all intents and purposes, are pretty much out of it. They might not even know that they're out of it, but their customers and investors do.

This book helps you guide and lead your organization to break away from the pack—and stay ahead of it. I offer you a winning blueprint for the race that your competitors (especially those who are mired in the pack) will find puzzling or will deride as crazy. If you take this book's injunctions seriously and have the courage to act on them (I give you advice on that, too), you will be able to help your organization achieve genuine market leadership and sustained competitive success.

First, a little more about "the pack." No metaphor is perfect, and I must emphasize a few caveats. Typical races, whether Olympic trials, NASCAR heats, or corporate charity runs, have one defined endpoint and one linear path toward victory. In business, there is no finish line. Having market advantage today doesn't mean you can relax and remain the star runner for the next decade. The mechanical rabbit stays in front of the greyhounds forever, and the lead dog doesn't necessarily remain in the forefront. For decades, powerful AT&T owned the telecommunications space in the U.S. In 2005, after hemorrhaging in a deregulated environment, AT&T was finally devoured by its Baby Bell offspring SBC. As I demonstrate repeatedly in this book, nothing stays the same.[1] Those who can't evolve, or who believe that they're too big or powerful to need to evolve, fall behind quickly.

Not only is there no one "end," but there is no linearity in the race itself. That's great news for you because that means there's no one prescribed path to victory. Think of today's competitive arena as a big bubble within which competitors constantly maneuver. In the global race, the winners are those who have figured out that while everyone else is dutifully running the race on the same track at the same speed in the same direction (a.k.a. industry conventional wisdom), there is no rule mandating it. And that means that any organization can successfully burst out of the round-and-round-we-go pack-mentality bubble, and do so in any direction, as long as that direction has a radically compelling value proposition, hard economic logic, and fast efficient execution.

Any one or more companies can break away from the pack and win with alternative paths that contribute to their victories. IBM, Dell, and Apple began as hardware computer companies that morphed into three entirely different and successful business models: e-business services at IBM, low-cost manufacturing and distribution efficiencies at Dell, and media/fashion/entertainment at Apple. Nickelodeon, Marvel Entertainment, Electronic Arts, and Pixar Studios are all in the business of animation, but with vastly different approaches and products. All are very successful. Wal-Mart, Nordstrom, Target, and Zara are all successful retailers with quite different business philosophies and value propositions.

Again, that's good news: no one strategy for success, no one winner, plenty of opportunities to push ahead in a variety of directions. The bad news is that in a global free market, with these sorts of opportunities, the pack is bigger than ever before—and continues to get bigger as the race progresses! In every industry, more players from more countries are jumping into the race—especially in markets that appear to be lucrative and fast growing. With technological advances, waves of global capital seeking better returns, and myriad possibilities for networks and alliances around the world, conventional barriers to entry are becoming less relevant, even in more capital-intensive businesses. So the pack grows, more players run earnestly, the racers constantly check each other out, and they mimic each other's movements. As like-minded leaders of diverse organizations generate "me-too" strategies, the organizations become tepid, unexciting, and overly cautious. They also become indistinguishable from competitors, as perceived by customers and investors. All that, in turn, pushes them into mediocrity and raises serious adverse consequences for profits, earnings, customer loyalty, market buzz, employee innovation, and investor confidence.

The result is what I call the Copycat Economy, an arena marked by "me-too" mimicry and lots of commoditized products and services.

As a leader, helping your organization stand out and win in a Copycat Economy is the most important strategic challenge you will face during the remainder of this decade.

If that's not challenging enough, the race itself has become increasingly unruly and unpredictable. Business guru Tom Peters has described the business world as "a brawl with no rules." That is too extreme a characterization, especially in the post-Enron environment of ethical caution and increased public and governmental scrutiny. But it's safe to say that it's becoming increasingly futile to try to predict the outcome of the race through rational strategic planning and statistical linearity. Boeing and Airbus have each made enormous bets in fundamentally different directions about the future of global air travel, Boeing in favor of the middle-market, middle-size (200- to 300-seat), long-haul 787 Dreamliner, and Airbus with its enormous two-story, 555-person A380. You could easily make a case for either strategic choice. In 2005, Airbus and Boeing booked 1,055 and 1,002 new orders, respectively. With the aid of these new products, Boeing and Airbus enjoyed a combined, record-breaking 2,057 orders, a sum that leapt over the industry's previous best record of 1,631 orders (set in 1989).[2] Will one company ultimately prevail? That's hard to say, especially since it might take up to ten years before real profits from current sales come through. There's nothing certain or predictable in today's business climate.

In today's market environment, chaos often trumps predictability. Rich Walker, Executive Vice President of the American Architectural Manufacturers Association, told me, "Two years ago, our companies never anticipated the Asian challenge we face today." Lee Raymond, the recently retired CEO of ExxonMobil, confesses that, in spite of the mammoth sums that ExxonMobil has traditionally spent on predictive modeling, he basically gave up trying to predict oil price fluctuations.

In the marketplace of 20 years ago, there was more stability, predictability, and routine: finite and known competitors, customers with limited choices and options, long-standing and accepted "rules of the game," and entrenched good-old-boy networks for raising capital, distributing goods, building sales, and so on. All of these "givens" are under assault today. Industries and value chains are in upheaval. The assault on the norms of doing business will only accelerate over the next 10 years. That's what happens when you have global free markets, new media for commerce such as broadband and wireless, and billions of dollars in fresh capital seeking good ideas every day.

It is nearly impossible for us to delineate exactly who will be the market leaders in ten years, what products and services will be seen as value-creating, what the global environment will look like (currently, half the world's population earns, on average, $2 a day, and less than 30 percent have immediate access to a telephone), and what jobs will be up for grabs. Executives I consult for tell me that well over 50 percent of the jobs needed for competitive success in 10 years haven't been invented yet.

In your business, therefore, the race is very real, very unruly, and very unpredictable. Breaking from the pack to create your own economic destiny is a bigger imperative than ever before.

Who Breaks From the Pack?

In the corporate race I witnessed that Sunday morning, I could safely predict that the athletes leading the procession would not fall back into the pack. But in business, frontrunners frequently fall behind and fail.

In 2003, the Krispy Kreme doughnut empire was lauded as *the* coolest brand in the U.S. By 2005, the company's share price had plummeted by 80 percent due to changes in consumer eating habits, corporate overexpansion, financial mismanagement, and ethical questions about the company's top executives. During those same years, the once highly acclaimed Blockbuster fell back into the pack as its entire videocassette rental business model was ravaged by a slew of copycat local rental shops, coupled with new competitors in online rentals of DVDs, discount retailing of cheap videocassettes and DVDs, video-on-demand and pay-per-view services, and digital video recorders. In today's environment, no one is safe—not even current leaders.

In such uncertainty lies great possibility. In the corporate charity race, I could have been completely confident that nobody from the center of the pack would have been able to break through to join or overtake the leaders at the front. Fortunately, that's not true in the real race for business success.

In 2003 I could have ridiculed Motorola as a tired, buffoonish, red-ink giant doomed to large-scale mediocrity and a devastating legacy of having stuck to its familiar analog technology way too long, while lauding the nimble, highly focused Nokia as a company that took the honors in digital innovation, engineering quality, and financial metrics. Yet between 2003 and 2005, even as it clung to its number one position overall in the handset business, Nokia lost up to 20 percent of its market share in Europe; its global revenues dropped, and its share price at one point sank by nearly 40 percent. Why? Other players, including Sony Ericsson, Samsung, and, yes, Motorola, broke from the pack with more compelling innovations in design and features, product customization for corporate carriers, and a willingness to exploit a vast middle market of consumers. Nokia has struggled to maintain its leadership position, while a big—but leaner and more focused—Motorola is the high-momentum bigger margin company, with the "gotta have it" Razr and Slvr handsets, the elegant Q smartphone, and a new no. 1 position in Latin America. All this within two years.

So don't panic if your organization is currently stuck in the pack. You can break from it. I used to believe the old adage "If you ain't the lead dog, the scenery never changes." I don't anymore because in today's volatile environment, there's no "never." You can overtake today's lead dogs. Superb, courageous companies do it all the time. *Break From the Pack* shows you how. If you've already broken from the pack and are enjoying a market leadership position, I show you some very specific ways to maintain—and increase—your lead.

And for you personally as a leader, I will show that to help your organization break from the pack, you've got to act like a leader: change-driven, contrarian, passionate, courageous, committed, disciplined, inclusive, optimistic, honest, and performance-focused. This is especially true if your company's numbers are good today. Remember, your organization's numbers today are a scorecard of what you did yesterday. Obviously, if your numbers are bad, it's clear that important changes are in order, and you've got no choice but to aggressively pursue them, or else it's back to the back of the pack. On the other hand, if your numbers are good today, then after you celebrate and people feel comfortable and smug, you've still got to act like a leader: change-driven, contrarian, passionate, etc. Remember that good numbers today mean that you were smart enough, and lucky enough, to have made some good decisions yesterday. To take an attitude of "stay the course" or "why fix it if it ain't broke?" assumes, disastrously, that yesterday will be the same as tomorrow. It won't even be the same as today.

Rich Teerlink, ex-CEO of Harley-Davidson, said it best when he warned an executive team I was working with that it's not competitors who bring a company down. It is the fault of the company itself, specifically, the leaders' "complacency, arrogance, or greed."

The great historian Arnold Toynbee noted, "Civilizations die from suicide, not from murder." The same is true for organizations, which is why I am intrigued by Motorola CEO Ed Zander's self-proclaimed management philosophy: "Whack yourself before somebody whacks you."

Today the charge to differentiate and break from the pack with some new self-imposed whacks is essential if you want your organization to be positively regarded by customers and investors, regardless of whether you're publicly traded or privately held, regardless of whether you're for-profit or not-for-profit. This book tells you why you need to do it now, and how.

This book is divided into three parts. Part I (Chapters 1–4) is called "Resisting the Pull of the Pack." Here you're introduced to a place called Commodity Hell, the 10 things you're probably doing now that actually keep you stuck in the pack, a few critical lessons on success from Madonna and Willie Nelson, and why you should aim your organization toward a highly disciplined level of curiosity, coolness, and craziness. Consider Part I to be rigorous, pre-race training, to give you the mental and leadership conditioning you need to break from the pack.

Part II (Chapters 5–10) is called "How to Break From the Pack." It offers you six courses of action that you can take to copy-proof your organization and propel it beyond the pack. Here you're introduced to why and how to *dominate* a market; how to create a "higher cause" for your organization that will inspire and mobilize customers, employees and shareholders; how to build a "defiant" pipeline of cool, compelling products, regardless of the industry you're in; how to take your customers well beyond a place of "satisfaction" to a place they thought impossible; how to innovate in supposedly "dull" areas such as cost-efficiencies and supply chains; and how to avoid destructive mergers and instead "consolidate for cool."

Part III, "How *You* Can Lead the Pack," consists of one chapter that lays out a frank "12-step" recovery program to show you the kinds of behaviors you must demonstrate and the kinds of personal competencies you must possess if you want to lead the charge to help your organization break from the pack. Follow the 12 steps in this chapter and you'll also help your own career break from the pack.

As you now settle back to read, let me give you a couple assurances. First, I believe you will appreciate the practical nature of this book. Even as it challenges you to adopt a new mindset for transforming your organization and business, nearly every chapter is studded with specific actionable "do's and don'ts" that will squarely address the question of "what do I do Monday morning?" to make it all happen.

Yet even though this book is not an ivory tower tome, I also want to assure you that you are not reading a simplistic cookbook that was prepared in an intellectual vacuum. The content of this book, including all the "to-do's," is grounded in a foundation of validated theory and empirical research as well as my documented observations and investigations within many organizations around the world.[3]

In other words, even though what you will read in the subsequent chapters will occasionally sound outrageous or insane, I can assure you that every prescription I make has been battle tested in the field by leaders who have successfully navigated the treacherous waters of the Copycat Economy.

Bursting From the Bubble

Each chapter of this book presents an element of the "Break From the Pack" framework illustrated in Figure 1. This framework organizes the remainder of this book in a way that will help you understand the Copycat Economy and create an everyday action blueprint to capitalize on its opportunities.

As you can see, the circular "bubble" arena is the space where "the pack" of competitors in your business resides and competes. It's typically a space where convention and orthodoxy reign. It's a space where competitors share a common mental model of their business, where they "understand" the rules of the game and play by them. These attributes effectively keep rivals within the so-called "safe and familiar" boundaries of the bubble, and hence mired in the pack.

The bubble is anchored by the realities of the *Copycat Economy*. The roots of the Copycat Economy are *The Irrelevance of Time and Distance, Glass House Transparency, Customer Superpower, Cost-Crushing Technology, Fragmented Mobs of Competitors*, and a *"Zeitgeist" (or Climate) of Irreverence.*

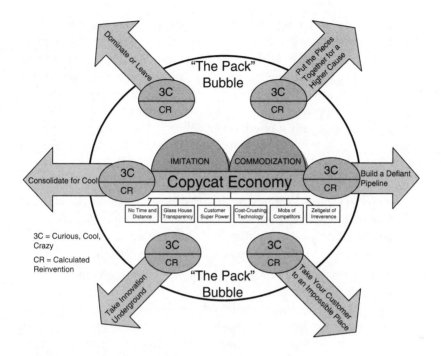

FIGURE 1 Break From the Pack conceptual framework

The Copycat Economy manifests itself with *Imitation and Commoditization*, both of which are spawning at an accelerated rate in today's marketplace. Today, the pervasiveness of imitation and commoditization is the primary strategic challenge for any leader and organization. Yet that same pervasiveness also gives the leader a precious opportunity to help his or her organization burst out of the bubble—that is, to defy orthodoxy and convention and break free of the straightjacket constraints of imitation and commoditization—and thereby *Break From the Pack*.

To break from the pack requires a metaphorical launching pad. That launching pad is a culture of disciplined *un*-orthodoxy where key decisions and actions that affect the organization's front-end (products, customer care, and value propositions) and back-end (cost efficiencies, operational effectiveness, and supply chain excellence) fit the "3C" criteria: *curious, cool,* and *crazy*.

The launching pad must be fueled by the mix of entrepreneurial spirit, foresight, and discretion necessary for *Calculated Reinvention*, or *CR*. The six launching pads can then propel the organization in six strategic directions: *Dominate or Leave, Rearrange the Pieces for a Higher Cause, Build a Defiant Pipeline, Take Your Customer to an Impossible Place, Take Innovation Underground,* and *Consolidate for Cool*. Each of these strategic choices generates its own set of specific action steps for optimal execution and achievement. As I'll note later, it is unlikely that any organization will excel in all six directions. However, the better the organization performs in each of the six paths, the more likely it will distance itself from the pack, and the more sustainable its advantage will be.

Keep the Figure 1 framework in mind as you read this book. It will help give meaning and urgency to the action blueprints that follow. It will also facilitate your adopting the habits of "break-from-the-pack" leaders described in the 12-step recovery program in Chapter 11.

At all times, remember this: It's not easy to guide your organization to break from the pull of the pack. Per the upcoming discussion in Chapter 2 you'll be continually seduced by the false and expedient lure of conventional-wisdom decisions that will most likely keep you mired in the pack. But also remember this: Breaking from the pack, no matter how difficult it is, is eminently doable, and it's absolutely necessary if you wish to add sustained value to your customers and investors. And as you'll see, it's personally rewarding for those of you who are striving for a richer and more lucrative career.

The "Break From the Pack" Attitude

It all begins with attitude. After a phenomenal career as a boxer, Oscar de la Hoya is building Golden Boy Promotions, a business whose mission is to clean up the corruption in the sport, rebuild its cachet with a new breed of products (fighters) and ethical promotional packages—and make some serious money in the process. Why build his own business? Why not join one of many already existing marketing and promotion organizations that would salivate to sign him on at a fat salary? For de la Hoya, the answer is simple: Boxing has been in a steady decline for years, and the conventional wisdom (here's how we've always done it) that grips existing "boxing organizations" is a big part of the problem. De la Hoya says, "Why am I going to be part of the bunch?" That's the attitude you want to begin with as you turn the page and begin your own quest for market leadership and competitive advantage.

Endnotes

[1] The notion that nothing stays the same was given fresh meaning by the fact that after swallowing AT&T, SBC changed its name to AT&T, and then attacked another former Baby Bell, BellSouth. More on this later.

[2] Of course, these numbers reflect orders for all types of planes, but the buzz is about the new products: the 379 orders for the Boeing 787 and the 159 orders for the Airbus A380, as of mid-2006. A side note: Throughout 2006, new orders for the 787 accelerated while those of the A380 declined, causing deep concerns for Airbus and suggesting that Boeing's view of the future might be correct. But who really knows for sure?

[3] For those of you who are interested, I lead a fairly schizophrenic professional life, with one leg in the world of university research and the other leg in the proverbial "real world" of business and leaders. In preparing this book, I put on my professor hat first. I sifted through the academic literature on competitive strategy. Likewise, I reviewed trends, cases, and analysis in a variety of daily and weekly business publications. Like a miner panning for gold and discarding the gravel and fool's gold, I eliminated the material that was inconsequential, irrelevant, banal, outdated, or arcane. I kept what I believe is the real gold—the material that clearly directs organizations to competitive advantage in today's unique market environment.

I then added the relevant highlights of my personal experiences with some of the most successful leaders and organizations in the world. To this I added the relevant information of my own consulting projects, survey data, interview data, field notes, client documents, and published works.

Lastly, I integrated and reshaped all the above pieces to create a new conceptual "break-from-the-pack" framework which forms the basis of this book.

PART I

RESISTING THE PULL OF THE PACK

1

WELCOME TO COMMODITY HELL: THE PERILS OF THE COPYCAT ECONOMY

Faster, Bigger, Harder

"Either you innovate or you're in commodity hell. If you do what everybody else does, you have a low-margin business. That's not where we want to be."

Sam Palmisano, CEO of IBM, uttered those words, and Robert Winquist would painfully agree. Winquist is CEO of Vending Supply, Inc. (VSi), one of the premier designers, manufacturers, and distributors of children's stickers and temporary tattoos. When your kids insert quarters to buy stickers or tattoos in vending machines at grocery stores or malls, they're probably buying a VSi product. Within two years of its launch in 1993, VSi was the fastest-growing, coolest player in what's known as the "flat vending industry." Before VSi, the industry was stagnant, dominated by big players churning out high-volume, look-alike stickers with conventional, bland images such as flowers, fairies, and smiling fish. VSi changed all that. Winquist and his partner, Sherry Backman, found edgy artists to create high-octane images such as smiling death heads, space aliens, and skateboard heroes. They pioneered the concept of third-party licensing for stickers, partnering with the World Wrestling Federation to create images of posturing wrestling celebrities. They also ran their business in unconventional ways: They hung out with 8- to 12-year-old kids to determine what was cool, they worked closely with the organizations that actually placed and operated the vending machines, they segmented their markets into Anglo and Latino, and they embraced the newest manufacturing technologies for speed and execution efficiencies. To entrenched players in the industry, their efforts were the work of arrogant and unwanted nut cases.

VSi's customers were thrilled. "We brought stickers to the forefront of cool," said Winquist, and the vending machine owners agreed, gladly paying VSi a premium to please the lucrative "tween" demographic. VSi grabbed margins and market share, while Winquist continued unleashing wicked designs. For eight years, VSi grew at a 30 percent rate, becoming one of the largest four players in the field. Every year, it improved its design, distribution, cost-efficiencies, and service. Much larger companies went bankrupt during that time. Pricing was not a big issue. Margins were big. Salaries were high. Life was good.

Then, says Winquist, "Our business began to fall. The decline was not in our volume; it was coming right from our bottom line. The reason is that everyone now is doing cool art. Everyone's hiring cool artists. Everyone's stickers and tattoos are so good that we all look pretty much the same. Stickers used to be a commodity before we came along. They are now a commodity again, but at a new level. The industry is glutted with cool product. Customers take it for granted."

VSi had to start competing on price. Because all the major players had copycatted VSi and were printing, outsourcing, and distributing more efficiently, there was little room to squeeze out more costs. In 2004, Winquist told me, "Today VSi is three times more creative and three times more efficient than we were ten years ago. That means we're nine times better. But our margins are one fifth what they used to be three years ago. *What's going on?*"

Welcome to Commodity Hell, Mr. Winquist. Or more accurately, welcome to the Copycat Economy, where everyone has access to the same resources and talent, where the Web is the great equalizer, and where the market's twin foundations are imitation and commoditization. It's a world marked by the "me-too" syndrome, where competing vendors benchmark, imitate, and build off each other, offering customers an ever-increasing array of choices, most of which look pretty much the same. VSi had exploded from the pack because its products, services, and processes were so outrageous that the company puzzled, angered, and intrigued competitors while exciting the hell out of the customer base. As Winquist explains, VSi's edge—and success—came about "because we violated a lot of industry rules."

But after several years of glory, the pack suddenly caught up. Within a two-year period, the edge that VSi had created, cultivated, and benefited from all but disappeared. Later in this book, I'll tell you what has happened to VSi, but for now I want to discuss the forces that pulled the company back into the pack.

First of all, keep in mind that it's not only stickers—or, for that matter, PCs and dishwashers and insurance policies and designer coffee—that become commodities. Every organization faces the challenge. IBM is discovering that even its traditional discrete consulting services are slowly becoming commoditized, a term IBM itself uses. Companies like Wipro—based in Bangalore, India—are replicating some of IBM's consultative offerings at much lower prices, which is why, to IBM's chagrin, companies like Louis Vuitton and Target are turning to Wipro for basic information technology and data-management expertise.

When I consulted at a major mutual fund a few years ago, I was told at the first meeting, "Oren, the first thing you have to know is that mutual funds are commodities." The company vice president said, "There are thousands of mutual funds that compete directly against ours, and over the long haul we pretty much have the same yields and performance, so our main job is to figure out how to differentiate ourselves so that investors will choose our products."

Twenty years ago, not many people even knew what mutual funds were, much less invested in them. Now millions of investors choose from more than 10,000 funds—a bigger number than the number of actual stocks traded on the New York Stock Exchange and Nasdaq combined. Small investors can pick one off as if they were shopping at Wal-Mart because mutual funds have become just another financial option with discounts and no-load fees. The same is true for hedge funds. Once they were instruments exclusive to those who could plunk down a couple million bucks and wait things out. Now every financial institution is offering its discount brands of McHedge funds to attract the masses of people who want to feel like they're special, too. Thus a once-special product line begins to lose its distinctiveness and vitality.

Two principles keep companies trapped in the pack and snared in the Copycat Economy, and make up the most challenging double whammy affecting your organization's competitiveness and very survival:

1. The inevitability of perpetual imitation

2. The commoditization of everything

These twin scourges are affecting every business at an accelerating pace. Old competitors find it easier to quickly imitate market leaders; new competitors find it easier to improve on them. Customers can choose among a glut of vendors who are basically offering similar products, quality, and services. "Buzz," prices, margins, and customer loyalty begin to drop as consumers shop around for the best deals. Some vendors might be "better" than others, but not enough to matter when the others are all "good enough."

Ultimately, customers—and investors, too—wind up concluding that the pack of fiercely warring competitors is bound by the same conventional approach. What happens then is fairly predictable. When customers see little difference in the availability and perceived quality of goods and services, they have a rational response: They buy what's cheapest.

When companies no longer can maintain their competitive edge, bad things start to happen over and above falling financials. Vital corporate intangibles like excitement, joy, and optimism begin to falter. Coming to work becomes less of an adventure, more of a grind. Attracting top talent becomes more difficult; in fact, the best and brightest on board begin to polish their resumes (always a good indicator of organizational decline). And companies make stupid, reflexive choices, like slashing any costs possible to make this quarter's numbers, or throwing budget, carrots, and whips at the sales and marketing people to jack up revenues—all compulsions that are meant to push them forward but actually mire them among their competitors, who are doing the same things. Dealing with other players in the value chain becomes less a creative, collaborative, value-creating process and more of an uphill battle focusing primarily on commodity discussions of price, specs, and contracts. All this happened to VSi, leading Winquist to sigh, "It's not fun like it used to be." Such are the traps of commoditization and imitation.

The Global Bazaar

Excess capacity, shakeouts, gluts, convergence, saturation, mature markets, and price wars—all these phenomena you've heard about are symptoms of the Copycat Economy. If you really want to understand their causes, skip over the microeconomic explanations and instead imagine yourself as a vendor in a large, cacophonous, open-air bazaar in a developing country.

Goods similar to yours are being sold in many stalls. As potential customers walk through, you and all the other vendors bombard them with "advertising," shouting enticements and invitations. The customers are overwhelmed with options and choices, and you know that they most likely view their success as a buyer by how low a price they can hammer out of you.

How can you differentiate yourself from the mob around you? How can you attract and retain customers while charging a reasonable price in this frenzied environment? How can you make your booth and your goods so extraordinary and appealing that you won't have to continually lower your price to differentiate yourself? And if you do something daring, what will you do when the vendors in the stalls all around you try to copy what you do? How do you avoid getting drowned in the noise and anonymity of an environment where your neighbor appears to be selling and yelling the same things you are?

Now imagine that bazaar on a worldwide scale, as the result of the "Perfect Storm" collision of globalization, deregulation, and technological advance. Imagine this phenomenon on a logarithmically accelerated, global, 24/7, physical and virtual basis across every product line in every industry. That's the essence of today's Copycat Economy. As you will see, the ravages of imitation and commoditization consistently flatten the financials and growth prospects of organizations in every industry, regardless of their size. Indeed, these factors left unchecked by leadership regularly cripple even the largest companies.

In the Prologue, I noted that an American icon was felled in 2005 when SBC purchased the legendary AT&T for the embarrassingly low price of $16 billion. The reason for the low price was, of course, a steep, steady decline in earnings, culminating in a 72 percent drop in stock value over the prior five years.

How did a colossal company, one that basically owned the entire telecommunications space before its court-ordered divestiture in 1984 and still maintained dominant size and market share throughout the 1990s, fail to avoid the freefall that led to its demise? We could point to a series of horribly executed and failed acquisitions into the wireless and Web arenas. We could point to a parade of CEOs who bought to the table more sizzle than steak. We could point to the lack of a cohesive strategy and the presence of a spirit-numbing bureau-cracy. All true, but more important was that AT&T's "soul"—and hence its infrastructure, sunk costs, budget allocations, legacy sys-tems, managers' comfort level and bias, and overall image—revolved around long-distance voice telecommunications. Long-distance voice used to be a lucrative, high-margin growth business, but when the protective wall of AT&T's semi-monopoly status was lifted and free-market competition in the field was permitted, long-distance voice gradually became a low margin commodity. New competitors, from Verizon to Vodafone, figured out new ways to deliver long-distance voice cheaper but profitably, even as advances in wireless and Internet telephony from companies like Nokia and Vonage rendered the field increasingly irrelevant.

I worked with AT&T leaders in the 1980s and 1990s, and I can assure you that they were smart, earnest people who understood these issues. But they did not approach their core problem with a sense of priority or urgency, nor were they prepared to do radical surgery on their business and organization. On the contrary, like the music indus-try's protect-the-past-at-all-cost response to the inevitable onslaught of digital music and file sharing (technologies that accelerated the com-moditization of the commercial CD), the reaction of many AT&T leaders was to circle the wagons to protect their cash cows by any means necessary: legal maneuvers, better advertising, better quality, re-engineering for efficiencies, acquisition for scale, and so on. As you will see in the next chapter, these sorts of reactive, incremental responses are worthwhile management principles, but when they're applied to a decaying business model, they become compulsions that show companies how to *lose*. At best, they buy organizations a little time, but they can't stop the descent into Commodity Hell.

What happened to the old AT&T is the most humiliating fate that the Copycat Economy can inflict on a company: Its flagship products became irrelevant, and, therefore, the company became irrelevant. It had nothing new and exciting to offer to replace its traditional prod-uct suites.[1] When I speak to corporate groups, I sometimes show a cartoon of an executive on the phone saying, "Actually, our products are so irrelevant that we don't have to worry about competition." Increasingly, the pressures of imitation and commoditization are turning up the volume of irrelevancy for many companies.

Commoditizing the "Good Enough"

The effects of imitation and commoditization are happening so quickly that we have started taking them for granted. Remember the first time you left the world of 28K and 56K modems for high-speed Internet access? It wasn't that long ago. Remember the rush, the "wow!" you felt? Now, however, aren't you starting to accept high-speed Internet as a given, whether in your business, your home, or your hotel room? It's becoming a yawner—an undifferentiated, routine service offered by many vendors and, accordingly, driven primarily by lower prices. A slew of small companies like Minneapolis-based Astound can challenge giants like Comcast with significantly lower prices for monthly cable access—and, unlike Comcast, they can make a profit off these lower prices because of their lower overhead and access to the most cutting-edge technologies. Large competitors like the "new" AT&T (the "old" SBC) can put together even cheaper $14.95 monthly packages as loss leaders for other products.[2] Moreover, in hundreds of communities, wireless high-speed Internet access is already offered nearly free. Although the cable and telecom companies argue that their quality and service is superior, customers themselves are saying, "Maybe so, but what we got for a near-free price is 'good enough.'"

In today's Copycat Economy, "good enough" is a frequent response from customers and investors—and, as it turns out, "good enough" is pretty darn good. Because they're overwhelmed with high-caliber options of goods and services, customers are no longer easily satisfied. They raise the bar on their minimum expectations of quality and service, and they expect to receive it.

My wife just bought a new dishwasher. I have no idea what brand it is, but the fact that it works perfectly doesn't fill me with delight—and it doesn't differentiate that dishwasher from the rest of the pack. My minimum, commodity-based expectation is that it work perfectly. If it does, I don't think about it. If it doesn't, I'm angry and vow a "never again" revenge on the manufacturer.

As more competitors rush to make incremental improvements of products and services, they get commoditized at a higher level, which leads many customers to conclude that "good enough" is really good enough. The fastest-growing wine in the history of America's wine industry is Bronco Wine Company's Charles Shaw wine. It is sold at the upscale Trader Joe's grocery chain, its customers are affluent and trendy, and its price is $1.99—hence its affectionate nickname "Two Buck Chuck." While Charles Shaw might not ever be confused with a vintage collector's wine, it's good enough for the discerning Trader Joe's customer seeking a casual drink. It's certainly good enough to have thoroughly cannibalized the sales of high-priced wines and skewed the industry's entire price structure. Small wonder that a *Wine Observer* article noted that the "terror of commoditization...is sweeping California's wine producers."

It used to be that if customers didn't pay a premium, they'd have to accept low quality in return. The low-price vendor was, by definition, the low-quality vendor. In the Copycat Economy, that's not true, and I'm not just talking about dishwashers or wine. Witness the financial success and growth rate of many companies as diverse as JetBlue, Progressive Insurance, and Men's Wearhouse, all of which couple low prices with surprisingly higher-end products and service. Rich Walker of the American Architectural Manufacturer's Association, in discussing Chinese imports, concedes, "It's not just that they're cheap. What's scary is that even though they charge one third to one half our price for window framing, they're exporting *good-quality* product." Last year a young executive at Morgan Stanley Dean Witter wrote me that "over the years, institutional and retail commissions for stock transactions have come down dramatically. Online and discount brokerage firms continue to offer *equivalent-quality executions* (my emphasis) at lower and lower price points."

The tentacles of the Copycat Economy extend throughout the market, even into "luxury" sectors, as anyone who has bought an authentic Picasso print at Costco will testify. An observer of the private jet market noted in 2002, "After a huge growth spurt in the jet market, the jet manufacturers find themselves with a ton of capacity and product .... Business jets are heading toward commoditization—meaning they are becoming essentially interchangeable—because of the large array of models with similar capabilities."

Other pricey items, even those with sentimental value, are now "good enough" to be commoditized. Caskets made in China now sell for 25 percent less than those built in the U.S., and among the six models of coffins you can now buy at Costco (!), one is priced at $925, which is less than half the price of a conventionally priced product.

Imitation and commoditization have always been part of a business environment, but they are now occurring at a scary unprecedented and accelerating pace. As one CEO of a small manufacturing company told me, "It used to be that if I came up with a terrific product, I could expect to enjoy five years of good returns on it. Now I'm lucky if I get 18 months." In many sectors, 18 months is an unheard-of luxury. In the online dating and matchmaking arena, the bigger sites tend to be interchangeable, and the competition is so intense that if one vendor introduces a new function, you can count on seeing the same option pop up almost immediately on rival sites. The very notion of a leisurely planning cycle has disappeared. And the old, reliable cash cows are dodos.

The bottom line? Imitation and commoditization are the most pressing strategic challenges that you will face for the duration of this decade.

The Causes of Commodity Hell

What's causing this rampant transformation of the market? Six key factors produce the Copycat Economy. Every leader must approach them with a combined sense of humility and urgency.

1. The Irrelevance of Time and Distance

Imitation can come from anywhere in the world. In an era of globalized free trade and accessible technologies, any organization from anywhere can combine local conditions (wages, tax, regulatory environment, and government incentives) with new technologies and new alliances to replicate what you're doing, often at lower costs.

Complete, unedited, free and low-priced downloadable bootleg copies of *Star Wars III: Revenge of the Sith* appeared on the Internet literally hours after the official release of the film on May 19, 2005. Talk about imitation and commoditization! On July 1, 2005, authorities (working under the appropriate moniker "Operation Copycat") arrested suspects in 11 different countries for masterminding a copyright piracy supply and distribution chain.

More than 90 percent of Microsoft products used in China are pirated—the ultimate form of imitation. Like the bootleg copies of the Star Wars film, freshly minted counterfeit copies of products like Windows 95 and XP were available in China *on the same day* they were launched by Microsoft in the U.S. Many computer retailers in China are gravitating toward Linux operating systems because their customers ask for Linux. And why are they asking? Because Linux is basically free (the ultimate form of commoditization), the total cost of the computer is less than if it was operated by XP. For some customers, that's "good enough." Others buy the computer, rip out the Linux operating system, and replace it with a counterfeit copy of XP. Even if you're a giant like Microsoft, these are pretty hefty challenges to overcome.

No time, no distance, huge impact. Low-cost manufacturing competition in Asia and Latin America creates havoc with higher-priced goods and jobs in Western countries, leading Patricia Panchak, the editor-in-chief of *Industry Week,* to note that for manufacturers, "the globalization of the marketplace means intense, low-cost competition, limited pricing power, and a high rate of structural change."

Global alliances and supplier relationships further accelerate the push to commoditization. In concert with international partners, some American companies are now manufacturing medical imaging equipment abroad and then designing, programming, and servicing it abroad, too—all at a fraction of the cost of doing it in the U.S. After American hospitals buy the equipment at reduced rates, they can, if they want, digitally zap x-ray or MRI images to reputable radiologists in India— reputable physicians who make their diagnoses and zap their conclusions back at one tenth the salary of their American counterparts.

At the same time, cross-border capital flows are funding corporate ventures and entrepreneurial start-ups that will force current market leaders into being commodity players. New VoIP (Voice over Internet Protocol) players like Skype (now part of eBay), Vonage (the fastest-growing phone company in the U.S.), VoicePulse, and Galaxy—all originally launched with international investment—have contributed to the commoditization of the entire long-distance telecommunications industry. More online music file-sharing sites, and Web gambling and sports-betting sites are moving to obscure international locations to escape the long arms of U.S. law and regulation. Their physical distance doesn't stop them from commoditizing the commercial CD to the point of irrelevance, or creating an easy-access low-cost gaming alternative to traveling to Las Vegas. Despite heavy pressure from American pharmaceutical companies and the FDA, Canadian companies like CanaRx and Canada Pharmacy allow American consumers to bypass the established drug supply chain and purchase quality-controlled generic and nongeneric prescription medication online at far lower prices.

2. The Rise of Glass House Transparency

Secrets, proprietary information, and closed-door management systems don't have the competitive edge they used to because new technologies have the capabilities to create total transparency. Today everybody has access to any information, talent, and resources, so it becomes a lot easier to copy anything, be it a product, a service, a marketing campaign, or an internal process.

Think about technologies like broadband, search engines, cable, e-mail, collaborative software, cellphones, satellite, fax, overnight delivery, browsers, file sharing, Wi-Fi, videotapes, video streams, videoconferencing, video discs, DVDs, Bluetooth, VoIP, cable TV, blogs, and podcasting. Think about the relentless movement toward global travel, free markets, and political democracy. Now imagine all these technological, social, and geopolitical forces converging to generate unfettered real-time news and information, and hence market transparency. All these factors make it easier for anyone, anywhere, to locate and access the information, talent, and resources they need at a better price. This, in turn, makes it easier for any current or potential competitor to copy, imitate, or improve a product or service—and leapfrog over any company's product, process, or marketing tactics.

Transparency relentlessly accelerates imitation and commoditization. The fabulously successful Apple iPod and Motorola Razr cellphone are spawning a slew of low-priced, ever-increasing-quality imitators because potential competitors can see the exact metrics of Apple's and Motorola's success every day, and they can readily deconstruct the entire business design and the underlying technologies. Low-cost private-label products in retail stores (with the same ingredients and similar packaging) are now formidable competitors to higher-priced brands. The fastest-growing segment of the pharmaceutical industry is the generic (i.e., copycat) drug business.

Competitors aren't the only ones profiting from the transparency and easy access of vital information. Customers benefit, too. Transparency allows them to find the most accurate and unvarnished information about any vendor or any product. The Web allows them to find the best deal anywhere, at any time, whether they're seeking a home loan or a car. The Web allows customers to read complimentary or scathing reviews of vendors and products—or post them, knowing that thousands or millions will read their comments. Such interactions wind up stripping away much of the high-gloss "value" that organizations believe ought to justify a higher price and brand loyalty.

Every business exists in a glass house, even when it tries to lower the blinds. In 2005, executives at both GM and Apple were shocked and infuriated when their ultra-top-secret new products were unveiled in magazines and on Web sites before their official launch. Why should they have been surprised? Secrets can't be kept in a market that is so transparent that pirates can access Microsoft's secret code and create counterfeit products at the same pace that Microsoft designs real ones.

The counterfeit trade is the ultimate, albeit corrupt, expression of imitation. It is fed and watered by transparency and is growing rapidly. Engineers and chemists in various countries can now reverse-engineer patented molecules to produce illegal pharmaceuticals and sell them at a fraction of what a legitimate drug company charges. In countries such as China, Vietnam, and Ukraine, the production of amazingly authentic-looking but bogus Calloway golf clubs, HP inkjet cartridges, Louis Vuitton handbags, Nokia cellphones, and Intel computer chips seems to grow exponentially. Ninety-one percent of DVDs and video discs in Chinese homes are counterfeit. The World Customs Organizations estimates that counterfeit products account for more than 7 percent of global merchandise trade, or $540 billion. None of this could occur without a glass house transparency effect in today's marketplace.

3. The Customer as Superpower

Customers, armed with the latest technologies and operating in a transparent environment, are now capable of reducing any well-promoted, well-packaged market offering to a bare-bones commodity. They can dig below the hype, bunch vendors together according to their generic products and services, and canvass the globe to find the best fit and cheapest prices.

Customers have taken full advantage of transparency-inducing information technology and increasingly open market climates. Individual customers now regularly bypass organizations' marketing plans and distribution channels, and instead compare, contrast, and critique products, prices, and companies on their own terms with a simple click of the mouse. The Online Publishers Association found that more than 90 percent of individuals between 18 and 54 years old turn to the Internet first for product information. The proliferation of Web sites has allowed customers to take more control over many sectors of the market, from travel booking and auto sales to music production and investment management.

As customers, we also collaborate on our own terms: With one click, we can e-mail messages and documents and files to a vast preset community of friends, family, and colleagues. We can create Web sites and interactive chat sites about products, prices, companies, issues, and trends. We can write opinion blogs and post commentary and dialogues with readers. We can podcast to get our ideas and creations to the immediate world. We can form ad hoc interest groups such as Angie's List, a virtual community of 425,000 subscribers who share critiques and recommendations about local service companies, like plumbers, car mechanics, and painters. In Shanghai, China, we can get together with other consumers in Internet chat rooms, agree to meet at a particular store (say, an appliance or furniture store), and then—as a group—converge on the store and haggle down everyone's price of a specific product up to 40 percent if everyone in our group buys that product.

All these activities yield more customer power and oversight over vendors, place higher expectations and demands on those vendors, and result in more beady-eyed assessment of their prices. As customers get smarter, they

- Raise the bar on "good enough" performance (which itself becomes quickly imitated by vendors who want to survive)

- Strip away the marketing hype of vendors and get to the unvarnished truth (how good is this product really, or this hospital, or this doctor?)

- eliminate the value-add of many vendors (do you need a travel agent or stock broker as often as you used to?)

- Reveal the hidden pricing foundation of many vendors (don't you know what that car dealer actually paid for that car on that lot?)

- Shop around for the best fit of product features and prices—or just the cheapest prices

- Get rid of middlemen entirely by ordering direct

- Sell goods themselves on online auctions

- Avoid online ads with pop-up blockers and TV ads with digital video recorders

- Exchange information with like-minded souls in digital communities like craigslist.org, Flickr, and MySpace.com.

Everything that consumers are now doing accelerates the demise of traditional sources of value and bunches vendors into a more homogeneous, look-alike horde with less differentiated, commoditized offerings.

Opportunities for corporate customer power have also exploded, leading *Industry Week's* Patricia Panchak to conclude that nowadays "the customers rule, making lowest cost, fastest delivery, and highest quality a *prerequisite* for success." Competition for corporate telecom business, for example, has become so frenetic that John White, CEO of the financial advisory Public Financial Management, told me that he now uses a reseller of long distance. He says it was easy to negotiate a cut of more than $100,000 from an annual $800,000 corporate headquarters telecom bill, while at the same time receiving an increase in communications speed and capacity from the same vendor. If he hadn't gotten the cut rate and service improvement, he was ready to find another provider because, he says, "They're all pretty much the same."

Corporate customer power forces vendors to make huge changes in their very products and services. Companies like SAP, Siebel, and IBM were staggered when customers told them they were no longer willing to be bound to a business model built around a massive, installed base of proprietary software systems. They wanted choices. They saw options like cheaper, Web-based, on-demand vendors like little salesforce.com, and they caused SAP, Siebel, and others to make mammoth changes in systems, services, and pricing.

4. Cost-Crushing Technology

New and existing technologies allow for radical cost-cutting and operational efficiencies, which, in turn, lower barriers to entry and create more competitors in the pack—who can profitably charge lower prices for the same goods and services.

Ricardo Greco, CEO of the Mendoza, Argentina-based management-education company Alta Direccion, went even further than

PFM's John White to reduce his company's telecom bill. He completely ignored the established vendors and installed peer-to-peer Skype Internet telephony in every Alta Direccion office throughout Latin America, thus reducing his company's annual telecom fee by more than 80 percent annually. Visiting Alta Direccion's Panama office, I was impressed by my ability to dial my family and my assistant back in the U.S. at local rates using a USB phone connected to a desktop computer. Had my home and office also been wired with easily downloadable Skype software, the calls would have been free. That's what I call cost reduction! It's also what I call the complete commoditization of conventional telecom's market offerings.

Small start-ups, bigger companies like JetBlue and Men's Wearhouse, and huge companies like Wal-Mart and Ikea are aggressively using state-of-the-art technologies to keep their cost structure down and thus profit from lower pricing. Coupling technology with low overhead (low wages, real estate prices, and local taxes in its Omaha, Nebraska, headquarters), Ameritrade's $9.95 Internet trade price showed it was actually profitable, and the company made life miserable for giant Morgan Stanley (with its key operations in expensive New York and San Francisco) and its Morgan Stanley Online.

Whether it's long-distance bills or many procurement and inventory-management charges, digitalization can reduce many costs to near-oblivion. New technologies can crush costs by breaking down old lines of distribution, bypassing middlemen and conncecting players at the end points to each other. Entire value chains can be eliminated. Using basic information technology tools, a musician can replicate and record the sounds of an entire orchestra. A publisher can create a low-cost, low-subscription-fee Web-based scientific publication that can effectively compete with a long-standing scientific journal with a $900 annual subscription—and, in fact, can surpass it because turnaround time for getting an article reviewed and posted, with analyses and commentary, is a fraction of what a physical journal requires. Intranets and expert systems can consolidate available knowledge to yield new innovations in cost reductions, not just revenue-line enhancement. ERP, CRM, and TLM software can radically reduce costs in back-office and administrative operations, customer relations, and product development, respectively. When these infrastructure changes occur, jobs and organizational functions that no longer add value are themselves commoditized; they can be eliminated in favor of cheaper automation and digitalization. (Yes, the pain of job loss to any individual is huge, but on the other hand, organizations that act prudently can eliminate fat and bureaucracy to become more cost-effective and agile—and thus eventually hire for more higher-end, higher-paying jobs.)

Barriers to entry crumble when startups such as JetBlue and the Canadian airline WestJet combine state-of-the-art technology with new management systems to unnerve huge, stumbling providers like United Airlines and Air Canada. Two-person shops with negligible overhead are accessing cheap, powerful technologies to become viable players in a variety of sectors, such as financial services, consulting, marketing, and publishing. They're building margins and market share even as they offer copycat services and lower prices than larger, higher-cost competitors.

There is also immense power in existing technologies when they are creatively applied. Fast-growing start-ups like netphone leader Vonage and search monster Google have been built on the backs of very cheap but very powerful servers and PCs cobbled together (and, in the case of Google, using free Linux software) instead of high-cost razzle-dazzle technologies that would quickly burn through precious capital.

The ultimate irony is that technology itself is getting cheaper. Critics like Nicholas Carr, author of the controversial book *Does I.T. Matter?*, point out three developments. First, software programs are quickly replicated by rival companies. Second, proprietary technologies are giving way to cheap open source infrastructures like Linux and Web-based applications like salesforce.com. Third, and most important, corporate customers are refusing to automatically pony up for pricey, glitzy next-generation products and forced upgrades because they don't see the value-add over today's "good enough." A brand manager at Sun Microsystems explained his company's woes: "Servers have become commodities and cheaper PCs have replaced $500 Sun servers for running applications. Customers are looking to our cheaper competitors to meet their IT needs."

Regardless of what products or services you're selling, *Forbes* publisher Rich Karlgaard believes that they will inevitably be part of what he calls "The Cheap Revolution." He says, "The industrial world has entered a period in which China, India, the Internet, and a tech glut will become platforms for shockingly cheap products and services." He's exactly right.

5. Mobs of Competitors

The interaction of deregulation, globalization, and technological advance breaks large, orderly, predictable homogenous market swaths into mobs of frenetic organizations seeking the same goals and trying desperately to avoid anonymity. Despite the efforts of some entrenched firms, markets are no longer ruled by a few huge players. Dell "owns" the global Personal Computer business, and its market share is a scant 13 percent. In the auto industry, Toyota's goal is a 15 percent global market share by 2010—a number which seems ridiculously modest but in that industry is positively audacious.

In industry after industry, the playing field has been fragmented as more players jump into the fray. The more lucrative and fast-growing the particular market, the more sharks are attracted to the waters. In these increasingly turbulent waters, barriers to entry slowly melt in response to the onslaught of technological advance, heightened availability of global capital, and the spawning of new partnerships and alliances around the world. One executive in a financial services firm told me that "the cost of entry in our business has become a phone, a computer, and a network of independent partners."

All this means an ever-growing number of competitors and a harder challenge to break free of them. Southwest Airlines' remarkable track record of multi-year profitability has spawned a growing, piranha-like cluster of low-cost, low-priced imitators who have doubled their collective market share to 15 percent over the past five years. Now add the low-cost imitation coming from the established big carriers, and suddenly Southwest is facing relentless pressures that it didn't have to deal with in the past. "There's a big bulls-eye painted on our backs" says one Southwest executive.

In the 1980s and early '90s, the music companies were on a roll. The marginal cost of producing a music CD was about 20¢, and the value chain was solid as a rock, delivering the product to Tower Records or Wherehouse, where customers would pony up $15 a pop for the privilege of hearing the one or two songs on the disc they actually liked. Multiply that CD by millions of products annually, all throwing off fat margins even after paying off artists and retailers. It was a darn good business if you were an executive, complete with the side benefits of hanging out with rock stars and wearing a ponytail even as you were balding.

The music labels became so fat and sassy that they began to consolidate to control the market completely. They did so for all the usual reasons: scale, scope, cross-marketing, and synergy. By the end of the 1990s, five companies controlled 75 percent of the market. The remainder they left for the scavengers: small, independent labels that scurried to find whatever business they could.

But ultimately, the darn market simply didn't cooperate with the music moguls' plans. New file-sharing and MP3 technologies—absorbed with delight by new obstreperous competitors and millions of customers—exploded their business model and reduced many of their assets to liabilities. Sales plummeted, market caps withered, and companies like Tower and Wherehouse sought bankruptcy protection. Today the entire music business is splintered into a manic mob of small and large competitors of every ilk, and the biggest players are now—when not suing somebody—desperately trying to shed "assets" and compete in a new ballgame.

Increasingly, that new ballgame in any industry is filled with more obstreperous competitors. The more players in the game, the faster traditional products and services become "me too" and lower-margin commodities.

The good news in the Copycat Economy: Anybody can play. The bad news in the Copycat Economy: Anybody *will* play.

6. A *Zeitgeist* of Irreverence

Zeitgeist is a German word meaning "the spirit of the times." The spirit of our times is irreverence, if not disrespect, for tradition, history, and the winners of prior battles. In your business, customers are constantly demanding, "What have you done for me lately?" Customer loyalty? You'll get it if you do a lot more and a lot more cheaply than the other provider can. Otherwise, you're gone. And that's true even if you've been your customer's supplier for 10 years.

And your competitors? Well, it's not simply that there are more of them; it's that so many are so darn irreverent. They don't play the game the way it's always been played. Vonage and Skype aren't interested in "improving" on what Sprint or Deutsche Telekom have always done; they're out to make the giants' business model irrelevant and to rewrite the rules. Skype's Web site says flatly that the company's goal is to reduce the price of a phone call to zero. By mid-2005, Skype had attracted more than 30 million users, adding 155,000 new users per day, which, no doubt, enticed eBay to buy the $60 million company for a substantial $2.6 billion later the same year.

Irreverance spills over into every market. Discount real-estate firms, commercial Web sites that cater to home bidders and FSBO's ("For Sale By Owners"), and companies that offer innovative referrals and rebates on sales are all launching grenades at the standard practices and the standard 6 percent commissions of conventional real-estate brokerages. Tiny Visto Corporation has built a wireless e-mail technology that aims to eliminate a lot of RIM's Blackberry value-add, letting people manage their e-mail on the cellphones at a significantly lower price. Already, Visto's technology is being rolled out by carriers like Vodafone and Nextel (a unit of Sprint).

Heart surgeons, who have seen their business drop by 20 percent, are unhappy with cardiologists, who historically have been their primary source of patient referrals. Many irreverent cardiologists have violated this cozy arrangement by treating patients themselves with a plethora of new medications, radical Dr. Dean Ornish–type diets, meditation and exercise regimens, and advancement in angioplasty and stent technologies that they can handle themselves. For patients and payers, that's a lot cheaper (and, in many situations, apparently, more effective) than open-heart surgery.

Small wonder that so many entrenched providers, when dealing with customers and competitors, feel like Rodney "I Get No Respect" Dangerfield. It's not simply that the pack has gotten bigger; the pack is irksome, iconoclastic, and unwilling to play the game the way it ought to be played, dammit! Many disrupters of various industries come from outside. The iPod/iTunes phenomenon came from Apple's Steve Jobs, a computer guy. Vonage founder Jeffrey Citron came from financial services. Skype's executive team started at Kazaa, the P2P music file-sharing company. Air Asia, which is offering JetBlue–type services in Asia, was founded by Tony Fernandez, also a refugee from the music industry. Industry insiders talk to each other in the same comfortable language, mimic each other politely, complain with one voice about insurmountable challenges that they all are dealing with the same way, and offer sympathetic excuses to each other as to why change is difficult. Meanwhile, full-blown crazies, often from outside the industry, come into the fray with no baggage, no excuses, and no preconceptions.

A Zeitgeist of irreverence creates dissatisfaction with the present, which spurs the spirit for genuine breakthroughs—which, in turn, accelerates the commoditization of everything that used to add value in the past. Combine this Zeitgeist with a meltdown of time and distance, glass house transparency, customer superpower, cost-crushing technology, and a mob of competitors, and you've got a nuclear-powered brew for imitation and commoditization.

Accepting the Challenge of the Copycat Economy

Managers like you are faced with massive and continuous challenges which could include some or all of the following:

- "Extreme" competition
- Excess capacity
- Mature and saturated markets
- Thinning margins
- Less customer loyalty
- Customers increasingly making buying decisions primarily by price
- Customers raising the bar on their minimal expectations regarding price, quality, and performance
- Analysts and investors growing pessimistic about corporate prospects
- For many companies, the real possibility of outright bankruptcy or liquidation

The challenges are daunting. But consider the payoff to breaking from the pack. When an organization's products and services are *not* commodities, when they're *not* seen as "me too," when they're viewed by investors as truly compelling, and when they're perceived by customers as truly value-adding, the correlates are also clear:

- A clear differentiation from competitors
- Rapid, sustained, and real growth (not the shaky kind that often results from megamergers)
- Higher margins
- Higher stock prices and market caps
- Boosts in market buzz

- Reputation as the employer and partner of choice
- More customer loyalty
- An optimistic and creative work environment
- A far easier sales and marketing effort
- An agile, aggressive infrastructure that is positioned for next-generation growth

Stakeholders are attracted to companies that break from the pack. Investors bet on companies that can increase future earnings and cash flows. Customers stay loyal and are often willing to pay a premium if they can count on unique, exciting price-value from a company's offerings. The best and brightest talent migrates to these companies because the climate is usually intellectually exciting and financially rewarding.

The implication is clear. In today's Copycat Economy, the primary strategic challenge for any leader and any organization is to *stop* and *reverse* the inevitable slide toward the commoditization and imitation of their current products and services.

And even that is not enough. Motorola's Ed Zander has correctly noted that "the market wants not just one good quarter. It doesn't even want a great quarter. It wants 6 good quarters or 10 good quarters or 12 good quarters." He's talking about sustainability, necessary to stay ahead of the pack. In today's Copycat Economy, those companies that are able to *continually decommoditize* and *unimitate* are the ones that will create sustained, accelerated value for their shareholders and customers. The remaining chapters show you how to achieve these goals.

There's an old joke about two hikers in the woods who come upon a huge grizzly bear. As the bear prepares to attack, one of the hikers reaches into his backpack and draws out a pair of running shoes. As he's putting them on, his colleague says, "Why are you doing that? You'll never be able to outrun a grizzly." Whereupon the first fellow replies, "I don't have to outrun the bear. I just have to outrun you."

It's not so funny anymore, for in the Copycat Economy, everyone seems to run at the same speed, and the bear catches up anyway. Regardless of whether you're in a "business to consumer" or "business to business" market, whether you're a for-profit or not-for-profit organization, whether you're in the private or public sector, you're under enormous expectations and pressures. There really is a grizzly bear in front of you—it's not a delusion. To outrun the bear, to break from the pack, you've got to run smarter, run a different path, run in a way that nobody's run before. You know the alternative.

The challenge is considerable. So are the opportunities. The trifecta of deregulation, globalization, and technological advance creates a wide-open, unexplored terrain that is right in front of anyone who has the gumption to explore it fearlessly and build upon it. No organization today, regardless of its current size and financial muscle, has a lock on the future, so the possibilities for you are huge.

Your goal, to paraphrase Barry Tarasoff, the research director at the midsize Wall Street firm S. G. Cowen, is to create something with unique value that cannot be easily duplicated. Your mission, to quote IBM's Sam Palmisano, is to lead with the spirit of breakthrough: "While they share many attributes, there is one thing that sets all great companies apart: They define and lead the agendas for their businesses."

Are you willing to be a new force in your industry? If you say yes, then you'll soon be sprinting from the starting line, and you're now ready to start eliminating bad training habits described in Chapter 2.

Endnotes

[1] Ironically, history has come full circle. Once SBC bought AT&T, it took on the name of its prey, and in 2006 the new AT&T bought BellSouth for $67 billion in stock and $23 billion in debt. Once again, AT&T is the nation's biggest telecom firm and the biggest long-distance provider. What's changed? According to *Newsweek* business columnist Allan Sloan, "not only is the AT&T name back. So is that old AT&T strategy...."

[2] The value-add for cable companies such as Comcast and phone companies such as AT&T is integrated bundles of voice, video, and Web services that are priced lower when the customer adds additional services. My point is that the individual services themselves, which were once unique and exciting, are now common and expected. Without regular reinvention, that will inevitably happen to the current bundles, too. Left unchecked, commoditization and imitation will also diminish customers' "switching costs."

2

HOW TO LOSE:
TEN COMPULSIONS
GUARANTEED TO KEEP
YOU MIRED IN THE PACK

Before we get to what we can do to break from the pack, we need to confront the things that keep us stuck in it. Faced with the twin plagues of commoditization and imitation, business leaders reflexively resort to ten courses of action that create a false, seductive, and temporary illusion of security—and plunge their companies further into the spiral of Commodity Hell. In this chapter, we explore ten compulsions that keep businesses trapped in the pack. I call these courses of action compulsions because even though they are counterproductive and dysfunctional, we persist in clinging to them anyway, perhaps because they worked in the past or perhaps because they reflect conventional wisdom. Either way, they won't do the trick for us in a Copycat Economy. As you read this chapter, ask yourself—does this compulsion describe how we do things in our organization?

1. The Compulsion to Cut Costs

Trying to stave off decline and beef up margins, many companies reflexively cut departmental budgets, sell off assets, lay off employees, and embrace any cheaper supplier. To be sure, cost-cutting efforts are useful and necessary, but only when part of a well-exe-cuted growth strategy. By itself, the frenzy of cost cutting is often a self-defeating compulsion, for several reasons.

- You can't shrink your way to success. After your budgets are slashed and the plants are closed and the bodies are hauled away, what exactly are you going to do to grow the business?

- You're not alone in your compulsion: Your competitors are also cutting costs for their own survival, and your company remains undifferentiated from others in the pack.

- Compulsive cost cutting often degenerates into intramural combat and backbiting. People scurry to salvage scraps of bud-get regardless of whether their actions create value, or they do whatever it takes to protect themselves from further cuts.

- Because your company still has no disciplined vision to break from the pack, your cost-cutting decisions can be strategically counterproductive: Some cuts might be grossly inefficient, leaving lots of fat, and others saw away your company's muscle and bone.

- If cost cutting gives your financials a temporary reprieve, you can be seduced into believing you don't need to make radical and truly efficacious changes.

- The cost-cutting compulsion is intermittent and unpredictable, like a smoker's resolution to quit. After the company discovers that—surprise!—the first cost cut didn't yield salvation, it cuts more, then more, then more, until it becomes a Chinese water torture for employees and investors.

- Employees (especially your best ones) become demoralized, catching on to the reality that the company lacks a coherent or inspiring alternative to the steady chop-chop-chop.

In early 2006, Ford—mired in deteriorating market share and "junk bond" status—announced another big restructuring plan. This one would slash 30,000 jobs, close 14 plants in the U.S. and Canada, and reduce capacity by 26 percent. These moves would generate $6 billion in savings through 2010. That's great. But will these steps unleash a fresh wave of capital, innovation, and employee commit-ment necessary to design, manufacture, and deliver sexy, high-quality, "gotta-have" cars with superb after-sale service? If the answer is yes,

Ford will rock. If the answer is no, the savings will be illusory. They'll be sucked up fast.

The ripple effects of a "cut-cost" compulsion are sad. I've spoken to disheartened employees of major airlines that are facing bankruptcy or are already in bankruptcy. They've got nothing to look forward to other than more slashes to assets, budgets, salaries, and pensions, with no exciting prospects for real growth. It reminds me of the story of the guy visiting a friend who lives on a farm and notices a pig with one wooden peg leg. He asks his friend about it.

"Oh, that pig is remarkable," the farmer replies. "He's friendly and obedient, and once while we were sleeping, he saved our lives by tapping on the bedroom window when he saw a fire start outside."

"But what about the peg leg?" asks the visitor.

"Come on now," admonishes the farmer. "A pig that special you don't eat all at once."

In 2005, Northwest Airlines mechanics went on strike and Delta pilots threatened to, even as the airlines continued their relentless southward slide. Perhaps even a peg-leg pig will eventually fight back. After all, what does he have to lose?

Of course, some argue that the solution is to cut costs rapidly and savagely. Forget the peg leg, they say—kill the pig right away. Use slash-and-burn tactics to eliminate as much cost and overhead debris as quickly as possible. Of course, the basic commodity product line, business model, and organization itself all remain intact: Everything is just "leaner." But it's "leaner" in a way that guarantees that performance will drop because there is no vision, investment, or support for sustained, break-from-the-pack growth. It's like the guy who says, "I'm training for a marathon race and need to lose 30 pounds fast, so I cut off my right leg."

A former MBA student of mine reported to me how this strategy worked with her employer, a public policy institute that responded to declining investment income with a sharp, across-the-board cost-cutting program. "Promising projects were cancelled in order to save money. Employee tasks were integrated, leading to overload. Fringe benefits such as Christmas parties, employee farewell parties, and annual company picnics were eliminated. In addition, employee raises were reduced substantially, and new hires got lower salaries than their predecessors. Within the first quarter of enacting the new 'leaner' policy, the number of research projects dropped, the scale and scope of the projects dropped, and 13 percent of the total staff (many of whom were the top researchers and rainmakers) left within the first six months."

As Frank Lorenzo showed in his emasculation of Eastern Airlines, and "Chainsaw Al" Dunlap demonstrated in his gutting of Scott Paper and Sunbeam, a "savage cuts" approach often leads to disaster—except for a very select group of top executives and investors. Most investors and employees lose. Eastern simply disappeared. Sunbeam wound up without the resources to build compelling new products and provide acceptable service quality—and its share price deteriorated accordingly. The result was a grotesque distortion of the idea of "creating shareholder value" because, in effect, certain shareholders were betting that Dunlap would eviscerate the companies he ran to carve up the carcass and sell them off at the most attractive prices. That's no way to prepare a company for competitive advantage.

2. The Compulsion to Cut Prices

Desperately lowering prices to keep customers from bolting—as when GM, Ford, and Chrysler regularly slash prices with discounts, interest deals, and rebates to woo buyers, keep volume up, and maintain market share—decimates a company's margins and trains customers to wait for another round of price cuts before buying. Moreover, when these companies offer zero percent financing, they're gutting their most lucrative source of profit: consumer financing. (GMAC Financial Services has been the most profitable staple of GM for so long that one could argue that GM has become a bank that uses cars as sales incentives.[1])

But the worst consequence is that by reflexively slashing prices while competitors like Toyota and BMW don't, GM and Ford are really conceding defeat. They're saying that the only way they can differentiate their products from those of their global competitors is not with higher quality, cooler design, better features, or great service, but with lower price. This step not only stamps "I'm a commodity" on every car they make, but it also slowly strangles their capacity to fund new product development and pay off a massive pension liability. It does nothing to address their enormous challenges: operational inefficiencies, legacy costs, unviable labor-management relations, and the fact that, as a *New York Times* analysis said, "not enough people like their cars."

When one competitor copies the other's price-cutting sales promotion, both fall prey to the Copycat Economy. Mark Thorsby, CEO of the International Carwash Association, tells me it drives him nuts when an owner of a carwash facility reflexively slashes prices to match the price offered by the facility down the block. "Instead of copying the lower price," says Thorsby, "the guy ought to be figuring out services and extras that will attract people who are willing to spend a couple more bucks on value. Even more, he ought to be trying to figure out ways to attract the owners of a hundred and seventy million vehicles in this country that aren't being serviced in carwashes at all!"

If blindly copying lower prices is ridiculous, just as ridiculous are the unanticipated consequences. A few years ago, Mitsubishi tried to crank up sales with a "zero-zero-zero" promotion, in which customers could buy a car with no money down, no interest charges, and no obligation to make any payment for a full year. So a lot of customers used this scheme to drive a car free of charge for an entire year and then let the car get repossessed. Mitsubishi lost hundreds of millions of dollars in the process.

Yes, there are times when it is strategically prudent to do a temporary price retreat in the face of difficult market conditions. In 2002 and 2003, the condition of the economy and the aftermath of the September 11 attacks hit the travel industry especially hard, so it made sense for hotels, cruise ships, car rental companies, and theme parks to offer generous discounts to woo customers—as long as they knew that this was a temporary solution, at best.

Likewise, Chapter 9 demonstrates that an organization can still enjoy profitable growth through price cuts *if* it can radically reinvent its cost structure. Unfortunately, most companies that fall into the price-cut compulsion keep their underlying costs fat and happy at worst, or compulsively less (see Compulsion #1) at best. A few years ago, when United Airlines simply attempted to "match" Southwest Airline's price structure with its ill-conceived, now defunct "United Express" in select western routes, the results were catastrophic in terms of on-time take-offs and arrivals, customer satisfaction, corporate image, and financial returns. United had simply dropped prices without tackling its underlying cost structure and inflexible bureaucracy. We can only hope that United's more recent venture into the low-priced airline market—"Ted" (a cute shortening of Uni-Ted)—will not be an instant replay.

Sensible, dynamic pricing is an effective management tool, especially when linked to cost-efficiencies and provocative innovations. Simply cutting prices to stave off market decline is a truly dysfunctional step. The commoditization continues; the company's freefall persists.

3. The Compulsion to Improve Current Products and Services

Making incremental improvement in whatever you're currently doing might help maintain your company's market share, revenue stream, and customer loyalty—for now. But if your market offerings are in a downward commodity spiral, rarely will you generate sharp or sustained increases in sales, margins, or buzz just by adding an extra zipper to your company's signature handbag. Your competitors will probably ape your improvement instantly, or your customers might not see the value or importance of the "improvement," or they'll be unwilling to pay for it.

If you want to *survive* in the pack, improving current products and services is a must. If you want to *thrive* beyond the pack, it's not enough. Some of my MBA students researched the effects of "incrementalism," the compulsion to make minor product enhancements that are not coupled with any breakthrough growth strategy. They found that focusing solely on making minor changes to current products and services

- Slows but does not stop the exodus of current customers

- Reinforces commoditization of a company's products and services

- Offers only temporary cost benefits

- Commits the organization's mindset and infrastructure to what are soon yesterday's products, making it more difficult to change later

- Aggravates corporate complacency

So why do corporate leaders compulsively resort to tinkering with current product/service offerings at the expense of new ones? In the short run, it's expedient; it's cheaper and faster to improve on what you're currently doing than to challenge and invest in something different. This is especially true when what is "different" might challenge the habits or cannibalize the products that have brought the leader success in the past. But although incremental improvements are easier to implement, pouring money and time into improving what are becoming commodities diverts management's attention from opportunities to take renewed command of the marketplace. What's the point in building a better buggy whip?

Until its about-face several years ago, Motorola lost billions in revenues and market capitalization to companies such as Nokia because it compulsively kept improving its market-leading but increasingly irrelevant analog technology in place of plunging into digital technology. Kodak put its muscle behind bolstering its traditional cash cow—the high-volume film business—and only recently came to it senses vis-à-vis digital imaging after suffering multibillion-dollar losses in revenues and market cap. These companies survived; many others came too late to the party and no longer exist.[2]

The compulsion of incrementalism appeals to a manager's aversion to risk and his or her fear of taking the first step into unchartered territory. But how can you break from the pack unless you're willing to risk breaking from the pack? As one executive told me, "I'm successful because I do things that my competitors think are risky, but I know it's riskier not to be doing these things." Propping up your business model rather than challenging it in a fast-changing Copycat Economy—that's the biggest risk of all.

4. The Compulsion to Concentrate on Marketing and Sales

First, let's agree that a truly revolutionary marketing concept can sometimes vault a company beyond the pack. Over the past few years, a tiny enterprise called And1 roared past giant Nike in the teen and young adult male basketball shoe market with a marketing effort that was mind-blowing and also hard to replicate. And1 scoured the country for phenomenally athletic and flashy urban street basketball players, putting them together for entertaining "streetball" competitive tours in parks and schoolyards throughout the U.S. The theatrics and skills of the 15 players (all African Americans except for one little white guy) were captured and sold in DVDs and on an ESPN "streetball" series. Thanks to its brand promotion, And1 now generates $180 million in annual revenues and sells its products in 125 countries. The And1 shoe might not be breakthrough, but its marketing package is. In fact, one could argue that the breakthrough product for And1 *is* its marketing.

And1 is an exception. Across industries, most marketing and sales efforts revolve around conventional, known parameters like high-profile endorsers, product placements, ad spots, and persistent sales forces. Do they work? Well, the old complaint "We waste 50 percent of our ad and promotion dollars—we just don't know which 50 percent" still holds true, but there's always hope.

That's why high-school basketball phenom LeBron James got endorsement deals worth more than $100 million with Nike, Upper Deck, Juice Batteries, and Coca-Cola before he played one game in the National Basketball Association. It's why hip-hop star Jay-Z, uber-model Elle Macpherson, and NASCAR idol Dale Earnhardt, Jr., get mega promotion deals. It's why Jimmy Choo shoes paid big-time for product placement on HBO's *Sex and the City*. It's why Sony differentially markets to consumer segments as diverse as Affluents, Alphas (early adopters), Gen X, Gen Y, "Zoomers" (post-55 empty-nesters), and SOHO (small office/home office). It's why CEOs Ed Zander of Motorola and Jonathan Perdue of software start-up Seabridge Software are fanatical about building an aggressive sales culture.

Even so, the track record of sales and marketing initiatives is, at best, mixed. Good marketing and sales efforts will definitely help boost the revenues of a great product, like Apple iPod or Toyota Prius. Huge ad and promotion budgets can sometimes help the sales of a mediocre product, like Budweiser Beer, or a nondescript product, such as Geico car insurance.

On the other hand, over the past decade, companies like GM, Levi Straus, and AOL budgeted huge sums for advertising and promotion and suffered dreadfully. Other giants, including many pharmaceutical, financial services, and full-service insurance companies, have focused substantial resources on aggressive marketing and selling and have seen flat, uninspiring returns. If that's not convincing enough, consider that some of the most popular and successful brands, like Starbucks, Google, Nickelodeon, and Zara, do hardly any advertising and promotion.

This means that despite our love affair with sales and marketing, their impact in a Copycat Economy is cloudy and often turns out nowhere near what we hope it will be. The reality is that pouring money into marketing and sales won't compensate for an uninteresting or commodity product for long. I reiterate: When a product is great and a service is special, innovative marketing and aggressive sales can turbo-charge the organization. But on their own, marketing and sales efforts are lousy predictors of break-from-the-pack success.

Why? First, it's the old "putting lipstick on the pig" problem. Lipstick won't change a sow into an eagle. Because the venerable Goodyear has lagged behind Michelin and Bridgestone in several quality ratings, it sells tires cheaper than its rivals, budgets heavily for promotion, and still trails in the pack. A few years ago, Goodyear's big $60 million ad budget generated some very entertaining commercials, like the one in which parents in different parts of the world were shown enduring their kids' whines in native languages of the universal "Are we there yet?" These were very charming commercials, but according to *The Wall Street Journal*, they didn't convince many people to desert Michelin. As one Goodyear dealer noted, "I didn't have people coming in and saying, 'I saw that cute commercial—let me see some of them tires.'"

Second, in today's Copycat Economy, there are simply too many ads, too many promotions. We're so bombarded by them that they become noise. We often seek to avoid them via TiVo, mute buttons, and pop-up blockers, or we simply turn the magazine page or ignore the billboard. Even when we actually pay attention to the ads, as when watching the Super Bowl, we might laugh with delight and then fail to remember the company or product. When it comes to LeBron, Elle, and those rare personalities whose name alone can carry a global brand, Marian Salzman, chief strategist at ad giant Euro RSCG Worldwide, has concluded, "People are becoming far less susceptible to the power of celebrities who are seen as shills for a brand." In other words, customers are getting a wee bit cynical—and not just about celebrity promoters, but also marketing rhetoric.

Even *where* to advertise is challenging vendors. For all the excitement about the potentials of broadband-based Yahoo!/Google targeted ads and Internet Protocol TV (with customized, on-demand capabilities), the ultimate impact of online marketing remains unclear. Only a tiny percentage of ad and marketing dollars is being dropped on broadband. Pepsi North America, for example, allocates only 5 percent of its total ad budget to online advertising.

Where does the rest of the budget go? Primarily to conventional TV, which is itself a problem. TV network audiences are decreasing, and the amount that advertisers pay to reach them grows. Scott

Donaton, editor of *Advertising Age*, is baffled about why so many companies copy each other by spending up to 80 percent of their ad budgets on network TV, thus sustaining what he calls a "corrupt" model. He rattles off the symptoms: a shrinking market, no guarantee that a TV show will be watched, and the possibility that a last-minute competitor will get ad space for less money. Why do companies do it? Fear and blind faith, Donaton says, both totally irrational.

To be sure, marketing and sales are important functions for any organization, but not to the point that they become "magic bullet" compulsions. The biggest problem with the compulsion to throw money at these functions is that it drains attention and urgency from the effort to develop break-from-the-pack products and services. For example, despite the growing onslaught of lower-priced generic drugs, many large, financially troubled pharmaceuticals have compulsively redoubled their heavy marketing efforts (more TV ads, more sales reps in doctors' offices) to prop up their higher priced products. It's not working well.

A bank executive tells me off the record that his bank would be better served by figuring out new compelling services than relying on me-too campaigns of "free" check writing, online banking, and 24/7 phone service, which the customer winds up paying for anyway via hidden charges. KFC would have been better off developing a truly healthful product line consistent with emerging eating trends rather than attempting a series of TV ads (short-circuited by consumer protest) that were underwhelmingly described by a KFC vice president this way: "Consumers will be surprised to learn that they can enjoy fried chicken as part of a healthy, balanced diet." Chrysler would have been better off focusing on making more appealing cars than spending big bucks for the ultimately scuttled "Lingerie Bowl 2004," a Super Bowl panty-football game played by fashion models in their underwear and coached by ex-NFL player and drug abuser Lawrence Taylor.

5. The Compulsion to Get Bigger

Growth is a terrific goal—when it's a natural consequence of a company's forward motion. But the compulsion to get bigger in the belief that if you're bigger you're better and more likely to steamroll through the pack is a myth in a Copycat Economy. If size was the best predictor of success, then GM, Kodak, and United Airlines would be at the top of the investment food chain.

The benefits of bigness—scale, scope, synergy, and cross-marketing—are genuine, and I've seen companies put them to good use. Nevertheless, the impact of these benefits has been grossly misunderstood and overestimated. Before the company's final collapse, AT&T president David Dorman sent out a memo declaring, "I've been preaching only one gospel, and that's the gospel of scale. We're going to use our size and scale and leverage it in ways no one else can match." Shortly thereafter, AT&T's market capitalization sank to a new low. Companies that have used size and scale to make and sell a me-too commodity a little more cheaply or market it with more resources and leverage buy a little time. But a sclerotic bureaucracy, runaway costs, declining profits, flat earnings, and dipping stock valuations are inevitable for most. Perhaps that is why more than 50 percent of 1980's Fortune 500 no longer exist.

When large companies do break from the pack, their success is often wrongly attributed to their size. A megacorporation like GE does reap benefits from distribution efficiencies and leverage with suppliers, but CEO Jeff Immelt has used its size primarily to propel innovation and contrarian thinking, not scale and marketing muscle. "We can take some risks because we've got enough size to keep reinvesting and ultimately be successful," Immelt has said.

That is simply not what many big companies do. As corporations get bigger, their leaders spend more time merely managing the organization. During the disastrous Carly Fiorina reign at HP, when the company's market cap sank 55 percent over a five-year span, a company veteran told me, "It used to be about the technology and the products; now I spend most of my time in Dilbert-like meetings about management." The sheer size and complexity of such companies make it easier to camouflage elements that are destroying value and harder to pinpoint small (but potentially big) opportunities that demand fast investment and rapid response.

In the pharmaceutical arena, for example, there used to exist hundreds of "major" drug companies. Now, as a result of incessant consolidation, there remain a few behemoths that expend most of their management attention and resources in heavy promotion and sales, minor modifications of existing drugs, and cost-cutting efforts. Instead of seeking rapid, incessant innovation based on hard research, imaginative intuition, and trial-and-error experimentation, they become obsessed with the organization itself: corporate finance, restructuring, merger and acquisition issues, business planning, human resources analysis, and marketing analysis. Unsurprisingly, the financial track record of the huge pharmas is generally poor. The plethora of smaller, more niche-oriented, risk-oriented biotech companies like Genentech, Amgen, NitroMed, and Genzyme has cornered a healthy chunk of the market on the breakthrough new drugs and therapies.

That's why Jack Welch, during his reign at GE, said that one of his biggest goals was to ensure that GE always have a "small company soul," and why Bill Gates has often said that one of his top priorities is to make sure that bureaucracy and size—the dis-economies of scale—don't kill Microsoft. Wells Fargo CEO Richard Kovacevich (whose company's profits are significantly higher than those of much larger players like J. P. Morgan Chase) concurs: "I don't believe in economies of scale. You don't get better by being bigger. You get worse."

As I explain in further detail in Chapter 10, the key predictors of corporate success and shareholder value are not the size of a company's tangible assets, but the size of its intangible assets like its speed in execution and customer care, its culture of constant innovation, and its mobility and agility in capitalizing on fresh, fleeting opportunities. As the Brookings Institution found, 80 percent of shareholder value generated by the S&P 500 can be traced to intangibles. In other words, to predict who's going to break from the pack, look at who's got the quickest adaptivity and imagination, not who's got the biggest numbers on the balance sheet.

If your company is small in tangibles but big in intangibles, you can skyrocket with venture capital and sales the way that Google and RIM (the Blackberry people) have done. If you're big on both tangibles and intangibles, as with Dell, GE, Samsung, Virgin, and Toyota, you can happily leverage the benefits of both factors. If you're big in tangibles and lousy on intangibles, all bets are off.

I recently consulted for a multibillion-dollar company whose tangibles were awe-inspiring: a gargantuan balance sheet, a substantial payroll, a huge capital budget, and an immense product line. But this company's intangibles are miniscule relative to its size. The company is marked by little innovation in product or delivery, paralysis in decision making, archaic information systems, glacial bureaucracy, conforming employees, and hypercautious top managers. The result: a net income loss for each of the last eight quarters and a market valuation significantly lower than that of many smaller but more adventurous competitors.

One last issue that many managers don't seem to "get": In general, success leads to bigger size, *not vice versa*. Companies that break from the pack get bigger naturally—and *then* they can enjoy the benefits of scale, synergy, and leverage as byproducts of their size, even as they continue to exploit their intangibles for further growth.

The compulsion to get bigger often manifests itself in mergers and acquisitions. Chapter 10 is devoted entirely to describing how to effectively use consolidation to break from the pack. But the reason the majority of big acquisitions fail to achieve their goals is that after the deal is done, the commodity remains intact. Nothing inherently changes when two dull companies selling commodities merge to form a larger, duller company selling more commodities. They might sell them a little more cheaply with more marketing muscle, but all they are doing is buying time—even as they wrestle with integration, debt, new costs, and bigger bureaucracies. When the external market changes, the newly bulked-up company finds it even more difficult to change.

"Get bigger" is a serious compulsion. Pundits, community leaders, media professionals, and business school professors often worship bigness and glorify people who run the most enormous enterprises, no matter how regularly those people fail to make their companies successful. As deposed executives as diverse as Carly Fiorina, George Shaheen (Webvan), and Jack Greenberg (McDonald's) have learned, a "bigger is better" mindset might lead to bigger, but it doesn't necessarily lead to better.

6. The Compulsion to Control

To revitalize your company, you've decided you're going to be "tough," a "no-nonsense leader" who will "take no prisoners." Your assumption is that a steady blast of autocracy will squeeze out inefficiencies and somehow force people to produce better output, which presumably will make your company overcome the impact of its commoditized products and copycatted services.

The compulsion to control, centralize, and apply pressure from the top appears alluringly professional but, in reality, is based on four erroneous, anachronistic, and fairly primitive premises.

1. Profitability issues are divorced from people issues.

2. Strong leadership means rigid hierarchy and domineering leadership.

3. "Empowering" people is okay as long as it doesn't interfere with effectively running a business—which really means "Run all decisions by me first."

4. Smart people at the top make smarter decisions than do people in the trenches or out in the field.

Perhaps these premises once made practical sense, when employees weren't expected to think, middle managers weren't called on to innovate, competition was limited and predictable, consumers' expectations were low and their choices circumscribed, technological breakthroughs were rare, and standardization and mass marketing of products made sound strategic sense. But today those assumptions make for complete dysfunction.

In a Copycat Economy, competitive vigor depends on the leaders' capacity to optimize employees' intellectual capital for bold, dramatic, and ruthlessly efficient effect. When Maury Myers engineered a dramatic turnaround at Waste Management in 2003, he declared that his first step would be regaining employees' trust. He did so by sharing sensitive corporate data with them and by including them in key decisions. Myers' advice: "Address employees' concerns before those of Wall Street. If they're not onboard, your turnaround will fail." The exact same mindset—involve employees in creating service value and performance gains—drove Gordon Bethune's remarkable turnaround of Continental Airlines from worst to best or near best in factors like on-time departures, baggage handling, customer satisfaction, employee satisfaction, and ultimately revenues and stock value.

Growing a business—and breaking from the pack—is all about mobilizing and encouraging people, not intimidating and suppressing them. As GE chairman Jeff Immelt says, "If you want to create a growth culture, you have to nurture people and not make them fight so goddam hard to get any idea through the door."

Are Myers, Bethune and Immelt "tough"? You bet. But like Carol Bartz of Autodesk; John Chambers of Cisco Systems; Herb Kelleher, who built Southwest Air; and Bernard Rapoport, who built the highly successful American Income Life Insurance company, they know that being "tough" doesn't mean intimidating people. It means having uncompromising standards and expecting people to take personal responsibility for their decisions. "Turning the screws" is not the same as nailing someone to the wall. Instead, it means ratcheting up everyone's sense of urgency and fostering collaborative effort in the face of openly discussed competitive pressures. "Professionalism" and "business savvy" are not limited to the corner office; they become everyone's objectives. Intuit CEO Steve Bennett has a blunt conclusion to this discussion: "Put people first and strategy second."

I have found more than a few managers (especially in privately held, family-run businesses) who still instinctively buy into the compulsion to control. In the short term, tightening controls and increasing pressure might indeed uncover some inefficiencies and get people to hustle, out of sheer fear. Short-term financials might actually improve. They did for a time even under the coercive reigns of Al Dunlap and Frank Lorenzo. Yet in the long run, such autocracy kills risk, initiative, and personal accountability—the very qualities you need to break from the pack. "What happens is that fear becomes the main driver," a manager who survived this kind of regime told me. "Everyone worries about their personal success. People become obsessed with 'process'—the details of where paper goes, how it is handled, following rules—rather than outcome." Even worse, after the company's health is destroyed, the "tough" leader is either dispatched with a multimillion-dollar severance package or gets a glorious new job where he can once again knock heads together and do damage.

But attitudes are changing. Where "tough" leaders used to be lionized, they are now being challenged, sometimes even ridiculed. Consider this employee memo written by Doug Monahan, the founder of marketing firm Sunset Direct, publicized by the magazine *Business 2.0:* "I expect my computers to be used for work only. I expect my phones to be used for work only. Should you receive a personal e-mail, I expect the e-mail either not be answered, or a brief note telling whoever is sending you e-mails at work to stop immediately. Should I go through machines, which I assure you, I will be doing, and I find anything to the contrary, you will be terminated immediately. For those who think I am kidding, and do not get with this program, I will promise you that by Christmas Eve 8:00 you will be gone." For this gem, *Business 2.0* declared Monahan the winner of the "worst human resource decision" of 2004.

7. The Compulsion to Ask Customers What They Want

Yes, every company should be keen to its customers' desires and attitudes. But the compulsion to ask customers what they want can leave you reactive and fossilized. Breaking from the pack requires you to lead customers to a place they didn't ask to go and didn't know existed.

When a company asks customers what they want out of its current products, many consumers provide a rational and useful response. They might suggest a more compact size, a new color, or a new feature that makes the product easier to use. Customer surveys led Heinz to change the design of bottles so that the opening is at the bottom of the bottle instead of the top, and that was helpful. Customer surveys helped Best Buy to design a proprietary PC. In both cases, the improvements led to a small increase in sales, although the results did not serve as a catalyst for newer, more radical products, and competitors quickly redesigned their products to match the improvements. Welcome back to Commodity Hell. Customers can tell you what they like today, and they can tell you their reactions to your current products. That is good information. But customers are lousy predictors of what they *will* like, prefer, expect, and need tomorrow, and that's where the gold lies.

Imagine if Fred Smith, the founder of FedEx, had run a focus group in the 1970s asking people if they'd be willing to spend $10 to get a letter to a recipient overnight instead of the dime they were spending to send a first-class letter to a destination in two or three days. Fifteen years ago, how many people would have volunteered that they would spend $300 for a Palm, or that they would even "need" a Palm, much less a Blackberry? Before Starbucks, how many consumers would have assured Howard Schultz they would stand in line to spend $4 for a cup of coffee in a paper cup? Who asked for Jiffy-Lube or ESPN before those concepts were introduced to us?[3]

As I reiterate throughout this book, market leaders who break from the pack pull the customer to new places. They don't simply respond to the consumer: They take some chances that push them past their market research. They don't always succeed, but they'll have enough pilots out there that overall they will turn out winners.

No industry does more consumer and market research than radio. Yet listenership is down, advertisers are nervous, and radio stock is soft. I submit that one of the major reasons is the "research."

Every station does the same research and gets the same results, which leads to me-too radio content, which means that stations in any given format sound pretty much the same. The research has contributed to risk-averse, predictable content, even as radio executives profess bafflement about why there is less brand loyalty to any station. Yet when the unpredictable, iconoclastic Howard Stern was on "terrestrial" (non-satellite) radio, he commanded up to 12 million fanatical listeners nationwide. As *Fortune* magazine has pointed out, "AM/FM radio has left itself vulnerable to satellite and other media not because it has too much out-of-control talent like Stern, but because it has too little on-air talent."

Consider a typical customer survey for an auto insurance firm. It would include questions like, "Are our premiums competitive? Did you receive good value? Would you prefer a different billing arrangement? Was our staff courteous? Was the claims adjuster knowledgeable? What was the overall quality of our service? What can we improve to better meet your needs?" Every insurance company asks these questions, and they get similar vanilla answers to them.

In 1995, Progressive Insurance discovered that these surveys were not helping stave off price wars and me-too competition. Accordingly, the company changed its approach. It reinvented itself with a unique business design built around radical and transparent speed in auto insurance, which included Web-based and 24/7 knowledge centers that give prospective customers fast, hassle-free customized rate quotes and real-time comparisons with prices from four leading competitors. Progressive invested in extensive employee training and advanced computer tools that allowed it to sharply reduce the hassle and time that customers spend submitting claims and waiting for checks. Progressive further upped the ante on claims speed to the point that when a damaged vehicle is brought to a Progressive service center, the policyholder receives a pager and keys to a rental car within minutes. The result of this obsession on speed? Progressive exploded from the auto insurance pack with sustained double-digit returns on capital, earnings per share, and market-cap growth. The key to its phenomenal growth, says one of my students who studied the company, is that "Progressive went beyond what the market stated it wanted or expected."

Expecting salvation from hiring a consultant or ad agency to ask customers what they want or what they'll buy is a very expensive way to feed a compulsion. "We become slaves to demographics, to market research, to focus groups," says media mogul Barry Diller. "We produce what the numbers tell us to produce. Gradually, in this dizzying chase, our senses lose feeling and our instincts dim, corroded with safe action"—which, of course, is anything but safe.

8. The Compulsion to Embrace Organizational Fads

When a company gets mired in the pack, nervous executives sometimes resort to adopting well-accepted, high-profile programs that revolve around "total quality," "diversity," "conflict management," and such. Behind the compulsion to embrace these fads is the unspoken assumption that these initiatives will somehow turn the company's fortunes around. If they don't, at least it appeared that management tried and was socially responsible to boot.

Research data shows that the success rate of such programs is about same as overweight people's success with get-thin-quick programs. Good intentions and organizational programs don't get you to the head of the pack, and many companies have failed even after investing in faddish initiatives.

I recognize that challenging this compulsion stirs strong reactions, many of them negative. As a monthly columnist for *Management Review* during the 1990s, I wrote an article called "Ten Reasons Why TQM Doesn't Work," an unsentimental critique of the Total Quality Management craze at the time. The whole idea of total quality, I argued, is really just plain effective management: doing whatever it takes to creatively, eclectically, courageously produce a quality organization, a quality culture, a quality product, and quality people. But "TQM" had become a slick billion-dollar industry with multiple products employing myriad high-priced salespeople and consultants. Research showed that only 20–30 percent of "TQM" interventions had produced significant or even tangible improvements in quality, productivity, competitiveness, or financial returns.

The column provoked a chorus of indignant howls from TQM trainers, consultants, program developers, and in-house "quality" staff. But real-live managers, those with direct profit-and-loss responsibility, loved my article. They complained they had to devote precious time and resources to comply with a rigid TQM bureaucracy without seeing any serious payoff.

There's more. All practicing managers know that quality is vitally important, but quality itself is no predictor of corporate success. "Zero defects" is simply the price of admission in a Copycat Economy. Customers *assume* that the products you provide them will work, that you'll meet specs, that you'll deliver on time, and that you'll be available for some help after sale. Without quality, you're doomed, but quality itself won't break you out of the pack. In my column, I quoted a consultant whose biting comments on quality programs still ring true: "Automobile manufacturers strive to improve fuel efficiency. Detergent makers become intent on improving the whitening power of their products. While these certainly are not unwise targets for improvement, they are unlikely to move a second-tier firm into a leadership position."

The same analysis can be applied to TQM's newer sibling, Six Sigma. For one thing, it's interesting that some companies like Xerox and Ford, both of whom trumpet their Six Sigma standards, have lower quality ratings than competitors Canon and Toyota, who don't invest in Six Sigma but are obsessive about quality as an integral part of their approach to the business. Even more damning is the fact that apart from a few well-known success stories like GE under Jack Welch, the data shows that very few Six Sigma interventions have any positive impact on stock value (one study suggests about 10 percent). Quality and Six Sigma are good things, but not if you compulsively view them as "magic bullet" saviors.[4]

This is all part and parcel of a bigger trend. The research shows that many other much-ballyhooed programs like reengineering, diversity, interpersonal communications, and conflict management have had very little impact on actual metrics of growth, profitability, and share price.

For example, despite the claim of the multibillion-dollar diversity industry that diversity yields higher performance and productivity, the evidence is anecdotal, highly questionable in its methodology, or not documented at all, even in corporations that spend big bucks on it. In fact, after reviewing the empirical literature, MIT's Thomas Keane concluded, "The business case rhetoric for diversity is simply naïve and overdone. There are no strong positive or negative effects of gender or racial diversity on business performance."

How can diversity not be important? After all, if you want to appeal to a Hispanic market, or a single female market, or an urban gay market, or a Christian music market, or a computer geek market, or a young tattooed-and-body-pierced market, doesn't it makes sense to have employees who are part of those subcultures and who can speak their languages? Well, it makes sense, but according to the research, it doesn't seem to make a significant difference in actual corporate success. For example, even an Anglo who has the initiative to study Spanish, learn about the Latino niche, and seek the right consultants and partners can appeal to the Hispanic market just as effectively, or more so, than someone with a Spanish surname whose grandparents emigrated to the U.S. from Peru 40 years ago.

Further, diversity, per se, doesn't automatically engender bold, innovative thinking and courageous execution. A "diverse" but unimaginative, hypercautious management team is not one you want to bet on.[5] Besides, because 70 percent of new hires in 2010 will be women, minorities, or immigrants (Canada's workforce is already there), there is an inevitability to all this even if no diversity programs are initiated.

Let's put it together hypothetically: In the music recording industry, Six Sigma and reengineering might help a music company improve the production efficiencies and quality of commercial CDs. Diversity might make its workforce ethnically varied. Open communication might reign among its management teams. But the music industry's basic business model is still dying. The commercial CD will still become economically irrelevant in a few years, and if they don't do something big about it, big recording companies will be another herd of dead dinosaurs in the timeline of free markets—faddish programs notwithstanding.

Advocates of many programs assume good things will somehow automatically happen if companies implement them. That's the sign of ideology, not disciplined business. As Colin Powell advised, "Fit no stereotypes. Don't chase the latest management fads." It's good advice for anyone seeking to simultaneously reverse the tide of commoditization and avoid the lure of compulsion.

9. The Compulsion to Use Legal and Political Force to Protect Your Business

If all else fails, invest in attack lawyers. That's what Big Music did. Or seek protectionism the way Big Steel did. Both industries are still in big trouble. To be sure, the realities of global competition mean that companies must aggressively litigate when competitors do something illegal. They are wise to support professional associations that exercise political influence with legislators. They are prudent to contribute to candidates for political office that are sympathetic to their problems. But if they rely primarily on legal and political force for competitive advantage, they are doomed.

I learned this truth firsthand in 1988 when I led a two-day seminar with members of the subcabinet of the Mexican government representing telecommunications, transportation, and the mail system. I spoke about the inevitabilities of open markets, the potentials of a then-proposed North American Free Trade Agreements, and the dangers to those who ignore them. The men (they were all men) reacted with blatant complacency. Gringo, you don't know Mexico, they implied. We've been cocooned by government protectionism and cronyism since our Revolution, so none of this free-market pap will affect us. Nothing I said— about global trends, the potential for economic and social development, or even the determination of their new president Carlos Salinas de Gortari to enforce privatization— swayed these men. Yet within two years, most were gone, victims of the upheaval that occurred as the protective blanket began to lift.

Lawsuit and protectionism strategies drain a company of resources, money, vision, and the urgency to challenge and reinvent itself in the face of new technological and competitive realities. Traditional barriers to entry, while still occurring, are becoming less obstructive in a global Copycat Economy. The capacity for any entrepreneur or organization to access global risk capital and emerging technologies—coupled with the enormous opportunities for outsourcing and global alliances—means that any company, regardless of size, even in capital-intensive businesses, can now become a player. Trying to build legal and protectionist fortresses around these realities almost invariably keeps you trapped within the fortress you created. Protectionism as a strategic weapon is illusory because its "victories" never last; worse, it keeps companies stuck. It's never a "temporary" strategy, either; it's like an addictive drug, with each dose increasingly less effective.

The same can be said for litigation. The music industry's lawsuits against grandmothers and 12-year-olds will stop some people from file sharing, and, yes, there is merit to pursuing the few exceptionally high-volume file-sharers. But then what? Every time the industry sues one group or shuts down a website, 20 new digital sources for file sharing pop up that are more legally and technologically bullet-proof. Besides, many of the sites are moving offshore, away from the long arm of U.S. law. At the end of the day, the *Wall Street Journal* has queried, "How viable is a business model based on suing your customers?" Not very viable. The legal attacks do little to stem the demise of a commoditized business, even as they do a lot to alienate potential customers.

In the case of music, I propose that many of those alienated customers will gravitate to any vendor that capitalizes on the technologies rather than defies them, and makes those technologies more user-friendly, hassle-free, and fun. The legal music platforms at Apple, Yahoo!, Napster, and Starbucks should be *starting points* in corporate innovations that embrace cutting-edge file-sharing technologies and take them to new (legal) realms that excite and delight customers. More computer-phobic people will start downloading authorized music for the first time—and paying. Gladly. Couple this with radically new alliances with artists and corporations to build new products, from branded clothing to branded artist tours, to cellular ring tones, to customized corporate music, to niche-oriented small-scale releases, to a wider menu of jukebox subscriptions, to wireless over-the-air (OTA) music sales, and you've got potentially big new revenue streams.

But if you're stuck in a lawyer/lobbyist compulsion, you won't aggressively go these routes. You won't even see the possibilities because you'll be forever protecting the shrink-wrapped CD. The alternative for Big Music, regardless of unanimous Supreme Court rulings against file-sharing sites, is grim. Recent data indicates that after all the litigation, illegal file sharing today is at an all-time high. Meanwhile, *Rolling Stone* reports that customers bought 48 million fewer albums in 2005 than in 2004, yielding a disastrous 21percent drop from the industry's peak in 2000. Under these circumstances, clinging to a lawyer/lobbyist mindset is lethal, regardless of which lawsuits you win. As singer Gwen Stefani's manager Jim Guerinot says: "The major (recording) labels want to say the glass is half full. I think everybody is getting the message: You better get a fucking smaller glass. The music business is a different game."

I'll wager that your business is now a different game, and attempts to deny it with lawsuits will inevitably fail regardless of your company's size. It was inevitable that Microsoft would stop its fruitless obsession with prosecuting software pirates in China. Today Microsoft continues the pursuit of particularly large, egregious thieves, but now most of the company's efforts lie in long-term product development and marketing alliances with Chinese partners, a much more lucrative alternative.

It was inevitable that big wireless carriers like Verizon and Sprint would, in the face of numerous consumer complaints and lawsuits, give up their legal blockades to cellphone number portability. Now that you and I can switch from one carrier to another and still keep our phone numbers, the carriers will have to figure out fresh, compelling ways to build customer loyalty.

It was inevitable that the National Association of Realtors, under threat of a Justice Department lawsuit, would have to drop the practice of limiting the home listings that some discount online brokers could display on their Web sites. Now intermediaries like the NAR will have to figure out new ways to create value for their customers.

Despite their huge lobbying muscle, it is inevitable that the giant telcos and cable companies will not be able to stop the growing movement of municipalities providing ultra-cheap Wi-Fi wireless high-speed Internet. Despite its armies of lobbyists, it is inevitable that American Airlines will not be able to preserve its long-haul flight monopoly against Southwest Air in the Dallas area. The protectionist Wright amendment, which prevents Southwest Air from launching domestic long-haul flights from its Love Field hub in the Dallas area, will be soon repealed.

A company that is serious about wanting to break from the pack always proceeds "as if" there is no "protection" anymore because, ultimately, there isn't. Feed your lawyers and lobbyists, but don't compulsively let them determine your strategy.

10. The Compulsion to Do Anything as Long as You're Doing Something

Many businesspeople respond to the Copycat Economy with manic bursts of action—any action, regardless of whether it's coherent, purposeful, disciplined, or inspiring, and regardless of whether it's copycat or break-from-the-pack. Such actions can be acquisitions, divestments, "back to basics" initiatives, restructuring, downsizing, outsourcing, new alliances, new technology purchases, customer surveys, or fresh ad campaigns. It doesn't matter whether there's any strategic discipline, due diligence, or follow-up execution, as long as action happens.

Incredibly, many boards of directors and industry pundits applaud this in the name of "making tough decisions" and "taking charge." But the whirlwind of action arrests real results. Opportunism and short-term fixes predominate as the leader tries a wild mixture of compulsions 1–9. Short-term spikes in performance sometimes occur, but they're not sustainable. Eventually, the chaos catches up.

Sometimes, in the name of "innovation," leaders advocate a "rip up the company" or "let's try anything" approach, abetted by management gurus who tell them to "start a revolution" or "blow up the organization." It's easier to sell and follow such advice than to confront the gritty detail work required to position an organization for breakthrough.

Sometimes the leader gives up any pretension of knowing what to do. His or her message to the troops becomes "Do whatever it takes to get me the numbers Wall Street wants." Well, one might as well pour gasoline on the fire of lousy management because at that point, one of two things will occur: One alternative was nicely put by the *Economist*'s description of troubled regional German bank WestLB in 2003: "In essence, WestLB has been a second-tier bank in an over-banked market, desperately seeking profits, whatever the source and whether or not it understood how they arose."

The second alternative is more pernicious: Telling the troops to do whatever it takes to get the numbers means the troops will do whatever it takes to get the numbers, whether or not it makes sense financially or legally. Creative product development might take second place to creative accounting. According to 2004 research performed by my colleague Nicole Jackson and me, across every industry, the message to "get the numbers" generated spurious inflation of key corporate financials with "innovations" like channel stuffing (forcing wholesalers to accept more goods to boost a vendor's sales data), phony off-balance sheet partnerships to hide debt, and imaginatively misleading financial statements that inflated profits.

Today this alternative is a bit less fashionable, but a recent survey indicated that more than 50 percent of CFOs in public companies still feel pressure from their CEOs to make the numbers, no questions asked. When a company goes down this track, it's exceedingly hard to stop the train; when the inevitable setbacks begin, the dysfunctional actions are accelerated at a frenzied rate, as occurred with Enron, Parmalat, and WorldCom.

It's no surprise that such whirlwind actions are dysfunctional and destructive. The effect is like a runner injecting himself with a shot of methedrine before the race. The consequences: a quick burst off the blocks, flashing glory, and collapse shortly thereafter. You can't even stay with the pack.

Beyond Compulsion

Remember that there's nothing inherently wrong with many of the actions described in this chapter. They ought to be part of any good manager's arsenal. But they become compulsions when you believe in their infallibility to propel you to the front of the pack. They will not. Only when you deviate from conventional wisdom, only when you challenge the status quo with exciting, meaningful alternatives will you break free of the pack and win in the Copycat Economy.

The remainder of this book tells you how do just that—by approaching your business in a vastly different manner and creating fresh, compelling, radical value for your customers and investors.

Endnotes

[1] GM's urgent cash flow needs in first quarter 2006 led the company to put up its majority stake in GMAC for sale.

[2] In an April 2006 interview with the *Wall Street Journal*, CEO Anne Mulcahey of Xerox described the necessity—and difficulty—of her company's transition from traditional copiers to new digital technologies. "It's always more attractive to stay in the old technology. Always. But you'll be going out of business."

[3] Once again, customer input should always be solicited, but leaders should remember that it is primarily a reactive attitude. I am helping a tiny startup software company in beta testing a potentially disruptive application product. Once the first beta sample of customers understood the product, they were truly impressed, and they offered some excellent suggestions on ways to make it more attractive to an end user. But the power of the product was that the customers didn't

expect it, didn't ask for it, didn't conceive of its possibilities, didn't initiate it—but now they're excited to test it in their workplace. And then they will give us more feedback.

[4] In fact, one study concluded that 91 percent of large companies with Six Sigma programs have trailed the S & P 500. Elsewhere, the July 24, 2006, issue of *Fortune Magazine* explained the poor returns this way: "One of the chief problems of Six Sigma is that it is narrowly designed to fix an existing process, allowing little room for new ideas or an entirely different approach. [Peoples' attentions are] devoted to driving defects down to 3.4 per million and not on coming up with new products or disruptive technologies."

[5] I suspect that a team that has members with diverse styles and backgrounds and a common commitment to audacious goals would be more likely to succeed than a team that simply fits conventional definitions of "diversity." Steve Jobs, in describing the early Macintosh breakthroughs, said: "I think part of what made Macintosh great was that the people working on it were musicians, and poets, and artists, and zoologists, and historians who also happened to be the best computer scientists in the world."

3

THE MADONNA EFFECT AND THE WILLIE NELSON PRINCIPLE: THE POWER OF CALCULATED REINVENTION

Learning from Madonna

Whether or not you're a Madonna fan, there's no denying the fact that, as an artistic enterprise, she's been spectacularly successful. Not only has she sold 140 million albums over the past 25 years, but she's also garnered mammoth sales from concerts, movies, books, and videos. In November 2005, when (according to the Drudge Report) she "stole the show" at the MTV Europe Music Awards, Robbie Williams—who won Best Male—said: "She's an absolute legend and makes us all look like amateurs."

All this in spite of the fact that she's not a particularly great singer, dancer, actor, or writer. Yet as one critic wrote recently, Madonna "still stands as the most durable pop symbol of her generation—and potentially the next." If you find her annoying, consider her annoying ability to elicit such a reaction after all these years. Consider her extraordinary staying power in a notoriously fickle, faddish, and imitative industry.

What is Madonna's secret? Despite what her critics say, it's not media manipulation, smoke-and-mirrors marketing, or shock. Sure, some of that exists to get the word out, but snazzy promotion isn't the reason for her success. The answer can be found in the title of her sold-out tour in 2004: "Reinvention." Alvin Hall of the 2003 BBC production *World's Most Powerful: Madonna or Oprah?* threw his final vote for Madonna based on her "extraordinary ability to reinvent herself *in anticipation* (my emphasis) of many fashions."

Madonna's brand relies on crossing over from mainstream to the margin and showing everyone else how to do it, too. She reinvents herself by keeping her antennae attuned to the culture, norms, and behaviors that interesting fringe groups are currently experimenting with, groups that represent the still-raw material for tomorrow's mass movements. She then discards her still-successful "products" and persona, puts her personal stamp on her new material, packages it with imagination and organizational finesse, and then leads the masses to it.

Throughout this process, she stays grounded and disciplined. She's market driven even as she drives the market. As she puts it: "You have to find a way to be creative and have the freedom to do what you want to do, while also being aware of what the market demands and what people like. It's a fine line to walk."

She's walked the line, and we all know the results: The world has watched Madonna evolve through the stages of "virgin," good girl gone bad, "material girl," "boy toy," Marilyn Monroe blond bombshell with body-armor lingerie, female power and sexuality figure (including everything from aerobics and weight training to erotic dominatrix imagery), media maven, androgyny, hard-charging career woman, AIDS and gay-rights activist, doting working mother and children's book writer, and spiritual seeker, among others. With each incarnation, Madonna takes her audience to the edge of conventional wisdom, far enough to be considered a rebel and iconoclast, but not so far ahead as to seem bizarre and irrelevant. She ushers us into an area that will become "conventional" one day but that for many isn't quite there yet. She leaves her audience thrilled, provoked, aroused, uncomfortable, outraged, overjoyed, incensed, or titillated—*but never indifferent.*

Jeffrey Katzenberg, the former head of Disney Studios and DreamWorks Animation, described Madonna this way: "She is always evolving; she never stands still. Every two years she comes up with a new look, a new way of presenting herself, a new attitude, a new act, and a new design. And every time it is successful. There is this constant genesis." That, my friends, is the protean mantra that applies to any business that wants to break from the pack over the next decade.

That is also why Madonna-type reinvention is much harder than it looks. It takes particular foresight and courage for any organization to let go of what's working today *before* it becomes imitated and commoditized, and forge a new identity consistent with emerging trends and opportunities. IBM CEO Sam Palmisano would probably be surprised to be compared favorably with a pop diva, but the leadership that he is attempting to provide at IBM with the massive e-business on-demand strategy is an example of what I call the "Madonna Effect."

When Lou Gerstner handed the reins of IBM to Palmisano in February 2002, the company was rejuvenated and prosperous. IBM's business model, designed around software, servers, and e-business technology services, was viable. Palmisano could have incrementally built on this business model for years, perhaps by employing some of the compulsions outlined in Chapter 2. The pack, including Dell, Wipro, HP, EDS, SAP, Oracle, Microsoft, BearingPoint, and Accenture, not to mention a thousand smaller niche outfits, would have eventually caught up with all or selected segments of IBM's business, but by then Palmisano would have been ready to retire with honors, leaving his successor to inherit the mess.

Instead, Palmisano has been working feverishly to transform a healthy IBM for future domination in a multitrillion-dollar information technology market. He refuses to sit idly and wait for the pack to catch up with IBM. "We have an opportunity to set the agenda in our industry," he says. As a 2005 *Business Week* online memo notes, "He's betting that by harnessing technology to improve clients' performance rather than simply hawking machines or providing routine tech services such as managing PCs, IBM won't be hobbled by the ongoing commoditization of tech and tech services." E-business on demand is just the sort of big-paradigm hook on which to hang a transformation of a $90 billion colossus like IBM. It integrates IBM with its partners, suppliers, and customers through a shared infrastructure that allows these stakeholders to access virtually any computational resource in IBM's arsenal. E-business on demand can potentially help IBM's corporate customers save huge amounts of money by standardizing all their computing needs and by allowing IBM to seamlessly deposit constant, cost-saving technological improvements into its customers' systems, while billing them only for actual time spent on IBM servers and other equipment—just the way a utility would. Corporate customers receive access to huge batches of IBM's industrial knowledge. Manufacturing companies can get help designing customized consumer products. Pharmaceutical companies can use IBM's resources to speed up their FDA approval cycle. Airlines can receive mathematically based marketing tools to boost repeat business among frequent flyers. IBM's current mainframe, software, server, and e-business consulting services will gradually become part of an enormous "grid" network that is transforming the way IBM operates and invests. Earnings reports show those plans are on track. In 2005, business-transformation services revenues rose 25 percent to $900 million, and bookings rose 192 percent.

Is it a problem that IBM is "ahead of the trend," as one analyst complained, and that "they've focused mostly on the part customers aren't so interested in yet"? I doubt it. As Cisco System CEO John Chambers puts it, "Sam is aiming to go where the market's going—not to where it's been."

This is the Madonna Effect. Not having to change, doing it anyway. Looking in the distance and aiming for where the market is going. Being willing to take some risk for huge potential payoffs tomorrow, knowing that not taking a risk means that inevitably the pack will catch up. Letting go of what won't work tomorrow even if it brings in sales today. Staying passionately persistent and honestly walking the talk in leading the enormous organizational changes in systems and processes. Being willing to tolerate the criticisms and potshots from those who think you're nuts.

Whatever your business is, you can employ the Madonna Effect. The winners who stay ahead of the pack over the long haul are following the path Madonna exemplifies, whether they know it or not. Here's a little self-test for you. Ask yourself how you would rate as a Madonna. If you were to emulate her business tactics, here is what you'd be doing:

- You'd be constantly changing, way before being "forced" to change by the marketplace. In fact, you'd be restless with sameness; you'd never allow yourself to get locked into any predictable persona or position. Customers and investors would agree that they don't know what you will come up with next, but they can hardly wait for the next iteration.

- You'd monitor trends in the distance, and you'd stay ahead of them. You'd capitalize on those trends to "get there first."

- You'd reinvent yourself even when your current products and services are popular, before others imitate and catch up. If the opportunities made sense, you wouldn't be afraid to change, even if it meant cannibalizing or abandoning what's making you successful today. You'd even be willing to risk losing that part of your "audience" that likes you as you are.

- You'd be constantly experimenting. You'd be stretching current parameters; you'd take chances. Observers would agree that the words *dated* and *safe* and *cautious* don't describe you.

- You'd always invite and challenge your customers to change with you, and you'd show them how.

- You'd be deliberately provocative. You'd try to stir people's reactions and emotions—from delight to fear to loathing, but not indifference. You'd understand that if there is no emotional reaction by the market to your products and services, you're not going far enough.

- You'd always be connected to reality. You'd stay enough to the edge, but not so far ahead that you'd lose your "audience."

- Whatever you'd do, you and your organization would do with passion and 100 percent commitment.

- Your tone would always be optimistic, upbeat, and fun loving. You'd work hard, and you'd enjoy it hard, too, and that would be obvious to people inside and outside the organization.

Looking to the Horizon

If I had to summarize the essence of the Madonna Effect in one phrase, I'd say, "Don't just respond to your customers; lead them."

Too many corporations are slaves to the familiar. They don't lead customers; they just follow them—or if they start to lead, they turn chicken and falter. Ford, GM, and Chrysler began researching hybrid technology at about the same time Toyota and Honda did. Yet when the time came to actually make the cars, Detroit hesitated; there was no clear market-research data favoring hybrids. Besides, why change? At the time, fat-margin non-hybrid SUVs were hot sellers.

By contrast, Toyota and Honda—which, by the way, were far more financially viable than the Detroit Three and, according to conventional wisdom, should have been less inclined toward a risky new technology—accepted the Madonna Effect challenge. Leaders at those two companies recognized flickering evidence about what would one day become conventional wisdom: High energy costs would lead to higher gas prices, and consumers in developed countries would have a greater environmental awareness. Looking at the horizon, they broke from the pack with their cool little hybrid autos and received a rush of sales and huge public relations buzz—not to mention a head start in next-generation developments and applications. Although hybrids accounted for only 6 percent of the market in 2006, this fast-growing technology is acknowledged as the wave of the future.

Detroit was waiting for mass confirmation by customers that they wanted hybrids. Toyota and Honda looked at the trends in the distance and predicted that one day mass confirmation would happen, but they could help define and accelerate that process with products sporting zero defects, hassle-free maintenance (no electronic plug-ins at night), style, zip, and 50-mile-per-gallon performance. By 2005, Detroit's market research finally had its confirmation, but only because their Japanese competitors had planted the flag and raised public awareness with their leadership. And while Detroit is trying to catch up, Honda and Toyota are forging ahead. Toyota, which currently owns over 60 percent of the hybrid market, plans to offer 10 hybrid models by 2010 and anticipates that 25 percent of its U.S. sales will be hybrids by that time.

Some of you who have a delusion of risk-free management are asking, "If customers aren't demanding something, how do you know for sure that they'll buy what you make?" Well, you don't know. Palmisano doesn't know for sure. Neither does Madonna. There are no sure things in business, regardless of the decisions you make. Before it spent more than $10 billion developing the now hot-selling midsize 787 jet, Boeing had no sales guarantees that the market would be receptive to a superlight midsize plane made of low-maintenance, carbon-fiber-reinforced plastic and using 20 percent less fuel, and which could take small groups of passengers nonstop between any two airports on earth. Nor, as I mentioned in the last chapter, was there a mass demand for $10 overnight mail service or $4 cups of coffee until FedEx and Starbucks gave us what we finally realized we wanted.

In 2005, Adidas came up with a $250 running shoe. It's an "intelligent" shoe with a built-in computer that allows the shoe to adjust its heel cushioning to changes in the running surface. Speaking Madonna-like, chief shoe engineer Christian DeBenedetto said, "We knew we would have to rewrite the rules. But we knew it would be massive if we could pull it off." Can they pull it off? The jury is still out, though early results are encouraging. But remember, who would have predicted that when Nike was first launched, people who were accustomed to spending $7 for "sneakers" would pony up $50–100 for heavily engineered, heavily designed running shoes?

A more important question is: What's the cost of *not* reinventing? Wouldn't another conventional Adidas shoe style be running in the middle of the pack behind Nike? Wouldn't it have been a far bigger risk for Boeing to simply stick with "improving" its 747–767 line that was already beginning to lose favor with the major airlines, while allowing Airbus or a future consortium to develop a breakthrough product? If you wait for customers to tell you that they want something, you're already playing catch-up because someone else has already planted the flag and sensitized them to the possibilities that you've ignored.

The Willie Nelson Principle: Jumping in Front

When they look to the horizon and embrace the change they see, the best leaders—like Madonna herself—are disciplined and calculating. Whether they know it or not, they follow the leadership principle espoused by none other than the great Willie Nelson.

In the late 1950s and early '60s, Willie Nelson was a songwriter. His song "Crazy" had become a huge hit for superstar Patsy Cline, but as a singer, he was getting nowhere. Country music at the time was a minor, low-end, narrow-niche format—a mishmash of rockabilly, jug music, bluegrass, and smooth, clean-cut American ballads. Frustrated, Willie found himself becoming increasingly disillusioned by the "Nashville Sound," with its clean-cut country singers dressed in rhinestone and spangle-decorated cowboy suits. Nelson was itching to make his mark as a singer rather than as a songwriter, and he wanted to do it on his own terms.

Nelson and Waylon Jennings pioneered a major transformation in country music: "Outlaw Country." The singers grew their hair long, wore denim and leather, and looked like hippies or members of motorcycle gangs. Their songs were about drinking, drugs, hardworking men, and honky-tonk women. The music sounded more like rock and roll than old-fashioned country, with no sweet strings twanging in the background

Willie and Waylon were key forces in reconciling hip and redneck musical interests, thus restoring a rawness to country music and leading a new explosion of popular interest in the format, teaming up to top the country charts with "Good Hearted Woman (in Love with a Good Timin' Man)" in 1976, which was featured on country's first certified platinum album, the "Wanted: The Outlaws" compilation.

Country music has gone through various iterations since then (as has Willie himself), and although the "outlaw" sound is now just one more country music offering, at the time the movement not only catapulted Willie and Waylon into country music stardom, but it also transformed and popularized country music itself.

In the late 1980s, Willie was asked about how he and Waylon "knew" that their leadership on "outlaw" music would be so successful. In one of the most important quotes in this book, here is his reply:

"Being a good leader is finding a bunch of people going in one direction and jumping in front of them. That's what I did. I saw all these things happening, so I called Waylon and we came down to Austin and acted like we started the whole thing. We didn't start nothin'. It was going on."

Yes, there was no secret. It was going on: Some nutty fringe groups experimenting with a new kind of sound that a small slice of listeners were really getting excited about. Hank Williams Jr., David Allan Coe, The Marshall Tucker Band, The Charlie Daniels Band, even a group called The Outlaws—they and others were out there doing their own "outlaw" thing.

As someone who was involved with the country music radio industry in the 1980s and 1990s, I can assure you that Willie was *not* saying that his secret was to simply wait until some other maverick musician developed a following and then imitate him with some snazzy marketing. Unfortunately, too many companies believe their salvation lies in letting someone else develop a new concept and work out all the kinks, and then jumping in. In the Copycat Economy, that's a naïve fantasy, as GM and Ford have learned. Instead, like Willie and

Madonna, if you get a sense of what is small, radical, fringe, but potentially powerful and imminently extended, you can win a head start by shaping it with your own foresight and innovation, thereby building your own unique business model and brand around the trend. In the process, you'll excite customers and investors and thereby accelerate the development of the trend, while taking leadership of it at the same time.

Willie and Madonna (and, in the case of hybrids, former Toyota North America CEO "Tag" Taguchi) paid attention to the oddball but interesting stuff that was "goin' on"—stuff that was available to anyone who paid attention to it. They didn't wait for a mass movement or a market research study that would tell them that those once far-away clouds of dust had become a huge herd that would soon run roughshod over their business. They "jumped in front," using their talents and skills to lead the herd in a creative, passionate, and disciplined way.

That's how you lead the customer: You lead; you don't simply respond. And like Madonna, Sam Palmisano, and Tag Taguchi, you start when your current market offerings are successful because perpetual evolvement and forward movement is your strategic edge. You do it knowing that taking chances is part of the deal. You might stub your toe and stumble, but as long as you're stumbling forward, you're doing the right thing.

Finally, like Willie, like Madonna, you have fun doing it. Only over the past few years have I learned to take this concept of fun seriously. I've discovered that employees in trailblazing, pack-leading organizations work their butts off, but they have a great time doing it. It's a lot of fun to work with a team of passionate fellow crazies doing what everyone else says is ridiculous and impossible. By contrast, I've discovered that one of the best predictors of organizational decline is when employees—particularly the best ones—say, "It's not fun anymore." The work is routine, mundane, and uninspired; the organization is slow, bureaucratic, and risk averse. It's just not fun. In short, fun counts.

To summarize, a lot of "motivational" business books have it all wrong when they pontificate about how great leaders and great companies "swim against the current." It only looks that way. In reality, the winners have identified the future direction of the current and are swimming furiously in that direction, while everyone in the pack, to quote F. Scott Fitzgerald, is like "boats against the current, borne back ceaselessly into the past."

Calculated Reinvention in the Corporate World

Many companies other than IBM and Toyota have successfully enacted the Madonna Effect and the Willie Nelson Principle to break from the pack.

General Electric

Review GE's financials, and you'll quickly attribute its health primarily to the 30 percent revenue and operating profit growth rates in health-care information technology, bioscience, personalized medicine, water purification, security technology and services, wind-powered turbines, and Hispanic TV. These are the nascent "tomorrow" markets that GE targeted as "growth platforms" (predictions based on trends and data in the public domain, available to anyone), even as the company has divested itself of many enterprises that it defines as nongrowth businesses for GE, like mortgage and life insurance.

Apple

When Steve Jobs returned to the sputtering, declining Apple in 1997, he rejuvenated the company with products like the iMac, notable for cutting-edge designs and technologies. Jobs could have sat back and enjoyed the accolades, but he was restless. Dell was starting to imitate the multicolored iMacs, and, besides, despite their sizzle and brand identity, Apple computers remained stuck in a sub–4 percent market share.

Jobs took seriously something that was visible to anyone who looked closely. While music executives fiddled around the flames of their plunging CD business, music outsider Jobs saw the inevitability of the pesky, chaotic digital music scene. He and his team did what the music folks should have done years ago. They put together the available pieces—the artists, the recording companies, the software and hardware purveyors, the marketers, and the distributors—in a disciplined and imaginative manner to fashion a must-have product (the iPod) and a killer platform (iTunes). This allowed Apple to capture nearly 80 percent of the growing "legal, paying" download market. That translates into 2 million legal 99 cent iTunes downloads a day, and sales of 42 million high-margin iPods, 76 percent of them in 2005. Breakthroughs like the Nano and Video iPods keep the ball rolling.

Just as important, iPods and iTunes branded Apple as one of the coolest companies on earth, not to mention cranking up the company's total 2004–2005 revenues from $8.3 billion to $13.9 billion, its net profit from $276 million to $1.3 billion, and its share earnings from $0.37 to $1.65. Strategically, Apple's music foray generated openings in a wealth of new fast-growth multimedia products, which have begun to leapfrog over its pure computer products in corporate importance—though ironically, and unsurprisingly, the "buzz" around Apple has rippled to its computer business, which saw a 38 percent sales growth in 2005 over 2004.

UPS

Company executives saw two very different trends emerging on the horizon: the creeping commoditization of their core package-delivery business as imitators like FedEx, DHL, and the U.S. Post Office stepped up; and the small but steady growth of outsourcing, as companies tried to tighten their internal costs. To catapult over the first trend and capitalize on the second, UPS decided it could address the outsourcing phenomenon with its own core competencies around inventory management, logistics, and transportation.

A new business model was born. CEO Mike Eskew envisions UPS as corporate America's traffic manager of choice. It will employ its integrated systems, expertise, and technologies to help customers either streamline their supply chains from raw materials to finished product, or take over and manage the supply chains altogether. Already, for example, UPS transports every vehicle that is produced by Ford from factory door to dealership lot. "Why keep big, bloated, inefficient supply chain cost-centers in-house?" UPS asks corporations. The company's message to potential customers is: Your back-end costs are our front-end expertise, our value-add to our customers. Let us handle your inventory, your warehousing, your order fulfillment, your international trade management and customs brokerage, your delivery and distribution networks, your entire supply chain, if possible—we'll do it better, cheaper, and more innovatively because that's our business.

In 2002, the company moved to combine UPS Freight Services and UPS Logistics Group to form UPS Supply Chain Solutions, which, augmented by some tactical acquisitions, is now a multibillion-dollar subsidiary operating from more than 750 facilities in 120 countries worldwide (including 40 centers in China).

Remember that UPS customers didn't ask for this; in fact, many initially resisted the idea of surrendering such large chunks of their organization. UPS had to use its reputation and trust to educate and convince them—that is, it had to lead the customer.

Whole Foods Market

In 1978, John Mackey borrowed $10,000 from his father and opened Safer Way Natural Foods in Austin, Texas. In 1980, Safer Way merged with Clarksville Natural Grocery, and Whole Foods Market was born. It was successful; Mackey could have stopped there and enjoyed a pleasant life. But unfortunately for grocers like Albertson's and Safeway, Mackey trained his eye on the trends on the horizon. He bet on the big idea that the Whole Foods concept was scalable and that mainstream Americans—not just the affluent and the hippies—would be willing to spend more money on healthful foods. As it turned out, natural and organic foods retailing has become the fastest-growing segment in the U.S. grocery business. Whole Foods is now the world's fastest-growing and largest natural foods chain, with more than 180 stores in 30 states as well as Washington, D.C., and the United Kingdom and Canada. In 2005, the company broke into the Fortune 500 at 479, demonstrating, once again, what I noted in Chapter 2: Breaking from the pack leads to a healthy "bigness."

What's even more interesting, however, is that the company maintains this growth rate and intense customer loyalty, despite its high prices (it's often called "Whole Paycheck"), which have led to triple the industry margins. Just to annoy its competitors further, the Whole Foods store environment crackles with innovation in colors, theater, and fun, making it a magnet for free-spending customers and talented employees.

Enacting Reinvention

If the Madonna Effect and the Willie Nelson Principle have helped so many companies lead markets and evolve successfully, why do so many leaders focus so much on servicing yesterday's declining business or today's "mature" business rather than anticipating and capitalizing on tomorrow's growth opportunities?

McKinsey consultant Charles Roxburgh points to several nonrational tendencies among corporate decision makers that keep them from forging forward-looking strategies: the status quo bias ("people would rather leave things as they are"), the sunk cost effect ("otherwise known as 'throwing good money after bad'"), and the herding effect ("the desire to conform to the behavior and opinions of others"). My own work over the past decade suggests that we can add fear, complacency and arrogance to that list. What's truly amazing is how many companies that are in deep trouble resist the Madonna makeover, even though they have so much less to lose by taking some chances.

Whether your company is successful or in trouble, here is what you must do to execute a Madonna Effect and Willie Principle—and, quite bluntly, what will happen to you if you don't.

1. Take Those Small, In-the-Distance Trends Seriously

Moribund companies always look for a big miracle drug to revive them, but consistently healthy companies do not ignore tiny opportunities that might have substantial impact.

If you don't regularly peer into the horizon, you won't put a lot of energy or resources into studying those trends, understanding them, considering their danger to current business and potential, or positioning them as strategic priorities. This problem is more likely to occur when your organization is big and powerful and the horizon trend has a minor or negligible impact on your financials today. Although Kodak executives were aware in 2000 that digital cameras and support infrastructure were a relevant blip in the horizon, they didn't seriously explore and embrace this trend until their flagship film business was collapsing and the digital business (which they didn't own) was enjoying double-digit annual growth.

It's not that Kodak executives ignored the digital movement, In fact, Kodak "introduced" the first digital photo camera back in 1996. It's just that Kodak executives did not take digital imaging seriously as a business priority. Intellectually, they suspected digital would eventually threaten film, they just didn't expect how fast or how completely it would happen. They waited too long. They let competitors define the market rather than driving the market themselves with their own 1996 prototype.

The bottom line is that Kodak executives screwed up big time by ignoring the basic principle of Madonna and Willie: They followed rather than led their customers. As a result, despite the company's (finally!) aggressive foray into the digital space in 2003, Eastman Kodak remains a humbled giant. Sales remain flat, earnings are down, the stock in 2005 was off 67 percent from its 1997 peak, and an onslaught from a growing pack of unorthodox competitors like Canon, HP, and Yahoo! continues to torment the company.

The same failure to scan the horizon remains true in the music business. Most recently, says Peter Standish, a Warner Bros. Records vice president, the music industry faces a possible "next big thing": downloadable music for cellphone ring tones. It's a tiny market but a big opportunity, especially with 180 million handsets in the U.S. alone and a price of $1 to $3 per tone—and especially again since young people seem to like to have different tones for different friends' incoming calls and also like changing their own tones regularly. The possibilities on the horizon go beyond cellphones. Imagine individualized tones for anything with a microprocessor: laptops, digital cameras, PDAs, cars. Standish is excited about exploiting and building this burgeoning market, but will his peers in the business concur when it comes time to set budgets and hire staff?

From tones to timber, the issue is the same. I've sat in meetings with people in the hardwood and commercial window industries, and one small, distant, minority-thought trend keeps popping up: customers' desires for high-design, environmentally sound, solar-friendly buildings. Will these industries exploit and accelerate this little trend to stay at the top of the food chain?[1]

2. Be Willing to Regularly Challenge What Made You Successful in the Past

Living in the San Francisco Bay Area, I remember how the '49ers dominated the National Football League in the 1980s with a remarkable four Super Bowl victories. Fanatic '49ers football fans vilified coach Bill Walsh for trading players while they were still solid, even marquee names like Ronnie Lott, Roger Craig, Jerry Rice, and the incomparable Joe Montana. But Walsh's reasoning was that even though these players were still able to contribute to the team's successes, they had peaked and their talents had begun to ebb with age. Walsh always believed that it was essential to trade or release a player while he was still good, before the inevitable steep decline, to keep the roster fresh and sharp. When Walsh left, his strategy left with him. Perhaps that is one explanation for the precipitous decline of the '49ers over the last few years.

Kraft Foods is still fighting the battles it won yesterday, and that's precisely why, despite its $34 billion in sales, its net earnings and stock price stay flat. Kraft offers a big portfolio of well-recognized brands, such as Oreo cookies, Nabisco chips, Kraft Cheese, and Oscar Mayer meats. But American eating habits are changing to favor healthful eating, low-carb and low-fat diets, and ethnic fares. The company's primary response to its declining position has been to slash costs, reduce payroll, and boost advertising—compulsions that lead to losing. Kraft has also made small introductions of yogurt bars and South Beach diet cookies. Is this enough to move a $30 billion dollar barge toward a new horizon? As a result of the same trends, the stock of Interstate Bakers (which makes Twinkies, Wonder Bread, Ding Dongs, and Ho Ho's) declined 86 percent between 2003 and 2004 alone.[2]

I'm not suggesting that leaders have to jettison *all* suffering products. IBM, for example, is no longer a "mainframe company." But CEO Sam Palmisano is integrating the mainframe business into his future "on demand" vision because mainframes drive the vision. The power and capacity of mainframes fit the IBM future. But anything that doesn't fit the future goes, which is why IBM (successfully) sold its substantial personal computer hardware business to the Chinese firm Lenovo—despite objections from traditional IBMers, who predicted dire consequences.

Many large companies find themselves bolted to the past; sunk costs, legacy systems, corporate culture, and managers' egos are tied to what made the company great yesterday. It's hard to change even when the evidence is staring you in the face. Don't be afraid to challenge your current cash-cow businesses to prove their worth, even if it means making substantial and meaningful deviations from them. Otherwise, it doesn't matter how big and well known you are today; you'll still fall back into the pack, and maybe even farther back than that.

3. Be Willing to Change Long-Time Suppliers and Disrupt Current Supply Chains

It's hard to capitalize on distant trends with break-from-the-pack responses if your supply-chain management is still stuck in the pack. I've talked to executives who won't change their ERP back-office systems or their CRM customer-relations systems even though they've found a perfect trifecta of cheaper, faster, and better-fit alternatives. Why? Because the switching costs would be (short-term) painful, or because they are "comfortable" with their current vendor.

Not long ago, I asked a Levi Strauss manager why the company, mired in every conceivable decline, didn't fully capitalize on its technologies and its prior acquisition of Custom Clothing that allow direct built-to-order sales to customers. I noted that Levi Strauss provided only isolated opportunities for built-to-order in a few selected Levi Outpost stores. Why not expand the opportunities for customers to design their own clothing, I asked. Customers could use Levi Strauss templates and support to measure themselves digitally with Levi Strauss tools. Then the customers, using the Levi Strauss networks, could deal online directly with low-cost Levi Strauss factories abroad, which would mail the finished product directly to their homes.

The manager agreed that it would be a potentially large and lucrative business, one consistent with emerging trends toward direct, built-to-order sales, and one that could transform the company. Yet in a mirror reaction to Madonna, she added, "We can't really do it because our retailers would be very upset."

I suggested that Levi's performance was pretty upsetting to begin with, so why persist in defending a system that was broken? I even began to offer scenarios in which Levi's one lucrative relationship with giant Wal-Mart could remain intact, but other smart, progressive retailers could have new roles in a direct-sales paradigm. I got nowhere. If such necessary changes in supply chain management are deal breakers from the beginning, it's pretty hard to reinvent yourself.

4. Don't Become Paralyzed by the Fear of Going Too Far

True, the Madonna Effect is about not jumping too far ahead of customers. But that occasionally happens as part of the process, and you should be aware that even too-far failures can foster future success. At FedEx, chairman Fred Smith cheerfully admits the occasional misstep. In the 1980s, before fax machines became common, FedEx launched Zapmail, a program to transmit documents electronically between FedEx offices. The idea was a $400 million flop; it was too complicated and too far ahead of what people were capable of absorbing. However, the Zapmail technology became integral to accelerating FedEx's worldwide express-shipping network. What's more, in a speech to employees after the debacle, Smith reiterated that the Zapmail process, good and bad, was part of FedEx's entrepreneurial culture, and an entrepreneurial culture can't have a perfect 1.00 batting average. "I'm not afraid to take a swing and miss," says Smith.

5. Listen to the Crazy Customers

You must listen to today's customers to survive, but you must listen to tomorrow's customers to thrive. That means you have to listen carefully to the crazy 3 percent, the ones with their eyes on the horizon. The craziees are the consumers who bought VCRs before the first Blockbuster even existed, or who traded music files online using slow, clunky 28K and 56K modems and exposing themselves to every quality defect and computer virus imaginable.

Mercer Consulting chief and noted author Adrian Slywotsky puts it nicely: "Future-defining customers may account for only 2 to 3 percent of your total, but they represent a crucial window to the future."

The leaders of the Indiana Heart Hospital were crazy. They were willing to let GE Healthcare completely digitalize all the hospital's operations, provide notebook computers to all physicians, set up networks right into physicians' homes, and make transparent a lot of organizational information flow that used to be kept under wraps by higher-ups. These are the crazies, the early adopters, those who deviate from the bell curve, those pace setters who are willing to try something new and untested, those obstreperous scratchy customers (not the whiners, but the high-performance zealots) who are always complaining about the status quo products and services they receive from you and your vendors.

By definition, the 97 percent base is what conventional consumer research measures. Small wonder, then, that most companies imitate each other by appealing solely to the big bulk of customers rather than to the oddballs who represent the growth markets of the future.

6. Take Underserved Markets Seriously

I often find myself working with clients to see opportunities for applying their resources to a large untapped gold mine of underserved or completely unserved customers.

The frustration of Mark Thorsby of the International Carwash Association, who lamented about his fellow carwash owners copying each other by price slashing instead of figuring out how to bring in the nation's 170 million noncustomers, is shared by officials at another professional association, the National Spa and Pool Institute. Its officials go nuts when their members declare that the business is "mature" just because the industry is more than 50 years old. That's not how to measure maturity, officials told me, especially when there are 55 million financially qualified and untapped households that do not have either a pool or a Jacuzzi.

Ford executives told me that one of their priorities is to convince their dealers to take seriously the enormous multibillion-dollar Ford aftermarket of parts like starters, brakes, fenders, bumpers, air-conditioning components, and even transmissions and engines. Dealers would have to invest in facilities, people, and infrastructure to service that different kind of business. In spite of huge low-hanging fruit opportunities, many dealers haven't been willing to invest in what's necessary because it breaks habits and represents a financial risk into the "unknown." Meanwhile, it drives Ford executives crazy to see individual customers as well as institutional ones (like governments and car-rental fleet owners) go to competitors like PEP Boys, NAPA, and Autozone for Ford parts rather than to Ford dealers.

7. Take Emerging Demographics Very Seriously

Organizations that truly "get" demographic shifts will pour attention and resources in the right direction and reap opportunities. The market has changed a lot since the *Leave It to Beaver* days of the 1950s, but many companies give this truth only an intellectual nod. Recently I gave a seminar to a group of CEOs of homebuilder corporations looking to boost their businesses. I asked them a simple question: "Which company in your industry owns the Asian space?"

Dead silence. "Well," I reasoned, "it would seem to me that if I were building homes, I would want to get connected with the fastest-growing affluent population in the U.S. I'd sure want to understand the principles of feng shui, and I'd sure want to know the differences among what Indonesians, Thais, and Chinese expect from their homes."

I then asked my next question. "Which company in your industry owns the Hispanic space?"

Again, dead silence. I continued: "It would seem to me that if I were building homes, I would want to get connected with the fastest-growing demographic, period, in the U.S., and I'd sure want to know the differences among what Mexicans, Puerto Ricans, and Cubans expect from their homes. At 42 million, Hispanics are now the largest minority group in the U.S. So how many of you are learning Spanish, and having your front-line people learn Spanish, and marketing your services through Spanish distribution and sales channels?" Silence.

With 140 languages spoken among the Los Angeles Unified School District classrooms, it's clear that American customers are no longer just the Ward and June Cleavers. Yet in many companies, product development and marketing approaches often seem to assume a monolithic, homogeneous market. Companies talk a good game of diversity as it relates to employees. They ought to be talking about diversity as it relates to customers.

I might as well add yet another element to the mix: the 70 million neurotic, stay-young-at-all-costs baby boomers who will be retiring shortly. What sorts of products—homes, vacations, cars, investment packages—will companies be offering this very unique market? I should have asked the homebuilders who owns the aging space—or, for that matter, the single adult space, or the straight and gay "DINK" (dual income no kids) space. All of those segments have both sizable disposable incomes and sizable unique needs. I bet I would have gotten the same silent answer.

Kroger, the giant grocer, took seriously the Latino demographic shifts in Houston and the steady nibbling to their market share from little Latino niche stores in certain Houston neighborhoods. The company spent nearly $2 million to convert a 59,000-square-foot facility to an all-Hispanic supermercado, complete with all-Spanish staff and foods. Not only did the store's sales and traffic volume increase dramatically, and not only did the store serve as a model for similar ventures in other cities like Atlanta and Indianapolis, but it also spurred the company to create its very successful private label Buena Comida, with more than 100 different items. With Latino disposable income jumping 29 percent since 2001 and reaching nearly $700 billion in 2005, double the pace of the rest of the population, this trend on the horizon is ready to arrive.[3]

New and relevant demographics transcend the standard categories of race, gender, and age. For example, the steady rise of religious, faith-based, and spiritual interests (megachurches, "The Da

Vinci Code," "The Passion of the Christ," Deepak Chopra, the "Chicken Soup for the Soul" empire, etc.) and the increasing desire for interactive online communities (MySpace.com, Flickr, Facebook, YouTube, etc.) are just two of many emerging social phenomena that are both inevitable, and ripe for shaping by prescient leaders. Demographic trends are everywhere, but only the Madonna and Willie organizations are willing to take them seriously—and lead them.

8. Don't Be Panicked by Finicky Investors

Whether your company is publicly traded or privately held, you'd be a fool to ignore the wishes of your owners. But you'd be an even bigger fool to run your business in daily fear of their possible wrath because then you'd be too scared to make any Madonna-like moves that might ding your income statement today but rocket-launch your business tomorrow.

The statement "We can't do that because our investors are interested only in quarterly earnings" is a loser's lament, and it's not true. Sure, sometimes investors make stupid, myopic decisions, and the shorters and flippers among them don't care about your business to begin with. If investors don't believe in your vision and capacity to break from the pack, of course, they'll probably ding you at the first sign of trouble. All of which is perfectly understandable and quite rational because the whole point of investment is about projected earnings and tomorrow's cash flow.

But I've worked with enough institutional and angel investors to assure you that as long as they believe that you and your business model can help your organization break from the pack, they'll stick it out with you even through some hard times.

For inspiration, look at a company I've already maligned a few times: Kodak. In 2003, then-CEO Daniel Carp unveiled his grand plan to dump much of the cash-cow high-top-line film business (including all film cameras except for emerging markets in Asia and Latin America), cut annual dividend by 72 percent, and plow a minimum of $3 billion into the digital imaging market. A lot of investors howled, and the stock plunged. The reasoning, held by a surprising number of investors, was that because Kodak can never succeed in the digital world (too little, too late), it should use its free cash flow for dividends and for propping up its dying business as long as possible before liquidation or sell-off. To their credit, Kodak executives ignored their nay-saying "owners" and, determined to prove the skeptics wrong, proceeded aggressively toward their goals. In January 2006 current CEO Antonio Perez said, "In 2003 we announced a four-year plan...If I'm a long-distance runner, I am getting the second wind." Within three short, traumatic years, it is safe to say that Kodak has crawled back from a near-death experience. Kodak is still a company in serious transition, but because of better returns it's a player again. Its stock, while significantly off its 1997 peak, is at least 23 percent higher than it was last year. Kodak's back in the pack, and if the company's executives follow the prescriptions in this book, Kodak might actually break from it!

For double inspiration, look at Google, a company that took Warren Buffet's philosophy to heart from the beginning, even before its initial public offering. Here was the company's message to the investment public, even as it was seeking their dollars: We're not going to run our business with a knee-jerk reaction to you or your analysts. Invest in us if you believe in us, and invest only for the long haul. Otherwise, we don't want you. Brave. Bravo. From its auction IPO, which bypassed most of the good-old-boy Wall Street fraternity, to the company's unwillingness to split its stock even when it reached a ridiculous $475 a share on January 11, 2006, to its refusal to spend time figuring out earnings "guidance" for analyst—Google's M.O. is to concentrate solely on growing its business in a smart, provocative way, attracting a mountain of long-term investors anyway.

9. Have the Courage of Your Convictions

The whole concept of leadership assumes that you have a conviction, an underlying philosophy, an overarching strategic direction, a deep and compelling "vision." And it assumes that you have the integrity and fortitude to see it through. "Courage of conviction" is an empty phrase without willingness to engage in reinvention. Without a commitment to change, your effort at reinvention will manifest itself in an uninspiring, uncontroversial, me-too "vision statement," the kinds you see gathering cobwebs on corporate walls. Or, if you do come up with a bold, transformational, Madonna-like vision, if you don't have the courage of conviction to follow through, you'll find yourself quickly backpedaling when the inevitable resistance occurs.

Barry Diller gave a good piece of advice to a young Jeffrey Katzenberg years ago, before Katzenberg achieved fame and fortune at Disney and, as the force behind the *Shrek* empire, at DreamWorks.

"Your job is to go out and find ideas that interest you, that you love sufficiently to put your career on the line, to have a level of passion to want to make something, and to have the courage of your convictions. There is no way you will ever know what a housewife in Kansas or a businessman in Chicago wants to see. Your job is to find things that interest you. Then you say "Yes." You close your eyes, cross your fingers, and pray that there are millions of other people who feel the same way you do. Any time you presume what someone else will like, you will lose."

Combine that gut sentiment with the first eight propositions outlined here, and you'll join Madonna and Willie Nelson in the pantheon of reinvention and success.

Endnotes

[1] You can find examples in every industry. For years, Coca Cola focused on improving and diversifying its core soda lines, paying insufficient attention to strange little markets like sports drink, energy drink, and bottled water. Those decisions came to haunt Coke, because soda sales are flat while those "little" markets are now soaring, sometimes with 85 percent profit margins.

[2] This trend is actually growing in leaps and bounds. Last year PepsiCo reported that two thirds of its revenue growth came from healthier foods, and McDonald's Fruit & Walnut Salad has become so popular that the burger company is now the world's largest purchaser of apples.

[3] I recently spent two days working with a roundtable of executives in the roofing industry. To be perfectly candid, each of them was an older white male. I was impressed with their sincerity in learning about the Hispanic culture, building bilingual English-Spanish training programs and career paths for employees, and transforming many of their internal documents into bilingual English-Spanish. They weren't doing this to "celebrate diversity." These tough codgers were doing it as a business necessity. They see the handwriting on the wall: more and more of their employee base (and first line management base) are, and will be Hispanic. Apparently, it's getting harder and harder to find Gringos who will want to do that sort of work for any length of time.

4

CURIOUS, COOL, AND CRAZY: BUILDING A CULTURE OF DISCIPLINED LUNACY

If competitors aren't bewildered or infuriated by what you're doing, and if industry observers and even customers don't think you're a little nuts, then you're probably not doing anything that will break you from the grips of the Copycat Economy. In today's hypercompetitive environment, organizations which break from the pack have these characteristics:

- They're **Curious**—Possessed of a culture built around inquisitiveness, and willing to explore uncharted, unorthodox, and even controversial paths

- They're **Cool**—Exhibiting an organization-wide willingness to be edgy, unconventional, and even defiant

- They're **Crazy**—Eager to make decisions that seem insane but are also the result of calculated discipline—or what I call "disciplined lunacy"

Curious, cool, and crazy companies—and the leaders who run them—approach things so differently that outsiders sometimes seriously wonder whether they've gone bonkers. Of the companies that made its "most admired" list a few years ago, *Fortune* magazine said, "Their managers are willing to take some risks so bold they may cause shareholders, stock analysts, and employees to seriously question their sanity—at least until they turn out to have been right." Their craziness is always rigorously organized, however, and it's infused with a fundamental, adventurous interest in what's new, as well as delight in what's arrestingly fresh, fun, and cool.

Curious

Colin Powell, the former general and secretary of state, once declared, "You're a good leader when people follow only out of curiosity." When leaders direct an organization on an interesting, intriguing path, they attract interesting, intriguing people who want to join the caravan—to see what happens, to make something happen. When employees, investors, customers, and partners follow you because they're curious about the bizarrely compelling and potentially lucrative path you're exploring, and want to be part of it, you know you're on the way to breaking from the pack.

This is not just "motivational" pap. Increasingly, curiosity is being recognized as a vital component for lifting your organization toward the high-value top of the competitive food chain, thus staying ahead of imitators and avoiding the ravages of commoditization. Barry Diller, currently CEO of InterActiveCorp, boils down corporate competitive success to just two factors: serendipity and curiosity. Using Diller's logic, if a company doesn't just rely on luck, success is about the capacity of an organization and its people to approach the world and its opportunities with a fervor for "what if?" and "why not?" inquiry. In a similar vein, *Wall Street Journal* op-ed columnist Daniel Henninger argues that the "worst sin" in business is to take action that is dull.

Curiosity has three components: audacity, a "yes" culture, and passion.

Audacity

If the strategic direction of your organization can be described as willfully daring, calculatingly bold, and deliberately adventurous, then you're on the right track. I'm referring to much more than just the "audacious goals" as described by Jim Collins and Jerry Porhas in their book *Built to Last*. I'm describing the entire mindset and strategy of the kind that futurist Alvin Toffler noted when he said, "The manager who can't conceive of a radical alternative to the way things are being done…isn't going to survive very long."

SAP, the business software provider, is moving in an audacious path with its new software platform suite NetWeaver, which promises to revolutionize both the corporate software industry and how companies actually run their businesses. NetWeaver will allow companies to build their corporate software to order (from accounting and manufacturing to customer relations and supply chain), by having them pick and choose what they want and then putting the elements together, Lego-like. As one Cisco executive noted, "SAP is setting the standard that other application vendors will inevitably have to follow." SAP executive Shai Agassi echoed that sentiment: "We could have sat back and waited for the storm to pass, but it never will. Instead, we decided to lead it."

When leaders operate while wearing the Madonna-and-Willie glasses discussed in Chapter 3, they'll often be branded as audacious. So be it. Richard Branson, the head of the Virgin Group, has been known for audacious personal behavior—like jumping out of luggage bins to greet passengers on Virgin Air. But beneath that raucous exterior are his calculated strategic immersions into "out-in-the-horizon" opportunities. For example, with a $400 million investment in alternative cellulosic ethanol fuel, Branson aims to build Virgin Fuels into "a major competitor to oil companies." That's audacious![1] And what could be more audacious than Virgin's new, privately funded Virgin Galactic outer space tourism business? On the surface, it sounds ridiculous, but Branson's partner Burt Rutan oversaw the development of SpaceShipOne, which has already traveled twice to the edge of space. Furthermore, Branson is licensing the necessary technology from Mojave Aerospace, owned by Microsoft billionaire Paul Allen, who happens to be Rutan's partner. With private investment coupled with an initial ticket price of $210,000 (for the experience of a grand total of 3 minutes of weightlessness in space) that is collected by potential customers (and believe me, there are plenty of potential customers) two years before the first flight—even skeptics are beginning to believe that Branson's audacity reveals shrewd business logic.

A Culture of "Yes"

A corporate culture of "yes" sends a complex but clear message to every employee: "Yes, if you're willing to take accountability for performance;

if you're willing to do the due diligence; if you're willing to take the responsibility of putting together a business plan, project team, and economic logic; if you're willing to stand up and fight for your ideals, then, yeah! Go ahead! Even if it challenges what we've always done in the past! We want you to succeed! Go for it!"

In other companies, you can smell a culture of "no": Earnest people are working long hours but are possessed of a certain ennui, a passiveness amid a grim routine, an absence of urgency, a lack of passion, a dearth of sheer joy, a hesitation in trying things out, a fear in deviating from standard procedure—in short, a lack of the ingredients of curiosity. But in a company with a culture of "yes," there's vibrancy, optimism, excitement, and entrepreneurialism. It's not an irresponsible, "do whatever you want" recklessness that permeated failed companies like Enron or Webvan, but a curiosity accompanied by rigor, reason, and responsibility.

Do you have a culture of "yes" or a culture of "no" in your company? To find out, assess your company's *speed* in responding with innovation. How quickly and pervasively do interesting ideas pop up and percolate? How rapidly and aggressively do they get scrutinized? How swiftly and imaginatively do they get developed and executed? Speed is the engine driver of a culture of "yes." Yes, you need discussion, analysis, and due diligence. But all these can proceed fast or slow. In a culture of no, everything is slow.[2]

Several years ago, I suggested to a client, an executive at a large but stagnant industrial firm, that he fire me. I told him that we were all wasting a lot of time and he was wasting a lot of money. Repeatedly, I would work with his team of senior managers, and we would agree on some aggressive "to-do's." I would return a couple months later and find that nothing had been accomplished. The executive agreed with me that the lack of fast action was undoubtedly a pivotal cause of the company's declining financials, but because he wasn't yet prepared to confront the issue, he agreed to fire me. Before he did, he ruefully shared with me his assessment of his company's problem, a lovely summary of a culture of "no": *"We study a good idea until it becomes a bad idea."*

As you examine your organization's culture, ask how long it takes to do the following:

- Make an important decision. (I am consistently astonished by how much time it takes large companies in financial distress to make any decision—glacial pace and financial distress are not unrelated.)

- Initiate and implement a significant change in anything—like work processes, information technology, customer service, or supplier relations

- Put together a team or an alliance, or start an experiment

- Get data and feedback

- Follow up on the data and feed it back to the right people

- Launch a product

- Get to market

- Follow up with next steps

The longer it takes to accomplish these things, the more likely you're operating in a culture of "no."

Passion

Curiosity has a strong intellectual component, but it also has a strong emotional component. Passion is the "juice," the fuel, for curiosity. Breaking from the pack is heavily dependent on leaders and employees who are passionate about what they're doing and what they might accomplish. They're zealous about a path of action they're taking. They're turned on about a product they're developing. They're revved up by a potential service they can provide. Without passion, people come to work and "do their jobs"—maybe earnestly, maybe amiably, but for sure conventionally. In a Copycat Economy, that's a recipe for competitive decay.

For several years, Bob Lutz has been trying to incite passion into GM. In 2001, less than a month after taking over his position as vice chairman, Lutz shocked his staid colleagues by declaring in an in-house memo that a good planning process cannot robotically create a good future portfolio of cars and trucks. "There are no significant unfilled 'Consumer Needs' in the U.S. car and truck market," he wrote. "What there are are 'consumer turn-ons' that research alone won't find." But how likely is GM to deliver those turn-ons if its designers, engineers, and marketers aren't themselves "turned on"? Unlikely, thought Lutz: "Happy, contented employees, and an environment where nobody argues or disagrees, and everyone compromises because the other person has goals, too, is usually not the culture that produces great shareholder value."

Lutz has a point. One of the best predictors of organizational decline is a bloated payroll of nonpassionate "satisfied" employees and managers who are content with the status quo and who don't challenge each other because of some notion of being nice. When State Farm Insurance Senior Vice President Harold Gray began his exceptional turnaround of the company's Pacific Northwest region in 2004, he rocked his management team by proclaiming, "We fall in love with our people regardless of their performance and regardless of their contribution. I'm tired of seeing happy people high-fiving each other when the results stink. I want to see high-fives only for results."

It is not always pleasant to feel passion and act on it, but the uneasiness that comes from passionately pushing past your comfort level will lead you and your business to a more creative place. Changing routines, learning new skills, abandoning current products, entering new markets, forging new business directions—they're all uncomfortable. They're also intoxicating.

You might say, all this passion stuff is well and good if you're making movies or iPods, but our business is more mundane. Is it? Consider the supposedly mundane world of public finance. Jeff Pearsall is a managing director at Philadelphia-based Public Financial Management (PFM), a company that advises state and local governments about bonds, budgets, and money management. Pearsall is the ultimate left-brain "quant jock." His specialties are swaps, derivatives, and other structured financial products aimed at helping governments grow their capital base. He has little patience for the "soft" stuff of management. Yet in a conversation with me, he expressed palpable eagerness, his body literally quivering with excitement, about a new platform his team designed that he felt has breakthrough potential. Called SwapViewer, it allows PFM clients to log on any time to view their daily derivative transactions, the valuations that PFM has assigned to those transactions, and data regarding exposure and risk scenarios of alternative hedging decisions. Pearsall's expectation is that PFM's clients will be willing to pay from $5,000 to $20,000 annually for this product because it's tailored to public and nonprofit needs, and because they will be able to get instantaneous, customized, and proprietary information rather than paying a higher fee for a team of accountants to do the same work far more slowly. (In effect, PFM has commoditized the accountants' conventional value-add while enhancing its own.) Moreover, Pearsall told me, SwapViewer's potentials for building business within PFM's current client base, and beyond, is huge. Pearsall's physicalized passion for SwapViewer seemed itself integral to its success.

Ultimately, curiosity and its components create an environment that generates an emotional allure and thrill of inquiry, discovery, and possibility. It generates the corporate adrenaline that will help your organization break from the pack.

Cool

The new millennium economy is *hot*—a bubbling cauldron of new ideas, innovations, competitors, demographics, and sources of capital. How does any organization thrive in this searing environment? By being cool.

In a hot economy, value and capital flow toward cool. If you want to break from the pack, what you do, what you make, and how you do it all must be perceived and experienced as cool by your employees, your customers, and your investors.

But what exactly does "cool" mean?

- Excellence, superiority, "the baddest" (that is, the best)

- Nonconformity, nonmainstream, alternative, hip, defiant

- Being set above the crowd, and inspiring the desire to be associated with what's distinguished and edgy

- Being exclusive and not available to everyone, but being inclusive to those who "get it"

- Being so interesting, innovative, and unique that we raise an eyebrow in surprise

- Continually embracing change, being restless with the status quo, and seeking reinvention

Do the above words and phrases describe your company, its business strategy, and what it markets? They ought to. Cool products and services are imaginative and unconventional; they inspire customers to feel that "wow!" experience, the "I gotta have it, I gotta tell people about it" reaction, and the sense that "I now belong to a special community."

Customers, investors, and talented people are attracted to cool companies, because cool companies create environments in which interesting, imaginative, exciting, unconventional, groundbreaking, and even controversial events occur on a regular basis. Cool companies also demonstrate an obsession with delivering products and services with the kind of speed, cost-efficiency, and flair that dazzles their more conventional competitors. In other words, being cool on the front end (products, services, value proposition) is not enough; in a Copycat Economy, you've also got to be cool on the back end (operations, costs, supply chain management).

Zara is cool. The $5 billion Spanish retailer, a division of Inditex, boasts nearly 750 stores that sell modestly priced, affordable "ultratrendy" fashion goods in 48 countries, primarily in Europe and South America, but also in Israel, Jordan, Malaysia, Kuwait, Canada, and, recently, the U.S. What makes Zara cool is that it can do in 15 days what it takes its rivals 9 months: to find out the kind of look and trend that is exciting people, design something even more exciting around that trend, and get it into stores. That means there is a constant churn of interesting, provocative product in Zara stores, appearing twice a week on a very disciplined schedule. Because of that, if you're a customer, repeat visits are always spicy because you never know what you'll find. If you like something, you'd better buy it because it probably won't be there if you come back a month later (or sometimes even three days later). Besides, if you do buy it, you know you'll look pretty special because after a month nobody else will be able to obtain it and copy your look.

Small wonder that Zara spends only 0.3 percent of sales on advertising (the industry average is 3.5 percent); with its fanatically loyal customer base and its buzz, it doesn't need to. According to *Marie Claire* editor Marie O'Riordan, "With other high-street retailers, the risk is buying something and then bumping into somebody wearing the same thing, and it spoils the effect. With Zara, because the stock turnover is so fast, you have to get there on day one. It tends to sell out two days later, so you have a real chance of being a little bit exclusive, which is quite unusual for a high street."

Conventional wisdom in the retail industry is to try to predict trends, build a hell of a lot of product to capitalize on scale, beat the drums frenetically to sell it, figure out what to do with the leftovers, and then start the cycle again. Instead, Zara deliberately delivers a steady flow of small batches of cool new product based on the discipline of daily market scans. The process enhances its products' "rarity value"; avoids large, costly mistakes; and eliminates the need to sell excess inventory at discount. New lines are constantly replacing existing lines, so a given store might receive 11,000 different products in a year, whereas a rival store's number is more like a few hundred. Indeed, it is not uncommon for multiple stores within one city (say, Paris) to carry entirely different lines of goods.

Here are the "back-end" organizational ingredients that make Zara's coolness work: a brutally efficient production and distribution process, and state-of-the-art information technology to make sure departments and outlets the world over constantly know what is needed when and where, complete with specially designed handheld PDAs that allow Zara people to discuss not only what's selling, but what customers themselves are wearing that's interesting. To be cool on the back end of process and on the front end of product, Zara is dedicated to speed and performance rather than function and turf. Company spokeswoman Carmen Melon says that at the La Coruna, Spain, headquarters, collaboration is absolutely essential. "We have five different teams sharing the same space, so design people work together with product people and merchandising, as well as the people who provide the samples and patterns." Likewise, there is constant interaction among members of design, procurement, production, and distribution in order to move things along as quickly as possible—and, of course, all are passionate and curious about what's new and cool.

You don't have to be in retailing or fashion to be a cool company doing cool stuff. Anything that resonates with innovation and imagination—anything that is counterintuitive, controversial, and delightful—is cool. Jeff Pearsall would say SwapViewer is cool, and, in fact, that's exactly the word I exclaimed when he first described it to me.

Cool Design

Cool is about design. Design is about cool. If colors and shapes and ease of use make your product cool in the minds of customers, then design itself can help you break from the pack, as companies as different as Proctor & Gamble, Apple, BMW, and Target have discovered. Pundits are proclaiming design as the next big management phenomenon. Raymond Turner, the British Airport Authority Design Director, made an astute observation: "Design is one of the few tools that for every [dollar] you spend, you actually say something about your business." If you're committed to cool, then Turner's comment should help shape your business philosophy.

Cool design is like a magnet drawing curious admirers and committed customers. Pedestrians literally stop and gawk at BMW Mini-Coopers, and well-heeled parents pay up to $750 for a futuristic baby stroller made by the Norwegian company Stokke. Customers look at Bang & Olufsen speakers and want them as museum pieces in their living rooms, just like they wind up saving empty Arizona Iced Tea bottles to display in their homes. Critics write less about the iPod's engineering features and song capacity, and more about its design, lauding its "irresistible ease of use" and "eye-popping hues," and describing it as "elegant," "svelte," "sleek," and (my favorite) "yummy."

The trend is clear. Proctor & Gamble CEO A. G. Laffley gushes about design as a prime differentiator of consumer products, from the funny-shaped, multicolored Crest Spinbrush to the purple Prilosec packages. *Reason* editor Virginia Postrel lists numerous variations on toilet bowl brushes, from the lowly Rubbermaid $5 version to the cooler $8 Michael Graves toilet bowl brush selection at Target, to the coolest $32 Excalibur model designed by Philippe Starck. Even business schools are beginning to partner with design studios.

Minneapolis-based Anchor Wall Systems (AWS) produces about the most mundane product imaginable: retaining walls. Yet AWS, with manufacturing facilities and licensing partners in 13 countries around the world, dominates the commercial highway and driveway business, with more than 50 percent market share in a number of geographical areas and close to 100 percent dominance in the retail category, even though the company charges premium prices. How did they manage that? By offering cool wall materials. AWS offers more than 700 different colors and shapes of concrete blocks, ignoring the industry refrain, "You can have any block you want as long as it's gray and square." When President Glenn Bolles showed me models of AWS retaining walls, I was enchanted by their sculptural beauty; I actually had to touch and stroke and smell the…uh…walls.

AWS design innovations also permit easy-to-install, low-maintenance, pinless, mortarless retaining wall systems. The company provides software that helps customers design customized product for highways, fairways, waterways, and driveways. Listening to Bolles wax eloquent about technological innovation, patent portfolios, and the importance of leading change, it was easy for me to forget that he is supposed to be operating in an uninteresting commodity business.

Cool design transforms service businesses, too. Singapore Airlines deliberately appeals to all human senses by strategically mingling music, fragrance, and employee demeanor to present a cool and coherent image. Many people remember their Singapore Air experiences as pleasurable, which no doubt helps tremendously when the company has to compete with low-fare rivals such as Air Asia.

From products to service environments, design is about appealing to the senses. It is about targeting feelings and emotions through fits and finishes and colors and shapes, through smells and sounds, and via tactile, sensual, and fun experiences—whether you're fondling a Target toilet brush or savoring the wide-aisle, colorful atmosphere of Target itself, whether you're buying Nike shoes that feel and look great or roaming the nightclub-like Nike store itself, whether you're drinking an iced decaf skim double mocha latte at Starbucks or merely sitting in a Starbucks couch savoring the aromas. Consider how when you enter a Virgin Megastore, a Whole Foods grocery, or a Selkirks department store in Britain, you feel enveloped in coolness. The colors, textures, music, and tactile furniture are all consistent with the strategic message that these vendors are trying to convey.

To build cool design into your product or service requires imagination and commitment, but the payoff is huge. Or, as one pundit put it, "Design is about the orchestration of behavioral, sensory, and reminiscent needs. [The goal] is to inspire, educate, involve and entertain. The right combination creates insane loyalty."

Crazy

Is Sirius crazy? Compared to the 230 million listeners of terrestrial radio, the market for satellite radio is tiny: 7.5 million or so subscribers in 2005, dominated by two financially fragile companies, XM and Sirius. In 2004, with fewer than 600,000 subscribers and less than $70 million in revenues, Sirius Satellite Radio signed up Howard Stern for a five-year gig starting in January 2006. The company guaranteed Howard and his crew *$500 million.*

So, is Sirius crazy? Well, hold on a moment. "We should do something when people say it is crazy," said Hajime Mitarai, the late president of Canon. "If people say something is 'good,' then it means that someone else is already doing it." That mindset led Canon to create breakthroughs in the 35mm camera, the copier, the printer, liquid crystal display, and so on, while using its period of patent protection to achieve extraordinary economies of scale in manufacturing and distribution. Not bad for being crazy.

"You can't proceed in a calm, rational manner," said Jack Welch to the *Wall St. Journal*. "You've got to be out on the lunatic fringe."

When Mitarai and Welch use words such as *crazy* and *lunatic*, I think the real power behind their comments is statistical. Imagine a bell curve. Statistically, to deviate from the pack, your actions have to be two or three standard deviations from the mean (the "mean" reflects the average, where the big bulk of the bell curve resides). Since the average is statistically "normal," then two or three deviations from normal is the operational definition of lunacy. But in the world of business, today's lunacy is tomorrow's conventional wisdom, while today's conventional wisdom is mired in a big bell bulk of a Copycat Environment. For a "crazy" organization, what at the outset appears risky and irresponsible to supposedly "sane" observers might actually be ruthlessly prescient and well-researched initiatives. Consider Richard Branson's Galactic venture at Virgin, or Jeff Immelt's investment in windmills at GE.

Or consider Sirius. After the Stern announcement, my MBA students and I did a spreadsheet analysis of the deal. Howard Stern has between 8 million and 12 million fanatical listeners. We calculated that if just 800,000 of them enrolled at Sirius, the company would break even on the deal in two years. As it turned out, Sirius enjoyed a serious run-up in retail enrollment and revenues after the Stern announcement: By the end of 2005, Sirius reported that Stern was a significant force in driving up its customer base from 600,000 to 3.3 million. That translated into a triple-digit revenue growth to over $200 million. Tacked on to these numbers was a huge buzz and a multi-billion dollar capital infusion; the stock went up 16 percent upon the announcement of Stern's contract and kept on going north, gaining 70 percent. This enhanced Sirius's ability to sign up other big radio jocks and partners like Martha Stewart, the NFL, and NPR. I can't attribute all of this momentum to the Howard Stern signing, but it sure didn't hurt! In 2005, a Merrill Lynch analyst wrote, "We have consistently indicated that the arrival of Howard Stern would be a major catalyst" to Sirius's growth. That's apparently the case. Analysts predict nearly a further doubling of subscriptions and a revenue stream of $600 million in 2006. The beat goes on. What appeared crazy-dumb to conventional thinkers seems to be crazy like a fox.[3]

Is Toyota crazy? It has licensed its hybrid technology to other automakers, like Ford and Nissan. Why would Toyota do anything that "stupid"? Because Toyota is busy developing the next generation of hybrid vehicles while competitors are trying to catch up. Selling its current technology to competitors allows them (Toyota's competitors) the "privilege" of funding Toyota's R&D efforts and reduces their incentive to develop their own technologies. The licensing also moves the industry one step closer to standardization, with Toyota as the leader, rather like Microsoft with PC operating systems. It helps accelerate the growth of the entire hybrid market the company already leads. And it spurs its own employees to push themselves harder. What is fascinating is that the conventional-wisdom explanations for Toyota's decision—"It builds top-line revenue"—has little to do with its decision. Furthermore, the conventional wisdom—to keep the technology "secret"—is one that Toyota executives, knowing the realities of transparency and imitation, are shrewd enough to reject outright.

For the purveyors of conventional wisdom, the failure to act boldly is seen as good risk management, whereas in reality it's the riskiest decision of all. In 2005, former HUD Secretary Henry Cisneros told a group of city managers that they "can't manage for steady state anymore. There are too many changes going on outside." As he spoke, I remember thinking, "That's just as true in the private sector." As if on cue, a month later, Mike Bannister, CEO of Ford's credit and financing business, sent me a copy of a memo he sent his managers. In it, he wrote: "We are managing in a time of chaos. There is no cement under our feet. The situation is fluid and things will change. Leadership is key to how we respond to these challenges." Steady-state management is not a prudent approach when there's no cement under our feet.

Remember that in the theater of business, the stage set doesn't have to stay the same, repetitive "safe" way. The walls have wheels, and successful leaders are always considering how the set might be rearranged for a more unique production—understanding that the more radically they rearrange the set, the more likely they are to be derided as crazy by those who can't see beyond the pseudo-safety of the original set.

For Sirius, a persistent failure to act "crazily" would have left the company permanently subservient to its much larger competitor, XM, and maybe in a steady decline if enormous outsiders like Viacom and Fox continue to test the satellite market. That's especially pertinent because the market is expected to expand to 44 million by 2010. In fact, Sirius's action was *entrepreneurial*—path breaking on the surface and meticulously researched underneath.

Disciplined Lunacy: A Passion for Precision

I'd like to return to the notion of passion. As we've seen, passion for an idea is an essential ingredient for curiosity. But a great idea is nothing without great execution. As it turns out, passion is essential for execution.

If you examine the back-end operations at curious, cool, and crazy companies like Zara, FedEx, Dell, Southwest Air, Toyota, Amazon, Louis Vuitton, IKEA, and Starbucks, you will be surprised at the fanatic discipline with which their leaders approach the details of execution. Their *passion for precision* allows them to breathe life into their radical ideas and to build speed, cost-efficiency, flexibility, and profit margin in the process. There should never be any disconnect among innovation, execution, and accountability. Poor leaders are passionate about just one of these three elements and ignore the others. Great leaders are crazy about all three.

Consider the band of seven admirable maniacs who journeyed to Tibet in 2002 to kayak down the remote, deadly, hitherto undescended Tsangpo River. Journalist Peter Heller describes the Tsangpo as "one of the deepest river gorges on earth...a cauldron of savage white water and unrunnable rapids....The seven kayakers who launched their boats down its roaring throats...were either going to die—or emerge transformed." Giant boulders, huge lateral waves, massive hydraulics, freezing temperatures, and deadly eddy lines all ensured that anyone who got flipped out of his boat probably wouldn't survive. It had already thwarted or killed the few who had made the attempt.

Scott Lindgren, the expedition leader, spent more than three years studying the river and its terrain in minutia, assembling a team with the right skills and personalities, securing corporate sponsorship, bringing together nearly 100 local porters and ground support personnel, ensuring sufficient food and supplies for several weeks, and maneuvering endlessly through the bureaucracies in Beijing. During the trip itself, his team undertook careful scouting of particularly chaotic whitewater, followed by precise, urgent, and thorough progress and performance reviews at camp. Like a good business leader, Lindgren was absolutely engaged not only in his vision, but also in what lay below the surface. His passion was not simply a gung-ho "let's be-the-first-to-do it" enthusiasm. His passion was also in the execution of details. *Passion for purpose* and *passion for precision* were intertwined. The expedition succeeded.

A passion for precision should not generate images of conventionally grim, unimaginative green-visor "cost-cutting" efforts, or grim, bloodless data reviews. It's a passion that results in *breakthroughs* in efficiencies and cost-reduction.

To the initial puzzlement of outside observers and competitors, for example, furniture retailer IKEA has redesigned one of its best-selling mugs three times (so far) to squeeze more units onto a single pallet, going from 864 to 2,024 at last count. Such an effort might sound obsessive—and a waste of valuable resources—until you hear that, when spread over 25 million mugs sold each year, the cost savings drops millions of dollars straight to the bottom line, reinforces a corporate mindset of brutally innovative operational efficiency, applies the results to the quick-turnover presentation of another appealingly designed product in the store, and allows the company to maintain a can't-be-beat price.

IKEA has applied a disciplined lunacy to the care and feeding of the back end of its business. Only rarely do I come across leaders who show the same audacity, obsession, imagination, and love for what's backstage as they do for what is onstage. Too many leaders are either the self-proclaimed "visionary" who abdicates the nonvisionary trifles to "those who make it happen," or else the "numbers guy" who has no interest in "the vision thing," much less a crazy vision. Neither alternative suffices anymore.

Certain "visionary" top executives understand this, among them Amazon CEO Jeff Bezos. "When Bezos drops in on the factory, it's like a visit from the IRS," says one insider. "He arrives firing a barrage of inquiries about every detail." Toyota CEO Katsuaki Watanabe has been called "a demon at spotting unnecessary costs and eliminating redundancies." News Corp Chairman Rupert Murdoch is well known as a leader with powerful compelling visions, but an executive who worked for him told me that one of Murdoch's compelling strengths is that he also pays great attention to the myriad details of operations, pricing, and marketing throughout his empire. He knows what's going on.

Compare these leaders with some high-profile "visionaries" who have been accused of ethical and criminal malfeasance—people such as Bernie Ebbers of WorldCom, and Kenneth Lay and Jeffrey Skilling of Enron. Forget the trial verdicts for a moment and just consider the

absence of passion for precision. Skilling, known for his brilliant analytical mind and financial acumen, has blithely said that right up until
the end, he believed that Enron was in great shape, even when many
employees and a growing chorus of outside observers were declaring
that the company's financial foundation was rotten. While Skilling's
legal strategy played us for idiots, Lay's unfortunate strategy was to
present himself as an idiot. His defense, similar to Ebbers' "I'm a
numbskull" stratagem during his trial, was that he didn't understand
what was going on, that he was kept in the dark and that others
betrayed him, and so the company's collapse was not his fault. A leader
with a passion for precision reacts to these statements with horrified
disbelief.[4]

At the end of the day, organizations need a very healthy dose of
both passions—purpose and precision—if they hope to break from
the pack. Passion for purpose without passion for precision yields corporate recklessness and irresponsibility. Passion for precision without
passion for purpose yields conformity and stagnation. When neither
passion for purpose nor passion for precision is evident, the company
is in a world of hurt.

Becoming Curious, Cool, and Crazy: The "Ember" Model

So you have resolved to make your organization—and your leadership—curious, cool, and crazy. What do you do Monday morning? As
you weigh the pros and cons of any important management decision or
course of action, employ what I call the EMBER model. Ask yourself:

1. (E) Does it make us *extraordinary*?
2. (M) Does it *matter* to customers?
3. (B) Does it *break new ground*?
4. (E) Does it encourage *evolvement*?
5. (R) Is it *real*?

If the answer is a firm "yes" to each of these questions, then your
decision could ignite your business like oxygen to an ember in the
fire. If the answers are "no," that ember will die.

Consider the EMBER model letter by letter.

1. *Does It Make Us* Extraordinary?

Whatever you are doing and however you're doing it, the action you take should help make your organization stand out from the crowd. It should somehow help your organization be perceived as unique and special. This is exactly how Apple got its groove back, with iMacs and iPods, after Steve Jobs was reappointed CEO.

2. *Does It* Matter *to Customers?*

Whatever "extraordinary" things you do should matter to customers. Even when you "lead" your customers, they should ultimately be as excited as you are. If you're thrilled but customers aren't, then what you've done doesn't matter. Over the past few years, both HP and Microsoft have been able to boast of numerous patents and new products, but as a number of critics have noted, none of them is really a big, "gotta-have" hit with customers. A Morgan Stanley executive told me that high-wealth individuals should entrust his company with their portfolios because "the company spends over a billion dollars a year on equity, strategy, and economic research." That is all well and good, but do customers believe that the research is of unique and relevant value to them? Does it truly matter to them? If so, Morgan Stanley's EMBER vision will be fulfilled. Otherwise, it's just whistling in the dark.

3. *Does It* Break *New Ground?*

The action you are contemplating should be something compelling that hasn't been done before. It can be large, like IBM's "computing on demand" strategy, or it can be small, like JetBlue being the first to put TV screens on the back of each airplane seat. The only thing that counts is that it's significant, it makes a palpable impact—and it's first.

4. *Does It Encourage* Evolvement?

Your company's offerings might be extraordinary, might matter to the customer, and might break new ground, but is your organization geared toward making that product or service perpetually evolve? What are you doing to scale up and expand its reach? Are you adding features, spicing up the design or presentation, improving distribution, or ramping up service? What are you doing in terms of developing next-generation technologies, materials, and designs? How are you applying these technologies to new niches and unserved customers? How fast are you doing it? How are you ensuring that the evolvement is extraordinary and matters to customers?

In the Copycat Economy, value continually evolves, often in a discontinuous manner, as new technologies, competitors, and customers enter the market. That's why companies today must be built to change, not built to last. In fact, only by being built to change will they last. Vince McMahon has built World Wrestling Entertainment and the World Wrestling Federation into a multibillion-dollar empire. According to an admiring Hulk Hogan, Vince McMahon's way of doing business is to "ride the horse until it drops, shoot it, then eat it." Now *that's* evolvement!

Evolvement is a continuing challenge for even the most successful and adventurous companies. Two current darlings of the investment community are Google and Apple. Apple's sales growth—63 percent in 2005—is estimated to fall to 13 percent in 2006 as more iPod imitators enter the fray. Google is running into more resistance—and cost—as it attempts to catalog copyrighted books, TV shows, movies, and scholarly publications. Will these companies slip back into the pack, or will their evolvement be successful, with audacious new products that catapult them even further ahead than they are now?

5. *Is It* Real?

Is that new product or service you think you are succeeding with truly profitable, or is its effect chimerical, a matter of "creative accounting," an illusion of corporate smoke and mirrors? All strategies and their execution must be built on the fundamental premise that data, outcomes, and metrics are based on accurate information and intelligence, and are backed by reliable, accountable sources. If the execution of your crazy idea yields inaccurate or incomplete data—on factors like expenses, cost of capital, progress toward revenue targets, cost overruns, consumer confidence, employee morale, unintended consequences of consolidation efforts, or unanticipated changes in the competitive landscape—then you can count on facing unpleasant surprises, greater risk, poorer decisions, and impaired execution.

The failure to keep it real also has more ominous implications. As we're seeing with the ethical meltdowns and accounting shenanigans afflicting so many once-proud firms, a reliance on funny money and financial sleight-of-hand ultimately destroys companies—and careers. A *BusinessWeek* article asserted that nowadays "trust is more important than growth." I take that to mean that if investors, partners, and customers can't trust the company's numbers or its motives, the company's credibility and attractiveness plummet. "Closed doors" mindsets and "creative accounting" practices are ultimately losers' games, leading to shady behavior, dishonest corporate cultures, untrustworthy relationships, lost credibility, major earnings restatements, high-profile bankruptcies, and criminal indictments. The more opaque the financial reporting and the more secretive the methods by which results were determined, the more that accountability suffers and the more the integrity of the entire company is called into question—and rightfully so.

One last thing: The ultimate barometer of a corporation's *real* performance is true, no b.s., unvarnished profit. You can argue which profit metrics to use—net income, operating income, one of several variants of cash flow, economic value added, return on invested capital, return on assets, return on equity—but it must demonstrate that the company is, or will be, making real, no-nonsense profit (not just raising sales and market share) from its curious, cool, and crazy new ventures. That's the core of disciplined lunacy.

Final Lessons from the EMBER Model

The EMBER model will help you put into practice the precepts of Chapters 3 and 4: the power that comes from calculated reinvention and curious, cool, and crazy. So will the following axioms, which I have culled from a career analyzing how businesses and their leaders succeed:

- **Winners do strategy on the run.** The winners in the Copycat Economy are companies whose people are always scanning the environment and horizon for opportunities and agilely capitalizing on them, then quickly generating action plans, racing to execute them, and ultimately redefining themselves in line with changing market realities.

- **Intangibles are more important than tangibles.** Size, mass, tangible assets, and balance sheets can be leveraged, but they are less vital than intangibles like foresight, knowledge, talent, imagination, speed, flexibility, responsiveness, caring, courage, and innovation.

- **It's gotta be fun.** In the most successful companies, from fast-growing start-ups to established businesses, employees say, "I'm working my butt off, but I'm having a lot of fun." Fun can mean informality, humor, celebrations, and shenanigans at work. But the best fun comes when you're given the tools, training, freedom, and accountability to be imaginative, enact changes, and execute bold plans with fellow lunatics.

Now that we've reviewed how to resist the pull of the pack, we're ready to examine some specific paths that will spur your organization to pull away from it. For this, we turn to Part II.

Endnotes

[1] Apparently, Willie Nelson himself has put on the same Madonna-and-Willie glasses that Branson has. Not only is he on the board of directors of a tiny company called Earth Biofuels, he's also promoting his own BioWillie fuel, a mix of diesel and soybeans which powers his tour bus and is already being sold in selected filling stations. Like Branson, he's pointing to the inevitable rise of environmentalism, demand for cheaper alternatives to oil, and desires to reduce dependence on foreign oil.

[2] One Morgan Stanley executive attributed his firm's strangled decline under CEO Philip Purcell to what he labeled a slow, risk-averse "culture of no."

[3] In fact, by first quarter 2006, Sirius's subscriber base had grown to more than 4.2 million, and its growth rate exceeded that of XM for the first time. In addition to barreling toward a billion dollar revenue stream, Sirius will be generating cash by 2007, according to CEO Mel Karmazin.

[4] On July 5, 2006, shortly after receiving a "guilty" verdict in his trial, Ken Lay passed away. To those who might object to my critique of Lay as disrespecting the deceased, I point out that I am not evaluating Lay the man. I am evaluating his leadership; specifically, I am pointing out how a particularly flagrant dearth of "passion for precision" can lead to particularly tragic results.

PART II

HOW TO BREAK
FROM THE PACK

5

DOMINATE OR LEAVE

"Uh-oh," I thought, "this is not good."

I was getting my first peek at the strategic plan of a chemical products and services company whose financials had been flat for the past four years. The company intended to enter just about every market and niche imaginable. Business after business, region after region, demographic after demographic, product line after product line—all were targeted, with specific goals, action plans, and marketing initiatives. It looked terribly impressive, but I knew that this plan would only aggravate the company's problems.

To break from the pack, you must dominate some significant area of the market. In advising military brass on how to win in warfare, Colin Powell says, "Choose your battles *very selectively,* then go in with *overwhelming force.*" Leaders of successful organizations, whether military or corporate, know that the key to achieving victory is to narrow their scope of activities, attention, and priorities to the point that they can muster the critical mass they need to achieve true market leadership.

In today's Copycat Economy, you can't be great in *many* businesses, you can't be curious, cool and crazy in *many* businesses, and it's a fool's gambit even to try. You must choose your markets, your products, and your customers very carefully, then go in with tremendous creative and productive force until you dominate the arenas you've selected. The implications are twofold: One, don't enter any space you're not prepared to dominate. Two, once you figure out what you will dominate, exit everything else. Period.

I could end the chapter right now, but I know that this principle will strike many readers as so bizarre that we must start at the beginning with some basic fundamentals. First, it's important to remember that domination is not necessarily about being the biggest. Whopping balance sheets, stout sales figures, fat market shares, and big newspaper headlines are no indication that a company has taken command of its market, as executives of United Airlines, Kodak, and GM would ruefully admit.

On the other hand, you've probably never heard of Moldflow. But this small $65 million global purveyor of computer-aided design and engineering software dominates in one critical manufacturing process: the simulation of plastics injection molding. Its domination is so impressive that over the past few years its real growth has ranged from 30 to 50 percent annually and its profit growth has hit the double-to-quadruple mark annually.

Neither is domination about beating up a rival. Does it really matter if during this quarter Ford's earnings are bigger than GM's, or American Airlines' income surpasses Delta's? All four companies are in deep trouble. In contrast, while Moldflow tracks the movements of its rivals, it has no interest or expectation of demolishing them. Instead, as marketing manager Peter Ruzinski explains, the company's primary goal is to "be anywhere injection molding is done on earth."

So if a company doesn't automatically dominate by outweighing the competition, or by crushing it, then what are its benchmarks of success? Commenting about Apple, the *Wall Street Journal's* technology guru Walter Mossberg gives us some clues that point in the right direction: "The Mac's impact on the industry is vastly greater than its market share. Apple is the most innovative major computer maker... Almost everything it does is later copied by the Windows PC makers..."

Ah, there's the first clue. Dominant companies can be big or small, but what's important is that, like Apple and Moldflow, they have a market impact that is greater than their size or the number of units they sell. They are lauded as "the" innovative players who set the agenda for their industry. They demonstrate consistently visible forward momentum, they are recognized for excellence in execution, and they often have a reputation for cool. The ultimate indicators are their ultimate results: Dominant companies are the most likely to generate consistently impressive financial returns (especially profitability) and organic growth rates. They also are a magnet for the best and brightest talent.

Apple has dominated the space of design and "high" technology in its computer products, even though the company is much smaller than rivals like Dell and Sony. Over the past few years, Apple has carefully applied this expertise to thoroughly dominate the world of online music and portable MP3 audio and video players. This dominance has translated into extraordinary revenue and growth, as noted in Chapter 3, the company's revenue and profit growth has been extraordinary.

One more thing to keep in mind: Dominance is not limited to one player. In the PC business, Apple might dominate design, but Dell dominates manufacturing and distribution efficiencies. There's theoretically no limit to the number of dominant players in any industry, as long as they choose different spaces to lead and those spaces matter to customers.

One Size Doesn't Fit All: The Peril of Offering the All-Inclusive Menu

If there's one phrase I would eliminate from corporate strategy sessions, it's "one-stop shopping." This phrase is diabolical, for it can make otherwise sensible executives salivate with infantile glee. Their eyes glaze as they visualize hordes of customers spending gobs of money and never leaving for another competitor because the company magically provides them with an all-inclusive, integrated, A-to-Z menu of products and services that they absolutely must have, forever.

This vision is a destructive fantasy that demolishes any possibility of dominance. For one thing, customers will simply not comply with it. As one of my clients told me, "Just because I keep a couple checking and money market accounts for quick liquidity at Bank X, why would Bank X assume that I'll let them finance my home and manage my retirement portfolio?" When Phil Condit headed Boeing, he stated flatly, "We don't buy engines, auxiliary power units, and avionics on one purchase order, and we don't expect to in the future."

Instead, the company continues to scan the global marketplace for the suppliers that can provide the best price-value mix in each product line, and then buys accordingly.

The pre-2005 AT&T learned this lesson the hard way prior to its purchase by SBC. During its 1980s and 1990s debacles, AT&T's strategic premise was that customers wanted to buy all their telecom services (long distance, Internet, cable TV, web TV, cellular, and so on) from one provider. Trying to make this all-things-to-all-customers menu-building possible and scalable, AT&T binged on massive, debt-ridden acquisitions.

Unfortunately for AT&T, those darn customers didn't cooperate with the plan. Like intransigent children, individual customers insisted on picking and choosing different services from different providers, depending on where they'd get optimal value. Corporate customers became increasingly wary of tying their fortunes solely to one provider; they, too, chose AT&T for one or two things and found better alternatives for the remainder elsewhere.

To challenge the famous *Field of Dreams* dictum, if you keep on building it, they probably won't come. And then you're stuck with a big stadium.

Apart from those darn customers who insist on making their own decisions, there's another reason why "one-stop-shopping" is a fantasy. No matter what your consultants and investment bankers tell you, you can't be great in everything, you can't do it all, and if you try to do it all you'll wind up with a big diversified menu of undistinguished "me-too" products and services. Further, the wider the net you try to cast, the more cumbersome, costly, and complicated your organization will be, and the more your company's resources, management attention, creative capacity, and customer care will be spread thin.[1]

Forget trying to be all things to all people. Resist the temptation to acquire and diversify for the purpose of being in as many segments and sectors of the marketplace as you can. These are losers' strategies because companies that declare they intend to dominate everything wind up dominating nothing. From 2000 to 2005, CEO Carly Fiorina put HP into every conceivable sector of consumer-electronics products, high-technology products, and IT services, and to her last day she insisted that the company would dominate them all. Yet after years of acquisitions and every possible organizational gyration, HP dominated only printers and imaging, the same arenas that the company ruled before Fiorina took over. Despite all the bravado and capital investments, she failed to create even one new dominating sector during her tenure.

Even worse, in 2002, Fiorina justified the huge acquisition of Compaq by proudly announcing that HP was officially number one in the PC business. Yes, as a result of buying another deeply troubled company, HP was temporarily tops in sales and market share. But, in fact, it was the smaller Dell that was genuinely dominating in the world of PCs while HP was bleeding red ink on its investment. HP struggled to maintain its artificial lead position not by innovating, but by reflexively cutting prices to match Dell's, thereby accelerating its hemorrhage because its costs were so much higher than Dell's. Ultimately, the Compaq acquisition drained the life force out of HP, and Dell eventually gained the number one spot anyway.

Imagine what HP's printing and imaging groups could have accomplished if they had been freed from the burden of supporting the rest of the corporation and instead applied their market-dominating resources to new business opportunities. Imagine if HP didn't spread management attention and corporate capital to integrate its divisions after a dubious megamerger, or try to prop up so many commoditized and uninspired lines of business. HP could have conquered the new worlds of imaging—in health care, national security, telecom, new media. Fiorina could have retired a hero. Instead, her successor, Mark Hurd, has had to clean up the mess.

The same sad story happened to "co-CEOs" Charles Schwab and (now deposed) David Pottruck at Schwab. Once a pioneering dominator in its field, Schwab responded to the accelerating imitation and commoditization of its services not by enlarging its dominance of the discount brokerage market, but rather by enlarging its presence in diversified markets. After a series of acquisitions like U.S. Trust (high-end wealth management), Soundview Technologies (research and analysis), and CyberTrader (digital trading), Schwab declared itself a "full-services" financial supermarket.

Unable to properly execute this vague, diffuse corporate vision, Schwab couldn't dominate any sector it was in. It got battered on the low end by companies like Ameritrade, on the high end by companies like Fidelity, and in the middle by companies like Merrill Lynch. Not only was it not dominant anymore, but it was no longer even distinctive. Its brand and reputation suffered, its skills were overwhelmed, and, unsurprisingly, its stock price plunged even as the market rebounded from its 2000 low. Explaining the mess, a Motley Fool investment website commentary was right on target:

> "There is a certain truism about basic competitive strategy: There should be only one. It is nearly a sure sign of failure when a company that has spent its entire existence as a low-cost provider suddenly tries to become a provider of differentiated products as well. Schwab was essentially trying to service two different kinds of customers at various pricing tiers (three, if you count the company's hundred-billion-dollar mutual fund business)".

If the lure of the all-inclusive menu is perilous for large companies, it's doubly dangerous for small ones with far more limited resources. When Seabridge, Inc., founder Jaimie Pardi proclaimed that his startup company's customer-retention software was universally applicable, I told him that if he tried to be all things to all companies, he would fail, and that conventional CRM (customer relations management) products hawked by Siebel and Oracle would prevail. After burning through nearly all his initial capital, Pardi conceded that I might be right. He and CEO Jonathan Perdue went back to the drawing board and figured out the distinctive market space Seabridge could truly dominate: online fan-loyalty programs for professional sports franchises. Today, Seabridge digital products tantalize professional sports teams with features like cashless purchasing opportunities that reward their fans with redeemable points, a chance for prizes like free tickets, and face time with players. Simultaneously, Seabridge products reward teams with documented boosts in revenues, operational efficiencies, brand loyalty, and hitherto unattainable customer profile information for follow-up marketing. Now, after sharpening its strategic focus and deciding which sector it will "own," Seabridge has paying customers (like the Los Angeles Lakers and the Sacramento Rivercats), more investors, and a growing brand identity within the professional sports community of owners and general managers.

An Unusual Case Study

To further illustrate some of these points in a rather unexpected market, consider a company I briefly cited in Chapter 4: Public Financial Management. PFM commands a unique sector of the market. It provides independent financial advice to public-sector and nonprofit organizations. Even though PFM is in the same industry as global banking colossuses like Citigroup and UBS, this small, $85-million company dominates the public financial advisory space. With its 360 employees in 26 small offices around the country, PFM sets the agenda in public finance. It's closely watched and benchmarked by rivals. And in an arena marked by regular scandals, its reputation is sterling.

How is it possible for a small player to be so powerful? Part of the answer is PFM's highly focused business model. PFM is a public finance fiduciary. The company provides independent financial advice and management to state governments, local governments, and non-profit organizations like universities and hospitals. It offers personalized services as diverse as debt management, policy development, capital planning, revenue forecasting and evaluation, pension advice, strategic consulting, and money management. It is acknowledged as faster, more comprehensive, and more innovative than rivals.

Over the past decade, many investment banks got out of the public finance business. Some saw it as a nongrowth business lacking the allure of IPOs and mergers and acquisitions. Other banks were not able to resolve the conflicts of interest between their fiduciary businesses (the kind of independent financial advisories performed by PFM) and their transactional investment-banking businesses. Today, with a couple notable exceptions, the big investment banks have abandoned the fiduciary business in public finance and have concentrated on the high-volume, product-based transactional investment banking side of the business—specifically, structuring, underwriting, and distributing tax-exempt municipal securities.

That's not what PFM does. When PFM advises a city government on how to use debt financing to fund, say, a stadium, the company determines the optimal strategy but doesn't underwrite the bonds. PFM might represent the client on a negotiated basis and perhaps bring in an investment bank like Citi or Goldman Sachs as underwriter and partner. I use the term "partner" loosely because PFM, as advocate for the client, has an important voice in steering the client around the marketing chatter of the banks' salespeople. This doesn't thrill the big banks angling for the deal. And when PFM is given the power to conduct and manage a competitive sale, the banks are often even less happy.

When PFM integrates these advisory services with complementary asset management and financial strategy services, all specialized for government and nonprofits, all tailored to the individual client—

the company simply dominates. It differentiates its value from the tiny competitors who offer low-cost commodity services and from the big competitors who press for the big deals. That is why PFM has continued to grow at a steady 10 percent annual pace over the past 25 years, with increased profitability over the past few years, even as competitors large and small go through periodic upheavals and stay mired in the pack.

Why Davids Beat Goliaths

The fact that size and dominance are not one in the same is a strange notion that deserves a little more discussion. Let me describe a few smaller, dominant Davids and their much larger Goliath adversaries. In the following anecdotes, the Goliaths are so much more diversified than the Davids that the companies are often not competing in the same market space. My point is simply that any two companies I compare in each David-Goliath dyad overlap in certain markets, and when they do, the David dominates. It dominates with focus, innovation, speed, efficiencies, killer products, and "wow!" services that simply surpass those of its larger competitors. That, in turn, explains why the Davids are financially healthier than the Goliaths.

David Google and Goliath Microsoft

Google doesn't dominate Microsoft. Google dominates search. Microsoft's "one-stop-shopping" strategy has turned it into a steady, dividend-issuing mature company that the *Economist* likens to a utility, "safe for widows and orphans." Nothing wrong with that. There's also nothing wrong with the fact that over $40 billion in revenues, Microsoft is nearly ten times the size of Google, with a core quasi-monopoly product line called Windows and Office, all growing at 15 percent annually. We should all have such problems!

Yet Davids like Linux, Firefox, SimDesk, Yahoo, and Google continue to throw rocks that chip away at Goliaths like Microsoft, and the technology giant doesn't seem to possess sufficient weapons to fight back. Its huge R&D budget is applied in numerous directions, because the company is into just about everything digital: servers, videogames, media, telecom, photography, browsers, operating systems, office systems, and blogging. Despite all this frenetically dispersed activity, what keeps Microsoft afloat are its core Windows operating systems and the Office suite of applications.

Meanwhile, Google concentrates on excellence in every conceivable permutation of search. Keep in mind that when I say that Google dominates search, I don't mean that it is content to simply be a little search engine. Google wants to be the primary player in helping us search, organize, and customize all the available information on the Internet. And it is. The upshot? Goliath Microsoft is frantically following the lead of David Google—video file search, local area search, desktop search, search designed for cellphones, scholarly journal search, and so on. Google seems to offer a new direction in search, and in profitable advertising technology linked to search, every two months. It dominates. Small wonder that the company's 2005 profits soared 500 percent over 2004, its revenues doubled, and its share price briefly topped the astronomical $400 level. Moreover, the alarming exodus of talent from other software companies, including Microsoft, to Google, shows how dominant companies find it a lot easier to attract the best and brightest.

David Whole Foods and Goliath Kroger

The $5 billion Whole Foods Market doesn't dominate $60 billion Kroger. It dominates natural foods. Kroger sells natural foods too, but Whole Foods' entire brand, expertise, innovation, supply chain, and scale is built around this market segment. Its scope reaches into the very farming and preparation of everything from vegetables to chickens in order to ensure that the labels "natural" and "organic" are authentic, not just marketing ploys. In Chapter 3 I noted that Whole Foods' financials and growth far exceed the industry norm. In fact, at one point in 2005 Whole Foods' return on assets was 70 times greater than that of Kroger and its profit margin was six times greater. When it comes to investor confidence, the numbers separating the companies are equally dramatic. Whole Foods' market cap is nearly the same as Kroger's despite revenue that is one-twelfth as large. (Parenthetically, Whole Foods' market cap exceeds that of Safeway even though the latter company has sales that are nearly ten times bigger. In a similar vein, Winn-Dixie, with triple the sales and six times the number of stores, has a market cap that's only 10 percent of Whole Foods.) It should not be surprising that Goliaths like Kroger are copying as much of Whole Foods as they dare—not vice versa.

David JetBlue and Goliath United

At $1.6 billion dollars in 2005, JetBlue is no mom-and-pop company, but it is miniscule compared to the $16.6 billion United Airlines behemoth. Yet, over the past few years, while JetBlue was growing in leaps and bounds without megamerger (another clue to domination), United's sizable debt, cost-inefficiencies, and mismanagement threw the company into bankruptcy, from which it only painfully extricated itself in 2006. United's multi-billion dollar annual losses compare miserably with JetBlue's 18 consecutive quarters of profitability. Even more remarkable is that JetBlue grew available seat miles (the industry measure for capacity) by 33 percent while the other majors contracted or stood still.[2]

Why has United struggled? In large part because it's too unwieldy, and it tries to do everything and be everywhere. United and the other major airlines fly multiple types of aircrafts, which require different and costly kinds of service. They fly into multiple hubs and spokes—a costly process—while attempting to reach as many towns and cities as possible. And they do this while operating under rigid and costly labor-management contracts and liabilities.

In comparison, JetBlue concentrates on a relatively small set of carefully selected routes with profit potential; straightforward point-to-point travel; new planes that require less maintenance (all of them one type of plane [the Airbus 320][3], which means easier servicing and training); more coast-to-coast red eyes to keep more planes in the air; compensation built on lower wages with stock ownership; hands-on leadership (executives work on the planes to stay in touch with the business); non-unionized employees doing multiple jobs; amazing productivity (all hands helping results in a 50 percent faster turn-arounds at gate); high-tech customer service efficiencies, with 70 percent of tickets sold through the website; and flight agents who can work from home while equipped with company computers. Even the other major airlines concede that JetBlue's approach will be the wave of the future. The 2005 America West-US Airways merger is proclaimed to be built around the JetBlue business model.

On top of everything else, JetBlue is cool. There are fast queues in airports (an employee told me the lines are so speedy because the new technology requires only a couple strokes on the keyboard to take care of each person in line, as opposed to the endless tapping that rival agents are forced to undertake). There's cheerful banter between staff and passengers. There's the 36 channel DirecTV at every leather seat. All these factors combined to create something intangible. Motley Fool says that: "By offering customers an exceptional experience, JetBlue has fostered brand loyalty in what had become a commodity industry."

David Genentech and Goliath Pfizer

In another, often-sclerotic industry—pharmaceuticals—smaller and nimbler Davids can dominate their sectors with stunning success. At $6 billion in revenues, Genentech often outperforms the $55 billion Pfizer and all other giant, big-menu pharmaceuticals in product development, speed to market, growth rate, return on assets, and market value (in December, 2005, Genentech's market cap exceeded every other pharmaceutical's except Pfizer and Johnson and Johnson).[4] That's because Genentech doesn't seek to amass all scientific specialties toward developing one-size-fits-all, home-run blockbuster drugs in big established markets like Pfizer and many of the Goliaths try to do. Instead, Genentech focuses on biotechnology and applies it to three specific markets: oncology, immunology, and vascular biology. Within those markets, the company futher focuses its resources on "targeted therapies"—drugs aimed at highly defined subsets of diseases, like Avastin for colon cancer and Rituxan for non-Hodgkin's lymphoma. Ironically, both of these supposedly narrow-niche therapies quickly reached the $1 billion-plus blockbuster sales mark, and at a substantially lower cost base than drugs produced by the big all-things-for-all-people pharmaceutical companies. Rituxin is already the number one branded anti-tumor drug in the U.S., and Avastin alone added more than $15 billion to Genentech's market cap. CEO Arthur Levinson is now seeking to narrow Genentech's mission even further. He wants his company to dominate biotech-targeted therapies only for *specific cancers*, such as HER2-positive breast cancer, a particularly deadly form of the disease.

In an industry besieged by expiring drug patents, drying drug-development pipelines, regular scandals and lawsuits, product recalls, and costly clinical failures, Genentech's track record and prospects are remarkable: ten drugs on the market, twenty more in the pipeline, relatively low costs, the ability to charge a premium price for its products, and products that patients take year after year. The final impact is significant. For example, as of mid-2006, sales of Avastin and Herceptin (breast cancer treatment) were up 72 percent

118 BREAK FROM THE PACK

and 100 percent, respectively, raising corporate profits by 79 percent and earnings per share by 82 percent. 2005 metrics were very similar, propelling Genentech's value to 18 times revenue even as the stock value of many pharma Goliaths, including Pfizer, declined.[5]

Genentech's highly focused, dominating approach allows it to more sharply define and hire the "best fit" scientists. Because these scientists share a more focused mission, the company has fewer conflicting fiefdoms to manage and sees more breakthrough projects that spring up as common research efforts. (No doubt this climate contributed to Genentech's being named number one by *Fortune* magazine as "the best company to work for" in 2006.) And because it's so clear on what it seeks to dominate, Genentech finds it easier to identify great partners in those areas it doesn't seek to dominate. Genentech has forged over 100 licensing and joint-venture partnerships to accelerate product development, like the relationship with Idec Pharmaceuticals which resulted in Rituxin.

The continuous merger-acquisition feeding frenzy in the pharmaceutical industry has expanded many companies to enormous sizes. Pfizer, in fact, is a fusion of mergers, including the mega-acquisitions of American Home Products and Pharmacia. The Glaxo empire is a fusion of Glaxo and Wellcome, which then combined with SmithKlineBeecham (itself a merged composite) to form the giant, European-based GlaxoSmithKline in 2000. These kinds of acquisitions in the pharmaceutical industry have cranked up revenues, but they also have bloated the companies' costs, drained their earnings, and accelerated their frenzied efforts to come up with save-the-day blockbuster drugs—drugs that would be used to treat as many diseases as possible and thereby spew out tons of cash to pay off the companies' debts. Some Goliaths, like Novartis and Johnson and Johnson, while not boasting the returns of Davids like Genentech and Amgen, have managed to perform well by overcoming these impediments. Most have not. In fact, despite all the management gyrations and hyperactive sales efforts among the giants, most of the growth in the pharmaceutical industry as a whole has been in generics—copycat drugs that flood the market after patent protection expires. What that means is that when it comes to product development, the "returns on megamergers" have been, shall we say, disappointing. Meanwhile, Davids like Genentech continue to dominate.

David Pixar and Goliath Disney

Here's an "if you can't beat 'em, join 'em" case where the Goliath ultimately threw in the towel and enticed the David to join his Army. In January 2006, $31 billion Disney bought $342 million Pixar for nearly $7.5 billion in stock. The following explains why Pixar was so attractive a target.

From 1995 until the acquisition, Disney and Pixar enjoyed a lucrative partnership. Pixar made the movies, while Disney co-financed them and then took care of marketing and distribution. They split the proceeds. Yet the separate histories and track records of the two companies were quite dissimilar. During the term of their partnership, Pixar unleashed a remarkable six-for-six streak of block-buster films featuring dazzling animation technology and hugely memorable characters like Buzz Lightyear, Nemo, and Mr. Incredible. The $3.2 billion in worldwide box office sales garnered by the Pixar production dwarfed the comparable figures from Disney's own animation studios, which produced lackluster films like *Home On the Range*, *Brother Bear*, and *Treasure Planet*.

Taken as an entire company, Disney's sales and profit growth were negligible compared to Pixar's 50 percent annual sales and profit growth from 2003 to 2005. In fact, by 2005, pipsqueak Pixar was post-ing profit and operating margin percentages that were more than six times those of Disney. The smaller company's return on assets was double Disney's—even though Pixar didn't even release a new film in 2005. So much for the value of diversification and size.

What makes these Davids so nimble and strong and what factors render the Goliaths so sclerotic? Pixar focused its strategy and resources on creating breakthroughs in storylines and 3-D computer technology for feature animation films that appeal to both adults and children. It dominated a very distinct space. Disney's strategy, how-ever, has been to promote and market a bewildering one-stop-shop-ping array of enterprises all in the amorphous category of "entertainment": animation films, every other kind of film, theme parks, television, cable and radio stations, TV production and distrib-ution, music companies, newspaper and book publishing companies, travel divisions, a cruise line, retail stores, special effects and engi-neering firms, theatre productions, sports franchises, and so on.

But with the notable exception of ESPN (which truly dominates sports television) and its theme parks, Disney hasn't dominated anything. In fact, the company's sprawl has often generated serious problems among the myriad Disney businesses: a diffusion of priorities, confusing misallocation of resources, bloated costs, accelerating political dissent within management, an exodus of talented executives, and a blurring of the brand. Under the reign of CEO Michael Eisner, these problems adversely affected Disney's financials and led to wild stock gyrations. In contrast, the steady upward trajectory of Pixar's financials and brand once again shows the power of concentrated domination over dispersion and sheer size. Small wonder that new Disney CEO Bob Iger wanted his Goliath to permanently team up with David—and learn some slingshot skills in the process.

Is Big Always Bad? Is Diversity Always Dangerous?

The Goliaths I've discussed above aren't "bad" companies at all. In fact, Disney and Kroger remain viable players, Pfizer's numbers are relatively solid, United has emerged from bankruptcy, and Microsoft remains a huge force to be reckoned with. I could have made an even stronger case against sheer size, however, by deliberately choosing from a vast roster of large, failing companies or large, dead ones. Even so, the leaders of the Goliath companies I listed share a seductively dangerous misconception that cultivating more presence in more and more markets yields dominance. The David companies show us that the opposite is true. Unless they make some dramatic changes, they will perpetually be fixing internal messes and playing catch-up to companies that do dominate.

There's nothing inherently negative about size and diversification as long as they remain true to the spirit of dominance. Dell is smaller than HP, but at nearly $60 billion is certainly no little computer shop down the block. Further, Dell has diversified so much beyond computers that it dropped "Computer" from its corporate name. Neither "big" nor "diversified" are four-letter words at Dell. But keep in mind that because Dell has diversified only in carefully selected high-growth sectors, from flat panel TV monitors to servers, the company is certain it can ultimately dominate. If Dell can't apply its low-cost business model to dominate a given niche, and if it is not prepared to go in with overwhelming force, it won't go there at all—even if some promised revenues and market share are enticing. Like a panther, the company slowly circles and scouts the field, and when it's certain it can dominate, it pounces.

Giant diversified GE is another case in point. Remember that under Jack Welch, any division had to be number one or number two in its industry in order to avoid liquidation. Many observers misinterpreted Welch's dictum as meaning he simply demanded the highest revenues. In fact, Welch mandated that each division's goals be carefully defined in terms of cost, net income, and growth. Simply being big in a buggy whip market—or growing revenue and market share by buying other buggy whip companies—wouldn't cut it. Under Jeff Immelt, metrics like net income, new product introductions, and growth performance for each division are now even more important than sheer revenue; that's why Immelt is more focused on fostering domination than with just making the company bigger. Under Immelt, GE divests what it can't dominate (like its insurance business), and pursues only the growth areas it believes it can dominate (like wind energy). It then insists on excellence in execution, using uniform corporate standards of quality and cultural values.

One last and very important point for you to keep in mind: the multi-billion dollar companies that dominate—like Dell, Whole Foods, JetBlue, Genentech, Wal-Mart, and Toyota—don't dominate because they got big. They got big *because* they dominated. These companies provided such sustained value that they literally grew the very size of their market slices. They did all this steadily, deliberately, and quietly while tightening their grip every step of the way.

The Seven Steps to Dominating

Now that you've seen that domination is essential to helping your company break from the pack, here are seven steps that will show you how to do it:

1. Choose to Dominate

Whether you're part of a start-up or a leader of an established business, the first step is to choose dominance over size. In fact, choose dominance over growth itself. Whatever sector you enter, you must be committed to being the premier provider, reaching the top of the food chain in excellence and innovation, and winning a reputation for being the coolest and most provocative provider. You'll find that it's a lot easier for your organization to innovate and stay streamlined when you're focused on dominance than when you're trying to simply "manage" an unruly array of enterprises. You'll also find that the business growth you seek will be the consequence of your dominance.

Resist the temptations to go for the easy buck or the size-at-any-cost opportunism. PFM, for example, stays true to its dominating mission. It does not seek private sector financial advisory clients even though they are a potential source of revenue. They don't fit PFM's persona, they blur its focus, and therefore they are a potentially dangerous distraction from dominance.

Remember, choosing to dominate means committing to going in "with overwhelming force." Dabbling with an opportunity—as Motorola did with digital technology while Nokia committed fully to it—is choosing to fail. Going in with overwhelming force is about committing to make all decisions—including resources of capital allocation, management time and attention, budgeting, hiring, and even selective acquisitions—for domination, not for size.

The bottom line is simple: Don't venture into any market space unless you can demonstrate—the way you would if you were a start-up seeking the capital approval of tough-minded venture capitalists—that you have the capacity and the will to set the agenda for it.

2. Be a Laser, Not a Floorlamp

Make sure your growth strategy is laser-like: simply stated, easy to convey, highly concentrated, and precisely focused on the arenas you'll dominate. If you find your strategy looking like a floorlamp—diffusing light over big chunks of carpeting and floorboords, with too many directions and with too many unconnected markets and targets and with too many priorities that are hard to ascertain—and if you require lots of words, generalities, caveats, and exceptions to explain your goals, then, to be blunt, you need to narrow the light beam and turn up the intensity.

Being a laser also means avoiding the temptation to seek the big broad spotlight. By that, I mean—consistent with my comments in Step 1—you must avoid the urge to get greedy and pursue revenues that are not aligned with your precise mission, even if the opportunity appears alluring. If you're a Disney, just because you can dominate theme parks doesn't mean you can dominate sports franchises. (Unsurprisingly, Disney finally unloaded the California Angels baseball team and the Mighty Ducks hockey team.) Even if you're a colossus like Wal-Mart, just because you can dominate the high-volume, low-price retail sector doesn't mean you can simultaneously dominate the high-design, discount-upscale sector just because Target does.

You'll face numerous seductive appeals to broaden the laser to a nice, warm, diffuse and expedient floorlamp that covers more and more unrelated ground. Don't do it. Laserlike dominance requires the discipline to just say no to floorlamp strategies.

3. Make Sure the Laser Is Exciting

You need to concentrate your efforts on a compelling and intriguing growth area, or an area you believe your company can ignite into growth. You must also ensure that you and your colleagues are personally passionate about the direction you're pursuing.

Remember how many investment banks got out of public finance because it was ostensibly a dull, no-growth sector? Well, the folks at PFM begged to differ. They thought public finance had great potential, and they liked doing it! They still think it's cool.

Talk to the management team at Ortho-McNeil Neurologics (OMN), and you'll be blown away by the collective, and targeted, passion. OMN, a Johnson & Johnson company formed in 2004, is pure laser beam: It's the only major health-care company focused exclusively on neurology. With products aimed at migraines, epilepsy, and Alzheimer's, the company already boasts more than a billion dollars in revenue. When I met the management team, what impressed me was the obvious commitment of the team toward alleviating the pain of the sufferers of these three diseases. So many big pharma meetings revolve around more detached issues of management, cost-control, synergies, sales, and product portfolios. Because OMN is not a humongous, diversified company, the managers were also able to put their arms around fewer issues while demonstrating a compassion for the customers they serve and a "love" for the market slice they intended to dominate. There's a human resonance there that is missing in many companies. If OMN were publicly traded, I'm sure this resonance would be an important plus for investors.

124 BREAK FROM THE PACK

4. Be Willing to Subtract

Remember that chemical company I cited at the beginning of this chapter? Ultimately, its corporate-planning group agreed with me that the company was trying to get into too many market sectors and that it couldn't meet its performance goals, much less excel, by trying to succeed in all of them. The executive team then pruned the number of market segments significantly. My job is to get them to prune by another 50 percent. Only then can they even think about domination.

Subtraction is hard to accomplish but essential to success. You have to be as committed to subtraction as you are addition. Too many companies get bogged down with a load of what retired Scandinavian Air CEO Jan Carlzon referred to as "bad business": products and services that have become low-margin commodities, niches that yield a lousy return on investment and ought to be abandoned, customers who yield a lousy return on investment and ought to be fired, dog divisions that might have been lucrative in the past but now ought to be sold, and costly internal functions that ought to be digitalized, outsourced, or divested entirely.

Back in the early 1980s, Carlzon turned around an ailing Scandinavian Air and made it the premier European business traveler airline. He did it by honing in on the routes, planes, and services important to business travelers. Simultaneously, and in spite of much criticism and admonition, he subtracted what wasn't important to business travelers. He dumped long-held routes, grounded and sold wrong-size planes, and curtailed irrelevant services. If tour groups and tourists wanted to use SAS, that was fine, but his investments went almost exclusively toward what he called "good business"—in his case, the business traveler market. Carlzon's unambiguous laser-like decisions made SAS sharply focused and clearly branded.

When Franck Riboud took over French company Danone in 1996, the company was in a wide array of food businesses: pasta, baby food, beer, sauces, ready meals, and so on. He dumped everything except water, biscuits, and dairy products. Since then, Danone has been a dominator in water (Evian) and yogurt, and despite (rather, *because* of) the pruning, its 2005 revenue of $16.4 billion was greater than it was when the company was much more diversified, its organic growth rate is a faster 5.7 percent clip, and its $39-billion market cap is far healthier than it ever was. CFO Antoine d'Estaing argues that what's important is not the company's overall size, but that it's big in the areas it chooses to compete in (domination!); he argues that diversified companies pay less attention to the kind of detail necessary for excellence.

Many people believe that in contrast to Motorola in the 1980s, Nokia was a start-up that found it easy to jump into digital because it had no legacies to protect. Hardly. Nokia was a midsize, diversified conglomerate making products like cables, rubber boots, toilet paper, televisions, and telephones. When it made the decision to break from the pack in digital cellphones, it shed nearly all its product lines to achieve the laser focus on digital mobile telephony. Motorola didn't—and suffered.

Leaders don't like subtracting any business, even if it's "bad business," because it means getting rid of customers, revenues, internal fiefdoms, legacies, and individual comfort zones. That's why it took Target Corporation a long time to sell its underperforming units, Mervyn's and Marshall Fields. Bob Ulrich, CEO of Target, finally bit the bullet, and now Target is focused successfully on a core objective of dominating the retail space of hip products at low prices in a high-design environment.

Nokia, SAS, Danone, and Target are exceptions. Leaders have few problems adding functions, product lines, market sectors, staff, and entire divisions, but getting them to seriously discuss eliminating them when they no longer create value is nearly impossible. In 2005, for example, the International Olympic Committee considered a proposal to add a few sports like golf and rugby to its menu, but its bylaws state that to do that, the IOC must eliminate the same number of current Olympic sports. According to *Sports Illustrated,* "the proposal stirred up such a hornet's nest that it never came to a vote.... The episode proved again that while the Olympic family has been terrific at broadening its program to include everything from tae kwon do to circus events such as synchronized swimming and trampoline, it has been incapable of seriously considering whether those, or other sports, really belong in the Games. No sport has been removed from the Olympics since polo got the ax after the 1936 Games."

Businesspeople hate subtraction not just for Olympic-size decisions involving entire divisions or market niches, but even for the so-called small stuff. At PFM, managing director Keith Curry says, "What used to be 'good business' for us—a small bond issue without the clear potential for big subsequent issues or for other services like investment management—well, that's now a drain on our resources. We shouldn't compete with the little shops for that business, and if the business is already on our books, we have to examine whether it's worth our while to continue having it on our books. But how do you convince our people of that while they're trying to build up their own book of business in preparation for performance review?"

Leaders in all organizations have to learn to subtract and encourage their employees to see the value of doing it too, even if it means abandoning traditional markets and comfortable products, and even if it means firing customers who no longer fit the new strategy and who longer help the organization dominate.

5. Choose Metrics That Dominate

Mercer Consulting head Adrian Slywotsky has flatly declared, "Market share is dead." By this he does not mean that market share is unimportant. Certainly, any company gains leverage and clout with share, and diminishing share—like that experienced over the past few years by, say, GM and Nokia—is a danger sign that must be attended to.

However, any leader who obsesses over the metrics of market-share growth, or who defines success by market-share growth, will make decisions guaranteed to stall his or her company. The same can be said for leaders obsessed with the size of revenues, the totals on the balance sheet, and the length of their personnel roster. All the window dressing and consultant-speak in the world can't camouflage the reality that size of market share, top-line revenue, and balance sheet is no predictor of dominance.

What is the alternative to a metrics that measures size? Well, how about metrics that revolve around *profit*?

I continue to be taken aback that measuring profitability remains a learning point for otherwise astute executives. In 1998, the newly arrived Boeing CFO Deborah Hopkins was shocked that so many of her top executives did not know how to project or measure profitability. I remain amazed how often an initiative is proposed in senior management meetings with the underlying logic that it will yield more market share, more sales, better leverage, more scale, better cross-selling opportunities, higher market "presence," less duplication, lower costs, higher employee morale, better relationship with the community, and so on—but with no mention of profitability. If you press the question—asking approximately when might this initiative possibly yield the kind of margins, net income, operating cash flow, or return on invested capital that would justify the investment— you get vague responses or blank, hostile stares. But as you've seen in earlier chapters, profitability is one of the most important differentiators between firms that break from the pack and those that stay mired in it. In the absence of profit metrics, all the other measures mask performance problems. There's a great *Dilbert* cartoon that hits the nail on the head. In a meeting with Dilbert and Wally, the boss declares, "We need a clear strategy. Does anyone have a suggestion?" Dilbert replies, "Let's figure out what makes us the most profit, and then do more of it."

The boss responds, "It needs to be less clear than that."

(Wally chimes in: "Can it be illegal?")

John Lumelleau suggests three other important metrics for domination. Lumelleau is the president of Lockton Companies, the largest independently owned insurance brokerage firm in the U.S., and the eleventh largest such firm overall. Lockton's customers include some of the biggest names in the Fortune 1000. At $400 million, it's a much smaller company than its gargantuan rivals, like Aon and Marsh & McLennan, which have diversified into other arenas, like financial services, mutual funds, and consulting. Yet I submit that Lockton, which focuses solely on insurance brokerage, dominates the business. While the Marsh & McLennan website crows that "the firm has beaten out Aon to become the world's largest insurance brokerage company," Lumelleau gains his satisfaction from the fact that Lockton rates best in the industry on year-to-year organic growth rate, customer retention rate, and rate of retention of its professional employees. And it does so without the financially catastrophic ethics scandals that have rocked some of its Goliath rivals.

So, along with metrics of *profitability,* you can add measures of *organic growth, customer retention,* and *retention of top talent.* Don't those criteria make sense? It's a far greater challenge to dominate in these metrics than to concentrate solely on revenue and market-share metrics.

A few caveats: First of all, while I celebrate the metrics of a company's organic growth, I'm not discounting the appropriateness of judicious acquisitions to help fuel dominance, a point I expand on in Chapter 10. But if your company is really the best in breed with the most powerful momentum, your main growth source will be your company itself, not your ability to paste a collage of disparate companies together in one big hopeful lump. Second, when I applaud customer retention, I'm talking about customers you want to keep, grow, and enlist as your word-of-mouth de facto salespeople. I'm not talking about retaining "bad business" customers who you ought to fire even if they currently boost your sales a little. Third, when I talk about keeping top talent, note the word *top*. If you're attracting and retaining merely adequate or mediocre talent, you're in trouble. And if your best and brightest are looking elsewhere and polishing up their resumes, you're entering a world of hurt.

6. Ensure That Your Organization's Talent and Skills Stay Dominant

No more lip service and empty slogans such as, "Our people are our most important assets." No more viewing corporate training budgets as onerous "costs." You've got to purposely seek and select the best people for your team. Then you've got to nurture them and invest in them, providing constant development, a sense of inclusion and empowerment, and attractive compensation. Recruiting the cheapest or most opportunistically available employees and partners is a loser's strategy. So is scrimping on the kinds of tools, technologies, and nurturing necessary to continually build peoples' expertise, capabilities, and accountabilities.

To maintain company dominance, PFM employees must constantly maintain cutting-edge expertise in areas like debt refinancing, derivative products, lease transactions, fixed-income portfolio management, and government budgeting. They must be the very best at understanding the intricacies of specific governmental businesses like airports, power plants, wastewater systems, and stadium facilities. For PFM partners, therefore, it becomes a business priority to attract, retain, and continually develop the skills of very talented individuals.

Just as no firm can be dominant in all sectors of an industry, no firm can be dominant in all skills and talents. Dominating an industry means picking only the specific *people* and *competencies* needed to succeed. Dell does very little pure research and development; its leaders know their dominance lies in operations and distribution, and that's what they concentrate on.

Further, to stay lean and focused, a dominating company sources out the areas it doesn't dominate to partner organizations who do. As ex-Boeing CEO Harry Stonecipher noted, "Boeing is moving up the value chain and focusing on just a few core competencies. That means it focuses on high-end design, engineering, and systems integration, and lets suppliers do the rest. There are advantages in *not* trying to take a product (let alone all the elements in a complex system) from start to finish. Instead of a closed and vertically integrated structure, a supply chain of innovative companies that are best in class will let each party focus on its core competencies and create added value."

7. Build a Dominating Culture

As a leader, figure out what it takes for your corporate culture to be powerfully dominating internally and built for dominance externally. For CEO John White, a dominating culture at PFM is about transparency and collaboration. Any piece of information, from the most obscure financial data about the firm's performance to partners' performance reviews and compensation, is available to all. Any partner, including White, is accessible to consult with employees at all levels. For White, transparency enhances collaboration, which is his particular obsession. He believes that the company's collective wisdom and integrated expertise allow PFM to stay ahead of the pack. "Partners who do not use each others' expertise waste money," he declares, "even if they stay in cheap hotels and are religious about using FedEx second-day air."

In a 2005 memo to the 53 managing directors (MDs), the most senior people in the company, White wrote:

> Culture is the main thing that binds us together and has made us successful as PFM has grown from a firm of 2 people to one of nearly 400. I say this fully understanding that a minority of MDs are either uncomfortable discussing culture or think such discussions are something between outright bullshit and a waste of time that needs to be tolerated to get through peer reviews and receive the bonus their hard work so richly deserves. Those MDs are, at best, simply wrong and, at worst, causing a deterioration in our culture that will ultimately render this organization unpleasant as a place to work and unsuccessful as a business. They need to either get with the program or find another place to continue their career.

White's comments are applicable to any organization that wishes to dominate. White's comments are applicable to any organization. Shape the culture that will help you promote dominance, and then take it seriously. And if you do, you'll hire people who seriously "fit"

the culture. If they don't fit, don't hire them, and certainly don't promote them. Don't even recruit people who may have great creden-
tials but are a lousy match with the mission and values of the culture.
Both PFM and Genentech have strong cultures marked by collaboration, openness, caring, and performance accountability. Both companies are getting better at consciously rejecting strong job candidates
who come across as overly concerned with rank, salary, and personal
power. The bottom line for you is this: Don't be expedient. Patiently
seek high-talent *and* high-fit people for your organization. Don't
lower the bar just because you need a warm body to fill a job. Talent
counts. Culture counts. Take culture seriously.

Let's summarize. In a Copycat Economy, it's simply impossible to
be curious, cool, and crazy about many things. You have to pick and
choose, and then act with overwhelming force. Regardless of your
organization's size, you must focus obsessively on doing select things in
an imaginatively awesome way for select customers who will see genuine price-value in what you offer them. Simultaneously, you must
dump activities, markets, and customers that don't fit in with your
tight, laserlike focus, even if they're currently bringing in top-line revenues. Do this repeatedly, and you'll see your business expand organically and exponentially. That's what I mean by "dominate or leave."

If you conscientiously follow the seven steps outlined, you will
position your company for dominance. You'll grow and prosper with
less clutter, less waste, less ambiguity, and less internal political crap.
You'll be able to better focus on new market opportunities to extend
your dominance, and you'll have sufficient funds, resources, and
attention to execute your plans with excellence. You'll be able to
mobilize people to commit to a well-defined direction. On top of
everything else, you'll have a better time doing it. Dominating—and
breaking from the pack—is a lot more fun than trying to keep up with
someone else.

Endnotes

[1] In my March 7, 2006 blog entitled "New AT&T, Old AT&T," I wrote:

I'm sure this won't be the last big deal we read about, because AT&T CEO Ed Whitacre's "M.O." is pretty clear:

- *Grow via serial acquisition*
- *Pay premium prices for prey*
- *Aim to be a one-stop-shopping telecommunications mecca*

I noted in the blog that the first two bulleted factors are good predictors of organizational decline (more on this in Chapter 10), and the third factor is more often a dream than reality. I concluded with this warning:

So AT&T's acquisitions make good copy. Newspapers love them. But at the end of the day, what will the new AT&T look like? A huge, unwieldy, costly, creaky, one-stop-shopping bureaucracy glutted with mini-empires offering a slew of "me-too," commoditized, often-mediocre products and services. Hmm, doesn't that sound like the old AT&T?

It will be interesting to see whether the new AT&T will use the principles in this book to break away from the pack, or whether it will simply fall back to its "family tradition."

[2] In 2005, confronted with skyrocketing oil prices, Jet Blue posted its first loss since going public. The company, however, remains vibrant and is poised to recapture profitability by end of 2006.

[3] JetBlue has bought 100 Embraer 100-seat planes for short routes, and, as discussed in Chapter 9, it has maintained operational efficiencies.

[4] That's no plaudit for Pfizer. Its labs have produced no new blockbusters since Viagra in 1998, the company's profits were down 30 percent in 2005, and its stock value dropped 40 percent between 2001 and mid-2006.

6

PUT THE PIECES TOGETHER FOR A HIGHER CAUSE

I love Jamba Juice!

When I'm at a shopping center, at my university, or in an airport, I often find myself waiting in line to order one of their latest concoctions of fruit or veggie smoothies, usually in the extra-large 24-ounce cup. It's so-o-o good.

I'm not the only one who loves Jamba Juice. Founded in 1990, Jamba Juice (the name means "to celebrate" in Swahili) now boasts more than 500 kiosks and small-store locations in 26 states, and net sales of $350 million. Average store sales per year are currently $650,000 and growing. Roughly half of all locations are franchised or partnered with other companies, such as Starbucks, Whole Foods, Safeway, and 24 Hour Fitness. The company is expanding rapidly through franchising and licensing agreements, currently rolling out a new location every five days or so, and has plans to go international. New spin-offs, like the expanded healthful snack-food menus and the Jamba Go-Go delivery and catering business, have sharply boosted annual revenues. The company anticipates this natural momentum to yield a $1 billion revenue stream by 2010.

Clearly, Jamba rocks. Although it has only 11 percent of the entire juice and smoothie bar market, it dominates. In fact, not only has the company continued to grow at a 25 percent annual pace, but it has also been able to finance its growth internally.[1]

What drives the leaders of Jamba Juice? What drives the dominance of the company to the point that it has broken from the pack? What drives its perpetual quest for further breakthrough in the increasingly crowded juice and smoothie bar industry, where smaller upstarts are constantly seeking to imitate the success of larger rivals?

Financial reward is one answer, of course, but if the research on entrepreneurs' motives is correct, it's only one piece of the puzzle. I submit that the deeper answer, and Jamba Juice's sustained success, is rooted in the company's *higher cause*. That cause transcends the kind of bland "we will make the best juices" vision statement that companies churn out all the time. The higher cause of Jamba Juice is, and I quote, to help us live a "healthier, balanced life"; a more "natural life"; a "fruitful life." In the eyes of its leaders, Jamba Juice is more than a portfolio of products to be managed. As they say, it's "a way to eat, a way to think, a way to live." It's a way to "celebrate the flavors of life." This is not simply marketing pap that can be copied by any Joe's Juice Bar. This is real.

Beyond the Mission Statement to a Higher Cause

Mission and vision statements are good things to have. But to break from the pack, a company would be wise to strive for something bigger than a mission and deeper than a vision. For starters, it must propound a cause, a "central idea" that people can rally around. In December 1981, a new CEO of GE named Jack Welch addressed a group of Wall Street analysts for the first time. He referred to a letter that he had recently read in *Fortune* magazine as something that fully captured his thinking on strategic planning. Referring to the great Prussian military strategist Carl von Clausewitz and his famous book *On War*, first published in 1832, here's what the letter stated:

> [According to von Clausewitz], men could not reduce strategy to a formula. Detailed planning necessarily failed, due to the inevitable frictions encountered: chance events, imperfections

in execution, and the independent will of the opposition. Instead, the human elements were paramount: leadership, morale, and the almost instinctive savvy of the best generals.

The Prussian general staff, under the elder von Moltke, perfected these concepts in practice. They did not expect a plan of operations to survive beyond the first contact with the enemy. They set only the broadest of objectives and emphasized seizing unforeseen opportunities as they arose. Strategy was not a lengthy action plan. It was the evolution of a central idea through continually changing circumstances.

The secret of strategic success, according to von Clausewitz and Welch, is not to try to figure out every possible contingency that might arise and linearly map out all operations thereafter—as if that was even possible. The secret is to have a "central idea" around which the entire organization revolves, and then develop quick plans around that central idea in response to fleeting opportunities in the marketplace.

Consequently, leaders who confront "central" questions about the nature of their organization are not simply engaging in intellectually interesting exercises; they are developing critical strategic priorities. "Central idea" questions include these:

• Who are we?

• What do we stand for?

• What's our agenda?

• What's our destination?

• Whom do we serve?

• Where are we going?

• Why do we exist?

• Why should we exist?

• What are our underlying philosophies and core values?[2]

The answers to these questions summon an organization to reach far more than the standard corporate mission statement that appears in the annual report and then is summarily ignored. The answers define a cause. That cause binds together all the disparate elements of an organization—people, decisions, systems, processes—and directs them onto the same path. It also allows employees to view the environment around them with the same eyes, and make rapid-fire decisions based on a common mental model.

I don't see genuine causes evident in many companies. I've seen overgeneralized, bland "vision statements" that meekly and unobtrusively hang on walls. I've seen thick, richly bound strategic plans with technologically whiz-bang PowerPoint presentations that are unclear, that don't differentiate the company, and that don't ignite peoples' passions. I've seen innumerable tough "no-nonsense" recitations of corporate goals, such as "We will capture market X," or "We will have an earnings growth of Y%," or "We will be a company of Z revenues in three years." Such objectives may be valid and worthy, but they still do not tell employees, customers, and investors how the company will act to achieve them, or why those objectives should matter to them.

None of the above alternatives is a cause. They do not illuminate a clear path that unites the people of an organization and sends them in a common direction with shared priorities. Nor do such statements necessarily even matter to anyone other than the executives and consultants who developed them.

Let's take it a step further. A central idea, or cause, will be essential if you want to have any sort of success in a Copycat Economy. But to improve your odds of truly breaking from the pack in a sustained way, you should consider going a step up, to a *higher* cause. A higher cause defines a noble and honorable purpose. A higher cause aims to leave a positive mark. It aims to change an entire market; in fact, it aims to change the world for the better. It's about somehow bettering the lot of human beings.

Don't confuse a higher cause with a mission statement. Most mission statements focus on the organization and its products, such as., "We will be the best provider of widgets (or "widget solutions") in the world." Higher causes focus on customers and potential customers: how they benefit and how their life or business will be elevated, all in a way that's fresh, compelling, unique, and, perhaps most important—uplifting and virtuous. The most powerful higher causes lead people to see how the world will be a better place, and how humanity will benefit anew.

Lest you think I'm urging you to turn hippie-dippie and sing "Kumbaya," consider that Google's unbelievable growth, domination, and innovation is in no small part due to its higher cause—which is to harness, organize, and categorize all the information on the planet so that each one of us can easily access it for our own unique needs in any medium we choose, whether text, audio, or video. Think of the opportunities that kind of higher cause opens up for dominance; think of the possibilities it inspires. Think about how it turns on customers and intrigues investors, too. Think about the kinds of strong visions, mission statements, strategic plans, and organizational commitments it can spawn if it's truly coherent, authentic, revolutionary, and evolutionary—terms we discuss later in this chapter. Think about the wealth that this process creates!

During the last segment of his illustrious career, Peter Drucker worked extensively with nonprofit organizations. He advised groups like the Girl Scouts and the American Red Cross to run themselves like a business, albeit a business that strives to "change lives" rather than maximize profits. Let me humbly suggest that this is a spurious "either-or" distinction, for two reasons. First, to achieve their missions, even nonprofits must maximize revenues over expenditures. They must do well in order to do good.

Second, the distinction is spurious even with for-profit organizations. "Maximizing profits" is a great goal, but when advanced in a strategic or ethical vacuum, it can easily lead to myopic, me-too, or compulsively destructive decisions. Savvy business leaders understand that in a Copycat Economy, the "either-or" becomes a "both-and": Companies that break from the pack will aim to *maximize profits by changing peoples' lives for the better.* That's what your company's higher cause should define for your customers.

Within the organization, a higher cause sharply defines an outcome and legacy that people who work in any organization would be proud of. As Virgin chairman Richard Branson noted, "I never, ever thought of myself as a businessman. I was interested in creating things I was proud of."

A higher cause takes employees far beyond their career ambitions to feed their most profound ambition: to lead meaningful lives. Microsoft CEO Steve Ballmer once described it this way: "What makes morale good or bad is the sense of the future. Are we working on something important? Are we changing the world? Is that an opportunity to benefit financially? Those are the kinds of things that make a difference to people."

A higher cause tells employees that their organization should not simply be an engine that provides "products and services at a fair price." It tells them that what they must do is far more important than

"a job." That's why a higher cause demands perpetual and collaborative innovation.

Jamba Juice's higher cause gives the company's workforce a moti-
vating dream. It drives the company's new drink introductions, the
spin-off businesses, the capital and budget allocations, the promotion
practices, the external partnerships, and the transparency with customers (the ingredients of every one of their products are readily
available to anyone who looks). When Jamba leaders say, "We care
about what goes into your smoothie and your body," you know they're
serious. It's their higher cause.

But how did Jamba get to the forefront of this business from the
beginning? How did Jamba get the big central ideas that led to the
higher cause? I sometimes talk to executives in so-called "mature"
businesses who wonder how those pesky new, disruptive, break-from-
the-pack competitors got their great ideas. I tell them that the leaders
of these disruptive companies are no smarter than they are. I tell
them that the only thing that separates them from those in the pack is
that they took off the conventional-wisdom blinders, looked at the
pieces out there in the horizon (remember Madonna and Willie
Nelson?), and put those pieces together in a new, fresh, compelling
way that they believed could change the world.

Several years ago, *New York Times* columnist Tom Friedman,
author of *The World Is Flat*, wrote an article about what separates
strong from weak national economies. His words were descriptive not
only of nations, but for all kinds of organizations. Substitute *organization* for *society* in the sentences that follow, and you'll see how a
vibrant and forward-looking organization can enact a higher cause:
"As globalization gives everyone the same information, resources,
technology, and markets, a society's ability to put those pieces
together in the fastest and most innovative manner increasingly separates winners from losers in the global economy."

There is nothing proprietary, secret, or patented about Jamba
Juice's constantly evolving smoothies and business extensions. Every
product ingredient and business element has been available to anyone
at anytime, but only Jamba put the pieces together in a way that
excited the heck out of people, who were motivated and organized by
the company's commitment to a big, worthy, and overarching purpose.

Scan the market landscape, and you'll see break-from-pack companies constantly rearranging the pieces in new, innovative ways, consistent with their higher causes. Proctor and Gamble's higher cause is

to help people solve every problem in the home. That dictate directs the company's efforts away from merely engineering improvements of its current discrete products, moving it instead toward breakthroughs that solve real issues and anxieties inside the home, from breakthrough mops to breakthrough teeth-whitening kits to breakthrough diapers.

At TiVo, the higher cause is about liberating people's time and power by giving them total control over their viewing. Its latest innovations (including technology that allows you to record shows via the Internet if you're not at home, or record programs onto a laptop, or burn them onto a DVD) stem from that commitment. At giant Samsung Electronics, the higher cause is "to make the Jetsons a reality," says one executive. Samsung aims to combine the company's resources in mobile phones, Flash memory, screen technology, chips, kitchen appliances, and digital media to fully network the home, all controlled by cellphones and in-house monitors—thereby making the home a more joyful experience. Motorola's higher cause of "seamless mobility" is about helping people use whatever products they want to use, wherever they are. It's about linking the company's electronic products for home, work, and automobile through a medium (as at Samsung, most likely a cellphone) that allows customers to access or use the products wherever they happen to be.

Diebold, with its 300,000 ATM machines in 60 countries, drives its new products and services under the higher cause of providing total security for peoples' financial self-services in a world marked by identity theft and terrorism. At Honda, the higher cause is an obsession with fuel efficiency to save people money and keep the environment safe. According to Honda's U.S. chief engineer, Charlie Baker, "Everyone at Honda views being in a company as being far more than just turning a profit. It's not that we're poor businessmen, but I think everybody at Honda is fired by the dream of creating great products that are the most efficient in their class." Small wonder that of the ten most fuel-efficient cars on the road today, Honda makes seven.

Launched in 2000, ING Direct USA already has more than two million customers and more than $30 billion in assets. The company is a direct bank. Its customers use the Internet, the phone, and direct mail to do all their banking. ING's higher cause, in the words of its president, Arkaidi Kuhlman, is "to lead Americans back to savings." With that spirit ("we want to show you how to save more"), ING Direct stands for an alternative to business as usual in the banking industry. With no high-overhead bricks-and-mortar branches, no

ATMs, no high-salary portfolio managers to push spending on new products, and a limited number of product offerings (savings accounts, a few CDs, and a few mutual funds), ING Direct's costs are as little as one-sixth those of its rivals. Here's the punchline: The company passes those savings to its customers in the form of higher interest rates (four times the industry average on deposits), thus encouraging savings.

A strong higher cause serves as an organization's strategic beacon, market brand, and organizational "soul." It drives all strategic and operational decisions. It demands collaborative excellence in performance. It pushes constant innovation in products and customer service. It spurs employees to continually reinvent and enhance the experience of customers. It improves the odds of leaving a positive, lasting legacy in the industry and the world.

Especially as organizations get larger, more complex, and more diffuse, having a central force to identify, unite, and galvanize all the pieces becomes even more essential, and that's what a higher cause can do. Without a genuine higher cause, what exactly do so many of today's huge, diversified corporations really stand for, other than trying to make money off a large menu of commodity products, an ability to scale them, and some vague allusions to excellence?

The Three Components of a Higher Cause

If you're serious about helping your organization discover its higher cause, remember that a potent, break-from-the-pack higher cause must contain three elements:

1. A Higher Cause Must Be Coherent

The central idea your company propounds must be clear, simple, edgy, easy to brag about, and able to inspire curiosity. The phenomenal track record of Starbucks is in no small part due to its higher cause. You may be surprised to learn that Starbucks' higher cause is not about coffee. Starbucks wants to create a place of "refuge" for people, where they can escape the woes and tribulations of the chaotic world outside, a place that is so safe and calming that it becomes the "third place" a customer spends time in (the first two places being home and office, though if a customer's priorities are screwed up and he or she wants to make Starbucks the first place, Starbucks is happy to oblige!). It is this higher cause of refuge that drives the ambience, the smells, the placement of furniture, the Wi-Fi accessibility, the unique Starbucks home music, the CD burning, the newspapers and accessories, and, of course, the rich array of constantly evolving coffees and teas. These factors, in turn, have driven the company's profitable growth to 10,000 stores worldwide, with the expectations of another 10,000 stores by 2010.

Starbucks' higher cause is quite coherent. It's clear, it's edgy (a "third place," a "refuge"? how arrogant!), it's easy to convey proudly, and it intrigues those who hear it (how exactly do you make a coffee bar a place of refuge?). It's also a cause that is coherent enough to inspire people to innovate continually with fresh new features. For example, like the Wi-Fi and the music, the Starbucks reloadable debit card was originally introduced to make the customer's experience more comfortable. Starbucks research indicated that customers spent 20-some seconds on each point-of-sale transaction, even more if they didn't use cash, but with debit cards they could cut that time to 4 seconds. The fact that the card also spewed a geyser of free cash flow and enhanced the Starbucks brand identity was simply a positive byproduct. The original motive was to innovatively operationalize the higher cause and make the store more of a refuge for customers.

Higher causes can't be vague, unclear, or bland. To matter—to have an impact on customers and to shape employee innovations—higher causes must be crisp, succinct, and sharply defined.

2. A Higher Cause Must Be Authentic

A couple years ago, I was chatting with Tom Grape, CEO of Benchmark Assisted Living, a large provider of senior living facilities, about what it takes to rev up an organization. In the past, he said, he thought that a mission statement would motivate a company. "But what happened was that we did all these mission and vision statements, and they always got filed away. Then we started to talk about authenticity. Who are we, *really*? What do we stand for, *really*? Where do we want to take our business, *really*? What could we do profitably that would make a *world of difference* to our elderly customers and their families, *really?* Once we started to discuss these things and come to a consensus, that's when things started to happen."

A higher cause must be real and pervasive if it is to have any substantive impact. It can't be a program of the month. It can't be marketing pap or catchy slogans. It's got to be real on a personal level and real on an institutional level.

How do we know a higher cause is *personally authentic* for a corporate leader? One answer, I believe, lies in business guru Tom Peters's phrases to describe passion: "It can't be faked, it happens 24/7, and it's what keeps you up at 4 a.m." For me, if the higher cause "grabs your soul," inspires your behavior, and defines your decisions, then you know it's personally authentic.

When a higher cause becomes *institutionally authentic*, it defines every element of the organization and is the central dictum by which everyone measures all the company's efforts. At Honda, chief U.S. engineer Charlie Baker talks about the corporate passion for fuel economy: "The answer is already clear: [At Honda] you are going to have the best fuel economy in class of any vehicle. Period. Have a nice day. You don't need to do any market research." If a higher cause is not authentic to the organization, it will have little impact and, worse, it will augment a collective sense of ambiguity and cynicism among all the organization's stakeholders.

Whole Foods Market actually has two higher causes, and they have both personal and institutional authenticity. First, CEO John Mackey points out that Americans love to shop and they love to eat, but they hate to shop for food. So the first higher cause for Whole Foods is to create an environment where people will enjoy food shopping. Whole Foods features a cacophony of colors and shapes of good, healthful fruits and vegetables and breads everywhere, so much so that *Forbes* magazine refers to the store environment as "food porn." The ovens with chefs cooking and discussing their recipes and methods with customers, the book nooks, the sushi bars, the open brick pizza ovens for pizza, the international foods, offered as in a bazaar— it's all theater, and it's fun, and it comes from an authentic place.

What is Whole Foods' "even higher" cause? "We want to change how America eats," says Mackey. Whole Foods' ultimate purpose is to get people to eat genuinely whole and organic foods because they taste better and are better for them and for the environment. Whole Foods is so successful because it remains authentically committed to this higher cause. Customers know the company is an obsessive, ethical "editor"; it does the dirty work to sift through all the products in the field to determine what's truly organic and what isn't, and drops suppliers who don't pass the test. You feel a sense of security shopping there because you know that everything there is real, per the higher cause of the company.

In January 2006, Google's institutional authenticity was questioned by many observers. As syndicated columnist Debra Saunders noted: "Google painted itself as heroic in refusing to help the U.S. Department of Justice's efforts to reinstate a 1998 federal Child Online Protection Act, then revealed that it was going to help the Chinese government suppress free speech." After defending the sanctity of open information and its customers' rights to privacy in the U.S., even in the matter of child pornography, Google then agreed to filter out sites that the Chinese government doesn't like—sites about Tibet, Taiwan, Tianamen Square protests, and such.

By being willing to censor itself and block politically sensitive information in order to gain a foothold in the lucrative Chinese market, Google seemed to be departing from its higher cause of organizing all the information of the world for the benefit of each user. Google's response was that the company's presence would benefit Chinese users more than its absence, and that "providing no information is more inconsistent with our mission." Many observers didn't buy that explanation, calling Google opportunistic rather than noble. My point is not to pass moral judgment on Google, but to observe that staying authentic to a higher cause is not easy. Your organization will be tested repeatedly as to its real commitment. Whole Foods is tested every day by the tantalizing come-ons of cheaper suppliers who are "kind-of" organic and by sexy products that are "pretty much" free of pesticides and artificial additives. The fact that Whole Foods hasn't succumbed yet is why its brand equity and momentum remain as strong as they are.

Institutional authenticity is hard to achieve, but on a day-to-day organizational basis, it's what separates good intentions from the real thing. The case of Atlanticare is a lesson for all of us. In a beleaguered health-care world marked by ballooning costs, overwhelmed resources, and megamerger mishaps, Atlanticare, a composite of two hospitals and a mix of health services, health plans, and related foundations, institutes, and community services, serves the southern New Jersey area with exceptional reputation and success. The flagship Regional Medical Center (an urban teaching hospital and a suburban campus) has received numerous peer-review accolades in the industry. It was named a J.D. Powers and Associates Distinguished Hospital two years in a row. Financially, the organization has gained a 72 percent share in its target markets while reducing cost-per-case by $1,500 less than those of competitors and posting a 9 percent real growth standard.

CEO George Lynn could have coasted on these accomplishments until retirement. But he had bigger ambitions. "We've proven we can effectively treat people with quality and compassion when they're sick," he says. "It's a reactive model. We wait until people come to us with specific problems, and then we take action. But imagine if we could use our knowledge to help them not get sick at all, or at least maintain their current health status without deterioration." Thus arose the Epidemic of Health (EOH), Atlanticare's revolutionary higher cause and the root for future dominance.

More than 75 percent of U.S. health-care costs can be attributed to chronic illnesses and diseases. Lynn's central idea is that systematic, research-based, preventative health-care services can create a *positive* epidemic, an epidemic of health rather than of disease, one that could significantly affect overall health-care utilization, outcomes, and costs. Lynn's initial task force identified several key principles that would underlie Atlanticare's higher cause:

- Emphasis on preventative medicine

- Emphasis on patients as full, responsible partners in their own health

- Seamless digital transparency to allow patients quick access to their personal information, as well as cataloged information about health

- Inclusion of nonmedical approaches to health, like diet, fitness training, yoga, and chiropractic

- Case managers to oversee and customize all EOH services

- A cost-effective, revenue-enhancing way that would attract insurers and employers, and brand Atlanticare as a unique provider

Six key target markets were chosen in 2004 to apply the EOH framework, with one project team of volunteer "champions" drawn from throughout the system for each market: MDs, Child Health, Women's Health, Employers, Patients, and Atlanticare Employees.

The champions grabbed whatever resources they could—capable staff, bits of budget, research findings, software, servers, and interested outsiders—and innovatively put them together. By 2005, each team was able to report back on impressive interventions and outcomes, including health kiosks, health and wellness software for both providers and patients; new digital and physical bulletin boards on health; new consultative services for patients and family members; community outreach programs; database development; electronic medical records; new call centers; educational interventions on weight management, nutrition, tobacco control, stress management, and disease state management; family health interventions for concerns like adult hypertension and childhood obesity; and a host of new alliances with employer groups and insurance companies.

But despite these impressive results, EOH remained a peripheral slice of Atlanticare, administered with a small budget, run by one full-time coordinator, and fueled almost entirely by the volunteer passion and talent of the small group of champions (fewer than 100 out of a workforce of 3,800) who were doing nearly all this on their own time. I was reminded of Peter Drucker's observation that organizations do something worthwhile only when a project is undertaken "by monomaniacs with a mission." Clearly, there is no questioning the personal authenticity at Atlanticare.

Atlanticare's current challenge is to fan institutional authenticity, pushing EOH down to the core of the business. George Lynn does not want to get bogged down in pilot study-ism indefinitely. "We need to push until we get that tipping point of acceptance inside our system and out in the community," he says. The company must now answer some formidable questions: How should EOH be budgeted and staffed? What sorts of performance metrics should apply to EOH? How can conventionally minded staff, physicians, and insurers be persuaded that the cause of preventive health care is worth pursuing financially as well as medically? Should EOH become Atlanticare's core offering or simply one more positive element in the company's brand? There are no simple answers to these questions. If Atlanticare leaders believe that EOH can become the wave of the future, then they will maneuver the *organization* to commit to it authentically. Stay tuned; even as it struggles with the issues of authenticity, the EOH initiative remains a truly exciting work in progress.

3. A Higher Cause Must Be Both Revolutionary and Evolutionary

A higher cause must have a distinct revolutionary component that, like Atlanticare's EOH, challenges conventional wisdom and jeopardizes the status quo. Otherwise, it's unlikely to inspire people or propel an organization ahead of the pack.

Historically, causes that have made a difference have always had an unambiguous tinge of anarchy and revolution. CNN's higher cause was to give people the power to access information when they wanted it, not when CBS and Walter Cronkite wanted it. FedEx's higher cause was not merely to get mail delivered a little faster than the post office could, but to provide people with a sense of total security that their documents would be delivered to a specific individual the very next day.

Most vision and mission statements, not to mention strategic plans, lack the stuff of revolution. They are conventional, orderly, linear, and acceptable to powers-that-be; they don't bug the people who protect the status quo. A higher cause must do all that, and because it's the seed from which break-from-pack mission statements and plans spring forth, it must do all that aggressively.

A higher cause also must continually demonstrate the capacity to evolve. Market conditions are continually changing, and the cause has to be relevant to those changes, even as it proves itself to be of enduring value. Certainly, you want your company's higher cause to be powerful enough to provide enduring value, but you also want to recognize that market conditions are in constant flux, and the cause must be able to capitalize on those changes. At IBM under Lou Gerstner, the higher cause evolved from an emphasis on hardware to one that emphasized software and services. Under successor Sam Palmisano, the higher cause evolved to "on demand." Both causes had a revolutionary tinge. Both evolved to fit the opportunities of the times.

Mike Corbett's story is also instructive. Although everyone now knows the word *outsourcing*, that wasn't always the case. Corbett was one of the first people to begin using the term and give it definition and meaning. In 1987, while working for IBM, he was one of the lead strategists who helped get IBM into its (now hugely successful) outsourcing business.

Corbett left IBM shortly thereafter and launched a research consortium (Michael F. Corbett and Associates) that began working with companies around the world with the higher cause of helping them understand the power and potential of this new approach to business. From 1989 to 1998, Corbett's team published some of the original market research studies on outsourcing and produced a series of conferences and training programs on the subject. By 2003, his company's global conference series, "The Outsourcing World Summit," had grown to become one of the world's most influential conference series on the topic, with more than 1,400 delegates, 150 speakers, and 75 corporate sponsors participating in four summits on three continents.

Instead of seeing his business continue on its exponential growth curve, attendance and revenue fell for the first time 2004. Why? Chalk it up to the Copycat Economy. The success of Mike Corbett's company and others like it had drawn the attention of much larger, better-funded corporate imitators. The market quickly became flooded with freshly minted experts, and, says Corbett, "outsourcing conferences themselves became commodities. When we went to China in 2001, we were one of the first groups to work with the Chinese government to produce business conferences on outsourcing. When we held our September 2004 event in Beijing, we were, unbelievably, just one of four outsourcing conferences being held in the city that month alone." Continuing in a business that was losing differentiation and was increasingly filled with much larger competitors was not the way to go. Corbett had to either go on a buying binge to bulk up or move to higher, more revolutionary ground.

In the spirit of this book, he chose the latter. In February 2005, Corbett relaunched his business as his field's first truly global professional membership organization devoted to the study and advocacy of outsourcing. The International Association of Outsourcing Professionals (IAOP) has the higher cause of *accelerating* the global outsourcing movement by *directly involving and networking* with outsourcing professionals around the world. The new cause evolved from the old one, and Corbett tells me that this new business model is already leapfrogging the old copycats, opening up new ways to connect with customers, and producing better results. In the first eight months of the changeover year, gross revenue was up 24 percent and net income was up more than 80 percent. Today, there are IAOP chapters all over the world, and enrollment for the Summits is 20 percent higher than it's been in the past.

Putting Coherence, Authenticity, and Revolution into Soul

When outsiders talk to tough-minded businesspeople like George Lynn and Mike Corbett, they often come away with the understanding that for those leaders, their companies are far more than a group of people making and selling things to people who buy things. There is, dare I say, a spiritual perspective on how they approach their leadership and how they use higher causes to imbue spirit and soul into their organizations. In this chapter, I've deliberately used cosmic terms such as "higher cause," "spirit," and "soul" because there is indeed a transcendent element to defining your organization's reason for being, and what it can strive for to deserve a position at the head of the pack.

Determining a higher cause is partly an analytical and intellectual exercise. You have to assess the external environment and your internal organization's capabilities, and you have to justify your decisions with economic logic. But ultimately, a higher cause is almost a spiritual aspiration, one that is deeply felt and sacred in a secular way.

A higher cause provides a deep personal purpose to you as a leader and to your colleagues, and it defines the deep purpose and persona, or soul, of your organization. When you as a leader can experience both analytical and spiritual elements as you determine future alternatives for your company, you're on your way toward defining a higher cause that will elevate your business to a new level.

Inquisitive, imaginative leaders can combine coherent soul, authentic soul, and revolutionary soul in any kind of organization, in any industry. Here are two brief case studies, one from a business that's supposedly too loopy to have a higher cause (the circus), the other in a business that's supposedly too mundane to have a higher cause (low-cost furniture).

Cirque du Soleil has the requisite clowns, acrobats, and stunts, but it's nothing like Ringling Brothers and Barnum & Bailey Circus—or any other circus, for that matter. Imagine daredevil acrobats and dancers, rich and lavish costumes, hypnotic music, breathtaking high-tech special effects, dazzlingly mobile sets and stages, and a thousand props—all converging to explore a theme that, depending on the specific production, might be spiritual duality, social transformation, or the interplay between East and West. Customers typically pony up from $100 to $200 per ticket to see any of the eight different touring productions around the world or one of the five different productions in residence in Las Vegas hotels and Disney resorts in Orlando. The venues for these productions seat up to 2,000 people and are often filled to capacity. Ken Feld, the owner of Ringling Bros. Circus, shakes his head in awe and says, "The economics are just staggering." With Cirque du Soleil planning new productions with cities like Montreal and Tokyo, and in concert with companies like Disney, Carnival Cruise, and the Beatles' record label, Apple Corp., the economics grow even more impressive.

How has this $600-million, Montreal-based enterprise completely rewritten the rules of the circus? Cirque du Soleil's business feats have not come from patents or proprietary technologies. Nor has it relied on high-priced consultants to shape a grand strategy. In fact, when Guy Lieberte launched Cirque du Soleil in 1984, he was a stilt-walking, fire-breathing street actor. He may not have had an MBA, but he had the ability to harness the elements of distinctive success that were all out there, untouched and unintegrated, in the public domain: extraordinarily talented gymnasts and dancers, high-impact media technology, dazzling design, controversial philosophical and political concepts, and unorthodox theatrical ideas. Lieberte integrated those elements in a curious, cool, and crazy way—one that would ultimately create a bigger "2 + 2 = 7" value proposition. The official "vision" of Cirque du Soleil is to provide customers with an "awe-inspiring encounter." But as is the case with Whole Foods, the vision statement doesn't do Cirque justice. Guy Lieberte says his personal cause is "to reinvent the circus." That tells us something, but still not enough. The organization Cirque has an even higher cause, one that is not written as an official document but can easily be inferred from the coherence and authenticity of its productions: to fully reignite adults' emotions and senses in ways they may have experienced as kids but never thought possible as adults. Raising customers' "awe quotient" to that level drives Cirque's obsessive insistence on raising the bar on innovation, yielding a steady evolutionary and revolutionary progression of extraordinarily elaborate and imaginative productions—each one completely different than the last.

One last thing: There are no animals in Cirque productions. That might be the most revolutionary element of all!

IKEA has had a higher cause from the very beginning. Founder Ingvar Kamprad, today one of the richest people in the world, began with the assumption that he would violate the "pack mentality" of the furniture retail business, which was to sell either high-quality attractive furniture at high prices or low-quality unattractive furniture at low prices. Kamprad has pointed out that his overarching goal is "a better life for many." That statement has translated to IKEA's higher cause: to provide a more enriched, more upscale everyday life to ordinary people. The company does so by providing high-quality, high-design, trendy furniture to those who couldn't afford it otherwise.

IKEA's authentication of its higher cause has led it to institute two vital innovations. First, it created revolutionary strategic supplier relationships, transforming its suppliers into partners. It included them in planning processes and provided them technical and engineering support as well as finance and management training so that they could meet stiff productivity and cost standards when they delivered their products. Second, IKEA has fostered revolutionary customer relationships. Rather than viewing customers as endpoints who bought products and did nothing more, IKEA utilized a process called "co-creation of value." The company transformed customers into active partners through the self-service, do-it-yourself (DIY) model. These customer-partners expected to assemble their own furniture as part of the high-quality, low-price deal. Thus, IKEA engaged customers directly into the production and distribution process and, in effect, converted warehouses into stores.

As a result of these two revolutionary innovations, IKEA realized significant cost savings, allowing the company to develop more popular high-end-like furniture at low price points and create more loyal customers. "When I have friends over, they think it looks expensive, but it's actually cheap," said one happy customer.

Ironically, just like the Mexican-brewed Corona beer, which is popular in the U.S. but perceived as a low-end beer in Mexico itself, in Scandinavia IKEA is perceived as a low-end, unfashionable brand. Not so in 180 stores in 23 other countries, however, where IKEA has become a cult brand. Its higher cause has led to phenomenal success: over $18 billion in annual sales, double-digit margins, and a track record that's remarkable when compared to other furniture companies. It boasts a 10-year (1994–2004) sales growth that's 10 times the industry norm (36 percent vs. 3.5 percent) and a 5-year (1999–2004) return on capital that's triple the industry norm (44.3 percent vs. 14.7 percent).

Six Steps to Help Your Organization Find Its Higher Cause

Higher causes arise from your willingness to carefully examine the horizon (using as models Madonna and Willie Nelson), figure out significant gaps in the emerging marketplace, get genuinely jump-up-and-down excited about an untapped opportunity to fill those gaps (especially when that opportunity changes the rules of the game), define how your next steps will make the world a better place as it makes your customers' lives better, truly believe that what you and your organization can do is very important and valuable, and articulate that in a way that inspires and mobilizes others. Here are a few concrete guidelines that will help you develop and execute a higher cause for your organization:

1. **Ask the deep questions about your organization.** Don't be afraid to wade into this space. Go deeper than conventional spreadsheets and quarterly goals. Really "know" what your organization is about right now. Reflect on what your organization could be. Think big, think bold. Be sure to initiate regular conversations with your people around the questions asked at the start of this chapter. Here are a few of them again, for easy reference: *Who are we? What do we stand for? What's our agenda? Whom do we serve? Where are we going? Where can we go? Why do we exist? Why should we exist? What are our underlying philosophies and core values? Do we offer any worthy value to the world? What worthy unique value could we offer? What possibilities excite us? Are we changing the world for the better? Are we improving peoples' lives significantly? Could we? How? What mark can we leave that sets us apart from everyone else? What can our legacy be?*

   When you ponder these questions, remember that a higher cause is not about your organization and its products. A higher cause is about customers and potential customers: how their lives will be elevated, and how the world will be better off too.

   Many managers in many companies function automatically and reactively, without really knowing why they do what they do or what they need to be doing instead. If you ask these questions regularly and then have conversations about what the answers signify for your business right now, you'll be amazed at how often there is initially no clue or no consensus about the answers among your team. But the more you ask them, the clearer the responses will become.

2. **Concentrate your attention on the horizon.** Asked the secret behind his great insights about future trends, Peter Drucker responded, "I look out the window." Start the conversations about what trends on the frontier of your industry might threaten your current business or offer it big opportunities. Dig into these analyses. Take the trends seriously. Map them out. Form groups to do quick studies on them and report back. Discuss the implications that intrigue you. Discuss the possibilities that excite you. You'll *feel* the higher cause emerging.

3. **Rearrange the pieces to make a *big* difference**. Push your people to talk about concrete possibilities that could be groundbreaking and that could make a *big* difference in the lives of your present (or potential) customers, and maybe even the world. Consider possibilities that might come from new technologies, new partners, new supply chains, new scientific advances, new sources of capital, and any new trends out in the marketplace. Talk about what it would take to match (or rebuild) your internal capabilities with those possibilities on the kind of scale and impact that would make a difference in the world—and make money for your organization. Start with the central idea that you want your organization to stand for. Don't water down your aspirations; keep raising them, even if your goals violate accepted practices in your industry, even if your goals sound impossible at first. Then start building a business case around those groundbreaking possibilities by rearranging the interesting pieces "out there" to make this big difference happen. Build on these initiatives with your team, discuss them together, contemplate them, and pretty soon you'll be talking about a higher cause.

4. **Don't let anyone else define coherence, authenticity, and revolution/evolution for you.** This is an effort you and your colleagues must provide yourselves, not delegate to outside consultants. If you allow a consultancy to determine your higher cause, you'll never truly embrace it because it will not resonate the way it will if you develop it yourselves.

Consultants might help you analyze the environment, the possibilities, and your organization's capabilities, but the soul you find must be your own.

5. **Enlist champions.** Find your monomaniacs who are committed to germinating your higher cause. Feed them, support them, reward them, and protect them. Help them find fellow crazies to work with. Encourage their creative fire, even as you help them maintain their commitment to acting responsibly and effectively. Avoid the career skeptics and stack the deck with people who share your cause and want to help it unfold.

6. **Learn to synthesize.** To put the pieces together for a higher cause, you and your colleagues will need to excel in synthesis skills. Most of us are great analyzers; we can break down a problem into bits. But being able to synthesize information, people, and opportunities is a vital skill in and of itself. Steve Jobs and his team reinvented Apple by putting together the pieces that existed in the public domain (songs, record labels, artists, lawyers, technologies, laws, programmers, marketing whizzes, and so on) in a fast, innovative, proprietary way that generated the hassle-free iTunes music mega-platform that fed virtual music into a killer MP3 player. The algorithms and the mathematical models that led to the creation of Google were already scattered in the public domain when Stanford students Sergey Brin and Larry Page harnessed them and creatively integrated them. On the most nuts-and-bolts level, college football coach Urban Meyer led the unheralded University of Utah Utes to a remarkable 12–0 season in 2004 with a radically new offensive strategy. As one sports reporter noted, "Nearly all the elements of his offense—the spread formation, the shotgun reads, the option pitches—were plucked from somewhere else. No team, however, had ever mixed them quite the way Utah did...." That's the kind of synthesis we want to see in leaders. That's the kind of skill you need to breathe life into any higher cause.

When you synthesize, remember the power that comes with Gestalt: The whole is more than the sum of its parts. When you rearrange the pieces, keep as your goal a bigger, richer, higher cause than is possible for your organization to accomplish today.

By doing this, you can achieve what your rivals think is impossible. Before Cirque du Soleil was born, the circus was a declining industry with many small quasi-sleazy players and one major but sputtering player who had been doing the same "Big Top" productions for a century. Today Cirque does not even consider Ringling Bros. a competitor. They're playing different games, and Cirque operates with a cause that is far, far higher. That's what happens with companies that break from the pack.

Endnote

[1] It's precisely this track record that attracted the attention of Ft. Lauderdale-based Services Acquisitions Corporation, which ultimately bought Jamba Juice in 2006. The goal of SAC is "to expand Jamba's footprint." As a Jamba Juice fan, I hope the new owner can do this without squeezing the soul out of Jamba in the process.

[2] Consistent with our discussions in Chapters 1–5, the answers to each of these questions should ultimately be framed as to how they help make your organization unique, special, and positioned to dominate. I reinforce this point in different ways throughout this chapter.

7

BUILD A DEFIANT
PIPELINE

We know about the power of a great product, as demonstrated by the waiting lists for the newest models of the Toyota Prius and Apple iPod, or the quasi-blockbuster status of Danone's Activia (a yogurt that helps digestion) and Actimel (a dairy drink that strengthens the immune system). But what makes Toyota, Apple, and Danone successful is not one killer product, which will ultimately be imitated and commoditized, but *steady pipelines* of cool, compelling products. Their pipelines—"defiant" as in defying conventional wisdom and challenging what everyone else is doing—are more than a steady supply of ordinary, same-old-same-old products. Instead, those pipelines provide steady waves of breakthrough stuff.

In this chapter, we dissect the process of developing your defiant pipeline and keeping it constantly replenished with percolating ideas, prototypes, interesting and intimate alliances, fast experiments, and cool design—all for the purpose of bringing to market break-from-the-pack products and services.

The Power of the Pipeline

As we've learned, in a Copycat Economy, an exceptional product is quickly imitated. When 3Com's Palm division came out with its PalmPilot and Internet-ready Palm VII in the 1990s, sales shot through the roof, and the estimated value of the tiny division soon exceeded that of its multibillion-dollar parent. But within two years, PDAs themselves had become commodities. In 1996, Bandai, a Japanese toy manufacturer, had an unprecedented hit with its tiny digital-pet Tamagotchi. Mass hysteria swept over Japanese teens and preteens for a "pet" that had to be digitally fed and comforted to be kept alive. After quickly selling a whopping 10 million Tamagotchis, Bandai manufactured more of them in anticipation of ever-increasing sales. But as competitors brought similar products to market, Bandai wound up carrying a massive amount of inventory as its sales began to slide. Even though the company ultimately wound up selling as many as 40 million units worldwide, and still continues to do so, overall its entire product line has barely broken even.

Even mighty Toyota is recognizing that its once-breakthrough, now-mainstay U.S. products like the Camry sedan, the Tundra pickup, and the Sequoia SUV are entering the latter phases of their product life cycle. Replenishing the pipeline is absolutely necessary if Toyota is to maintain its dominating position in the auto industry.

But to stay ahead of the pack, neither Toyota nor any other company can rely on a mundane pipeline filled with new but boring, "me-too" products. Nor can they rely on a pipeline of just one home-run product. To break from the pack, a company must develop a pipeline of continuously emerging products that defy and visibly transcend the weaker "me too" value of whatever is currently being offered by rivals, or by the company itself. Strong defiant pipelines have rejuvenated large companies like Procter & Gamble. For years, P&G owed its flat financials to its strong reliance on marketing strategies that emphasized "new improved" (a.k.a. dressing up old existing) products like Crest and Tide. Today, P&G concentrates more on strengthening a pipeline of hot, new, defiant products like Swiffer mops, CarpetFlick nonelectric "vacuum cleaners," Crest SpinBrushes, Home Café coffee makers, and Auto Dry car cleaners. This defiant pipeline is propelling substantial spurts in P&G's revenues, reputation, and market capitalization.

Defiant pipelines allow automobile parts suppliers like Johnson Controls to thrive in an environment where their institutional customers are obsessed with pricing. Johnson doesn't simply wait for orders from GM and Ford; it generates interesting auto-related products, like pulsating, massage-like seat cushions and devices that can simultaneously turn on house lights while opening garage doors. Because Johnson Controls comes up with innovations before its giant customers do, the company has both the pricing flexibility and the credibility to push its customers to outsource more of the cars' total interiors to Johnson.

Defiant pipelines allow companies like Puma AG, stuck in the midst of crowded mass markets, to differentiate themselves. The Puma pipeline includes "driving shoes," (which have an inner slipper within a sturdier outer shoe), 1950s boxing- and skating-style shoes, and martial arts types of unisex clothing.

Defiant pipelines are so potent that they help companies hedge errors. Electronic Arts (EA), the video game king, took a temporary hit on its *Sims* interactive online game by rushing it to market too quickly, with too high a price. Because of its strong, constantly replenished pipeline of games—*Madden NFL, NBA Live, Tiger Woods PGA Tour, Need for Speed* street racing, and constant new games based on blockbuster movies like *Harry Potter, Batman,* and *Spiderman*—the *Sims* setback was just a minor blip. In fact, Electronic Arts nearly made up the *Sims* $63 million impairment charge on *Pogo,* a downloadable family game that on its own boosted online revenue by $50 million.

A defiant pipeline allows companies to survive and ultimately thrive under seemingly impossible circumstances. For several years, even after Steve Jobs's return as CEO, Apple floundered, with a 3 percent share in the computer business. Despite repeated claims that the company was dead or irrelevant, it survived by supplying its tiny but fanatical customer base with a pipeline of cool, technologically exceptional multicolored iMacs and related software. In fact, writing in *InfoWorld* in 2003, a supposedly dark year for Apple, Tom Yager sang the praises of Apple's PowerBooks and OSX client and server operating systems, Safari Web browser, and Java platform. "Tracking the innovation coming from this dead, irrelevant company is wearing me out," he declared.

In contrast, mundane or stalled pipelines can lead companies to make bad decisions. Remember when ABC bled its successful *Who Wants to Be a Millionaire?* show to death by showing it three and four times a week, until it died from overexposure? That's what happens when your defiant pipeline is a trickle.

I am convinced that one of the reasons that Merck pushed Vioxx so extensively, even in the face of troubling data that suggested some nasty side effects, is because the company's pipeline was weaker than executives hoped for. When you're not confident about your new product pipeline, you market the hell out of anything that sells and pray for some deliverance later. That's a dangerous way to do business. Until the 2005 hit *Desperate Housewives* finally gave ABC a little lift, the company had dragged down its parent Disney's earnings for years. With the Vioxx debacle, the impending lawsuits, and the shrinking of replacement products, some analysts predict that Merck may not see any significant earnings growth for the remainder of this decade.

The Power of Defiance

Pipelines are powerful to the extent that their contents defy conventional wisdom, defy what everyone else is doing, and sometimes even defy what the company itself is currently doing. Defiant pipelines are loaded—and constantly reloaded—with transformational intellectual property, ideas that challenge tradition and dogma, provocative pilots and betas, controversial projects and alliances, and constant, quickly executed experiments to test potential new products and services.

Defiance reflects your company's unique, challenging, controversial, even shocking point of view about your business and your market. Defiant pipelines take a company—and, ultimately an industry—to a place of transformation. For example, with video game products like *The Sims,* a game that allows viewers in different locations to create and control an entire community, EA's technological breakthroughs in product after product are now becoming recognized by computer giants like IBM as the future of computing because they are visual, interactive, graphic, sensual, and immediate. Small wonder that from 1994 to 2004, EA's revenues and profits grew at an annual compound rate of more than 20 percent, while 2005 saw operating margins of 21 percent and return on invested capital of 60 percent.

While EA is definitely ahead of the pack, some observers of the video game business argue that the leader of the pack is an even more defiant Rockstar Games, the creator of notoriously violent hits like *Grand Theft Auto* and other products that have a distinct "gangsta" vibe. In developing products that allow up to six people to have a Wi-Fi gang war, one Rockstar executive explained, "We try to take stuff that hasn't been explored yet, and if others choose to follow, that's their business." That sounds defiant in spirit as well as in pipeline!

That is also why defiance is not about "benchmarking." Certainly, there are times to selectively imitate your rivals, especially when they're doing something that customers love. But to build an entire strategy around a copycat pipeline is to concede that your entire enterprise is simply a derivative of someone else's. That's why veteran industry analysts are sometimes acidic in their appraisals of GM's efforts to copy Toyota and Nissan ("They're only playing catch-up. There is nothing pro-active here," declares one analyst) or United's efforts to copy Southwest and JetBlue by starting its own low-cost airline ("Ted is a coat of paint and a press release. It has the same costs as United's planes," says another analyst).

One last point: Don't confuse a defiant pipeline with the number of patents you announce or the R&D dollars you spend. Building a defiant pipeline is about formulating, testing, and introducing real products that are cool, unique, and "gotta have." R&D and patents can certainly support defiant product pipelines, but on their own they don't define them. During Carly Fiorina's reign, HP rolled out patents and products left and right (one newspaper article recorded 158 new product announcements in one day), but they didn't do much good for the company. In contrast to the EMBER model described in Chapter 4, the patents and products didn't break significant new ground or matter enough to customers.

Microsoft's R&D budget is larger than most of its competitors' entire revenue stream—$6 billion in one year alone. Yet its return on those investments has been lousy, whereas companies like Google, Apple, TiVo, Sony, and Motorola have pioneered the breakthroughs that Microsoft hungers for and must play catch-up to compete with. The main problem is one of defiance, or lack of it. Microsoft's multibillion dollars in R&D expenditures since 1998, and its 2,000-plus new patents over the past five years do not sufficiently challenge and defy its own Windows in-house monopoly. On the contrary, as one Microsoft technology officer confesses, for every dollar the company spends on R&D, "probably something on the order of 90 percent is directly in line, or in service of, the existing business groups." That expenditure might lead to a pipeline, but not a defiant one.

Perhaps the greatest missed opportunity to establish a defiant pipeline was the Xerox PARC tragedy. In the 1970s, Xerox set up a lavishly funded Palo Alto Research Center to invent a future for the company beyond the photocopier. PARC scientists were allowed to create freely, and they did: the laser printer, the graphical user interface, the mouse, and typography language, to name just a few breakthroughs. But Xerox executives didn't aggressively put these great technological inventions into any pipeline because they weren't recognizable derivatives of the company's familiar product lines. Metaphorically, PARC products were little children who defied their parent Xerox. While Xerox told them to "shush!" other "parents" adopted those obstreperous little buggers. They took the PARC inventions and ran with them. Apple marketed graphics and the mouse, Canon and HP pioneered laser printers, and Adobe led the way with typography. Imagine how Xerox would have thrived if it had set up a defiant pipeline rather than recoiling from its offspring.

The 10 Commitments to the Defiant Pipeline

To help you create a defiant pipeline in your organization, here are "The 10 Commitments" that you'd be business-wise to follow:

1. Always Be Cannibalizing

You know the old "ABC" sales maxim "Always Be Closing?" In the Copycat Economy, a better maxim is "Always Be Cannibalizing." When you continually seek opportunities to cannibalize your current product offerings, you are taking the break-from-pack position of making your product offering obsolete before the market does.

It's the reason why Apple flagrantly cannibalized its ultrasuccessful Mini iPod in 2005, even though the Mini accounted for more than half of all iPod sales. The Nano iPod is not simply an "improvement" over the Mini; it's a device that runs on solid-state Flash memory instead of disk-drive storage, allowing for a much smaller and durable product.

Some said Apple's move to Nano was "risky" because the Mini iPod was so successful. "Why fix it if it ain't broke?" was their mentality, especially because the Nano required its own factories to make the product and because any delays in product launch would have damaged Apple revenue streams. But Steve Jobs, in the spirit of "ABC," has repeatedly urged his troops to take the risks rather than fall into the bigger risk of complacency in simply trying to "protect" the successful Mini.

You have to move past the reflex of circling the wagons to protect existing product lines that are inevitably being commoditized and imitated. Some protection certainly makes sense, but it's far better to concentrate on new products that supercede your current offerings. Always take the perspective that Google CEO Eric Schmidt describes as his company's source of success: "We're organized around taking advantage of technology discontinuities as they occur. That's our competitive advantage. You have to be set up to shift your focus quickly so that you spend most of your energies inventing the new business instead of blindly optimizing the old one."

Companies that get this ABC principle do things that sound insane. P&G licenses every one of its product patents to any outsider, as long as the patent has existed at least five years or has been in use in a P&G product for at least three years, whichever comes first. How does one explain this? P&G earns a little extra cash, but the main point of the process is to spur employees to stop clinging to current products and start developing new, defiant ones.

So call it *defiant cannibalism*—the process of continually replacing your own successful products or services with fundamentally new technologies and products, while providing a significant leap in customer value. Some competitors might edge up on you, but most will lack the awareness, expertise, or resources to compete. Defiant cannibalism allows you the potential to revolutionize the industry by providing a level of customer value far exceeding what has historically been possible.

Not only do you grow your own profitability and market share, but you can also grow the size of the entire market, thanks to the heightened value introduced by your discontinuous innovations. Expanding the market is a big part of the reasoning behind Toyota's hybrid cars and EA's "entertainment beyond games" approach. IBM gives away many of its software patents, believing that it helps enlarge the entire industry, which will lead to more higher-margin e-business-on-demand opportunities for the company.

2. Become an Anthropologist with Your Customers

Getting close to your customers means becoming an anthropologist with them, that is, observing and interacting with them as they do their work and live their lives. Being an anthropologist gets you deeply and viscerally in touch with the latent needs of your customers and the latent possibilities for defiant products.

As discussed in Chapter 3, this is not a matter of doing standard market-research analyses or asking customers what they want. Consumers often don't know what they want until you present them with options so arresting and revolutionary that they didn't conceive of them on their own. When they're asked about a company's current products, customers are indeed good at telling you what they like and don't like. In 2003, Motorola managers got a useful earful from focus groups of high school and college students, who bluntly told them that their mobile phones were boring and clunky, while those of Samsung "kicked ass." But customers are lousy at predicting what they will need or love in the future, and what future products and services they'll be willing to spend premium money on. That was Motorola's responsibility.

To get beyond customers' reflex responses, you would be wise to become an anthropologist and work in the field doing what in academe is called "participant-observer" research. You need to hang out with your customers and watch how they do their work and enjoy their leisure. What frustrates or angers them? What makes them happy? What do they wish they could do but can't? If you get enough employee-anthropologists coming back from their expeditions to share their "field notes," you'll have vital, direct data that will shape new, defiant products. Collect all this data carefully, synthesize it, and use it to create the new kinds of products that will make your customers' lives and jobs better in ways they couldn't have articulated, or anticipated.

For Bill George, the CEO of Medtronics from 1989 to 2001, customer anthropology was the secret to his company's ability to generate breakthrough health-care products so consistently that at any given point, more than 50 percent of revenues were coming from products that hadn't even existed two years earlier. Medtronics personnel would hang out at hospitals, chat with physicians, observe surgeries—all the while noticing what worked, what didn't work, and what might work for the health-care professionals who might not have been able to define what they needed now or in the future. Medtronics salespeople did the same thing, not just making sales, but spending a lot of time being participant-observers.

Every leader at Medtronics was expected to take part in regular anthropological expeditions on customer terrain and report back the results and implications. Bill George himself observed 1,200 multi-hour surgical procedures during his 12-year tenure as CEO. "I saw our products being used, and I saw how they could be better," he told me. "I saw what frustrated physicians during procedures, and I made notes about how we could solve that problem with an extension of our current product, or a new one."

When you are immersed with the customer, observing and caring, and not trying to sell, "all your senses are engaged," says George, not just your analytical prowess. That's how you get great ideas, and meaningful ones—by noticing a snag in the third hour of an open-heart surgery, or picking up an offhand remark from a physician during breakfast. "One time an angry doctor threw a faulty, bloody Medtronics catheter at me in the middle of a surgery," George recalls. "That got my attention about product quality better than any report could have!"

Did all this anthropology work pay off financially? During Bill George's tenure, revenues grew from $750 million in 1989 to $5 billion in 2001. The company's market capitalization rose from $1 billion to more than $60 billion, a 37.5 percent growth rate compounded annually. I'd say it worked!

Customer anthropology has become central to the success of Proctor & Gamble as a defiant pipeline machine. For its great ideas, P&G relies less on mass-market research studies except for general trends and demographics. The real payoffs come from three different processes:

- Many employees, including executives, including top leaders like CEO A. G. Laffly, spend time observing their customers (particularly female customers) carefully, in the customers' own homes whenever possible, seeking to understand their lives and domestic jobs, how they use products, and the challenges and delights they encounter on the home front.

- P&G leaders come together to analyze and share ideas about how to improve homemakers' lives based on the field observations, speculating on expanded solutions for today's customers and tomorrow's.

- They crank up some rapid prototypes based on the first two steps and start testing.

Like Bill George at Medtronics, P&G staffers find that this process engages all senses, allowing them valuable insights like breakthrough plastic container wraps that fully seal on contact and prevent icky spills; diapers with a nonplastic, cottony feel that make parents and babies happy; and colorful pop-up boxes of wipes that delight kids who are toilet-training.

Being an anthropologist with customers is a very different experience than being a market researcher with them. You're not wrapped up in a classic market-research paradigm that yields an experience described this way by media baron Barry Diller:

"We become slaves to demographics, to market research, to focus groups. We produce what the numbers tell us to produce. And gradually, in this dizzying chase, our senses lose feeling and our instincts dim, corroded with safe action."

Instead, as an anthropologist, you'll have a sense of sensuality and intimacy with your customers, you'll be immersed with their lives, and you'll be patient with the process of understanding who they really are. That's how you'll get defiant insights for your pipeline.

3. Be a NASCAR Racer, Not a Baseball Player

When I heard the roars of the engines after the announcer said, "Gentlemen, start your engines" at the Pepsi 400 NASCAR series in Daytona Beach, I felt a rush go through my entire body. NASCAR events are loud, boisterous, and *fast*. As a driver, you're going 180 miles an hour inside a 100°-heat four-wheel coffin, inches from rivals, who are themselves turbo-weaving through the heavy traffic of the pack, obsessively monitoring the track and making constant nanosecond decisions. As a driver, even the teamwork is blurrily fast: listening to your coach on your earphones, plotting split-second strategy, adjusting to teammates' positions while barreling down the track, executing team strategies for passing or "drafting." Of course, the pit crews are legendary; they can replace four tires in 12 seconds. The jostling among cars in the pack is incessant, leading to the frenetic last lap when, finally, someone breaks from the pack.

Compare NASCAR to baseball. Baseball is a game of lulls followed by a few seconds of frenetic action in response to a "crisis" (the sharp grounder hit to the shortstop, with a double-play possibility), and then more lulls. The game has athletic brilliance and dramatic tension, to be sure, but the real action comes in sudden, periodic spurts. In NASCAR, the action is constant and the stakes are higher: You can end up in a car wreck, or you can end up dead. The sport has no quality-speed "trade-off." Just like in markets.

To create a defiant pipeline, you've got to steer your business like a NASCAR driver. You've got to examine every part of your organization, from back office to customer interface, and ask: Are we built for speed and agility? When you're talking about the amount of time to do research or due diligence, gather and share data, build a prototype, launch a new product, assess market impact, and follow up with customers and in-house people, are you driving a race car or playing baseball?

If you do find that your company is playing baseball, you have to change things so that even as you maintain your quality standards, your turnaround cycles and speed-to-market cycles are reduced by *half*, for starters. I mean that literally. If you ask people to increase speed by 5 or 10 percent, they'll just start playing baseball a little faster. They'll do whatever they've always done, just a little faster, with fewer rest breaks and less time with their families, and they'll hate you more. But tell them you'll work with them to figure out how to increase speed of execution by a factor of 50 percent, and you set the stage for participation and teamwork in the pursuit of radical innovation. You'll all be asking, "What can we eliminate or change in order to meet this goal? What kinds of technologies, people, management, and commitment do we need to make this happen?" Those are the kinds of questions Samsung managers asked, and it led to the company's ability to reduce the average time to roll out new products from 14 months to 5 months.

When you drive like a NASCAR racer, amazing things happen. It took Apple only 13 months to come up with radically alternative solutions to both Napster and Microsoft Jukebox, make and integrate a small acquisition of a company called SoundJam to acquire the necessary talent to help achieve those solutions, build the first version of iTunes, show it off at the annual Macworld trade show, get a big critical mass of players (music labels and artists) to agree to be part of the new business model, develop the concept for a portable Walkman-like device that could store all MP3 files, and build a first version of the radically innovative iPod. I know of companies that after 13 months would just be getting the committees together to review the consultant's reports about the current state of the market.

Even worse, I know companies that would be paralyzed until the "crisis" of a rival's extra-base hit in the late innings would mobilize them to action. In a NASCAR market environment, that's too little, too late.

4. Become a Magnet for the Crazy Three Percent of Customers

As I discussed in Chapter 3, you need to seek out the crazy three percent of customers. They will help you build defiant pipelines. These customers are the key to your future because they are curious, cool, crazy, and impatient enough to give you invaluable insight into what the masses of tomorrow's customers will need, want, and expect. If they're institutional customers, they're the ones who themselves are more likely to break from the pack, and they can be part of your R&D efforts. Invite them to workshops and planning sessions. Ask them to participate in your teams.

IBM's new Cell chip is a thumbnail-size processor that, when combined with four others of equal size, equals the speed of a 1999 supercomputer. The idea for this remarkable product did not emerge from IBM's own research division, but from its customer Sony. Ken Kutaragi, who heads Sony's electronic games business, was looking for a computer that would allow Play Station gamers to experience a virtual reality *Matrix* type of environment. Engineers from IBM, Sony, and Toshiba worked together to develop the chip, which will now also be applied to next-generation Sony TV sets and could very well represent the next paradigm of computing.

The $7-billion computer-gaming industry is about highly visual, highly interactive contexts where the same image can be experienced and reshaped from numerous perspectives, and with the Cell chips, those contexts can be applied to numerous data-management business processes. Only because IBM people were willing to work with Kutaragi, that avatar of the crazy three percent, did this huge market potential emerge.

Public Financial Management is taking a similar tack with the SwapViewer financial derivatives valuation product described in Chapter 4. By closely partnering with a tiny, select group of "super-clients"—forward-looking "deviant" managers of government agencies who are willing to try radical new approaches to managing debt portfolios—PFM is working out the kinks in the product, getting valuable advice on technical features and business applications, and sowing the seeds for some serious word-of-mouth buzz in the industry. PFM project leader Alfred Mukunya describes it this way: "Concurrent development of features based on the client's priorities and business needs saves us enormous time and resources, as we reduce the 'back and forth.' Our super-clients see results faster too. We are building the mousetrap together."

5. Become a Magnet for the Crazy Three Percent of Employees

Breaking from the pack in a Copycat Economy requires the fuel of great talent. Great talent is about extreme competence, super initiative, crazy commitment, and absolute accountability. If you think about your employees in terms of "staffing," "labor costs," or "personnel management," then you are not going to get the innovative people you need.

Answer this question honestly: Are you and your organization truly *committed* to attracting and retaining the best, the brightest, the most inquisitive, the most impatient, and the most willing to challenge the status quo? Here are some precepts to help you enact that commitment:

- As noted in Chapter 6, don't accept "acceptable" employees at any level. Leave positions open until you find exceptional people who exude talent and "fit." And then gladly pay top dollar for them because you know that your ROI will be much greater than if you paid lower compensation for commodity labor. One Google vice president says that one top-talent engineer is worth "300 times more than the average one." That may be a little extreme, but it's a good mindset to have when you hire and promote.

- Hire and promote only those people who love the business you're in. When I worked with country music companies in the early 1990s, I was astonished that several of them hired "professional" (a.k.a. analytically detached) salespeople who didn't particularly like the music. On the other hand, at Quiksilver, a provider of very cool beach clothing and surfing apparel, CEO Bob McKnight is vocal that he hires only people with a passion for surfing and snowboarding. He can teach them the rest. Genetech hires people who love the science more than the stock options. PFM hires people who are more passionate about improving government than "doing deals." I don't care what your business is—you can find people who love it. I rarely have come across anyone as passionate about his business as John Bishop is about his, and he runs the claims function at State Farm Insurance's Pacific Northwest region; unsurprisingly, he runs it in a way that other insurance companies would be wise to emulate.

- Treat people as businessmen and businesswomen, not as managers and employees. In other words, ensure that they can access any information they need when they need it, whether it is financial or operational or related to customers or marketing. Your annual edited, filtered "state-of-the-company" presentations are well intentioned but insufficient. Simultaneously, ensure that people are involved in planning and operational discussions that affect their work. Ensure that each person is actively involved in running a whole piece of business, however small, either alone or as part of a team. Finally, hold your colleagues accountable with high-performance metrics and, ideally, some sort of profit-and-loss responsibility. If they succeed, make sure they receive some significant individual and team-based rewards for their performance, whether it's a bonus or promotion or, as at 3M and Johnson & Johnson, the opportunity to take over their thriving business unit as a general manager or vice president. Your rewards don't have to be as generous as Google's recent $12-million stock reward for two employees who developed a breakthrough technology, but they do have to be generous enough to discriminate among performance—and to matter to those who receive the rewards!

- Formulate a corporate culture that stresses collaboration, transparency, and "boundarilessness" so that it will be easy for your best people to find each other, talk to each other, and work with each other, no matter their rank or function. As part of this open culture, make sure people are equipped and trained in technologies that enhance collaboration for product development, like product life-cycle management (PLM) software, Instant Messenger technologies, and "wiki" pages where everyone can brainstorm, contribute, and edit on a common platform, even if they're in different continents.

- Commit to constant training, development, and career-enrichment opportunities. They are investments not only in keeping peoples' skills razor sharp, but also in ensuring a vibrant learning environment that will keep your top talent engaged.

- Assume the role of "servant leader." After you declare the height of the performance bar and the rules of the game, your job is to take on the philosophy of Jerry Anderson, president of Coldwell Banker's commercial real estate business, who told me that "to be a leader in today's marketplace, you have to provide people with a constant platform of support."

- Develop a tolerance for failure. You don't have to "celebrate" failure because nobody likes failure. But to build a defiant pipeline, you must openly tolerate mistakes and setbacks as inevitable byproducts on the road to breakthrough. The key is to coach people to be well prepared and to execute with discipline, in order to reduce dumb errors and learn something important from errors after they occur. Ultimately, you want to develop a culture of disciplined fearlessness, where the occasional failures are overwhelmed by the successes. Google vice president Marissa Mayer mentions Apple and Madonna as role models because they are fearless enough to accept the periodic setback that accompanies continuous innovation. "Nobody remembers the (Madonna's) *Sex* book or the (Apple) Newton," she says. "Consumers remember your average over time. That philosophy frees you from fear."

- Allow your professional and creative people time to devote to whatever projects they want to, no questions asked. At W.L. Gore and Associates, 10 percent of an employee's workweek is delegated to personal research; at 3M, the figure is 15 percent; and at Google and Genetech, it's 20 percent. Gore's successful entry into the cable and guitar string business began with one engineer tinkering with cables for his mountain bike, then bringing in a colleague who happened to play guitar to see how the technology might be applied elsewhere.

- Finally, as a leader, spend a *lot* of time on "people" stuff: recruitment, placement, performance assessment, pay and nonpay rewards, training, determining career paths. Jack Welch reckoned he spent literally 50 percent of his time as CEO of GE on these issues. If you want to make sure that you attract and retain the top three percent, doesn't it make sense to spend a lot of your time and energy on building the best possible teams?

6. Become a Magnet for the Crazy Three Percent Partners

Some commodity relationships with outsiders make sense. Delegating some commodity functions to cheap but competent suppliers is a prudent step in freeing up resources. But no matter how big or dominant your company is, you simply can't own all the value-adding uber-competencies, networks, and resources necessary to build and maintain a great pipeline. The solution is to search the planet for "the" state-of-the-art organizational partners—not the cheapest partners—to help you build a defiant pipeline.

There's a big difference between a supplier and a partner. Suppliers react to your orders. They provide what they are asked to provide, and not much else. Partners initiate ideas and resources to help you achieve your goals. They take a responsibility for the success of a project or product line. They are openly involved as collaborative team members. Anyone who can help you create a defiant pipeline— including anyone who has hitherto acted as a "supplier"—can become a bona fide partner. The principle here is to seek and find the top three percent competent, curious, cool, and crazy collaborators who have the resources and value-fit to help you build something special.

Harnessing the crazy three percent partners works only when you can trust them enough to work together in a transparent open environment, sharing plans, budgets, and people. Consider that even arch rivals Samsung and Sony are fostering this environment in developing and manufacturing next-generation liquid crystal display (LCD) panels. Samsung has dominated in technology, while Sony has dominated in consumer applications. After getting through their initial wariness, managers and engineers of both companies now acknowledge that they learn from each other by joining forces in a genuine and trusting way. I'm not suggesting you too should work with your "enemies" (though you could), but whoever you work with, you'd better be able to trust them enough to establish intimacy. If you can't do that with your "partners," then drop them regardless of their fee—or else figure out if you have a problem trusting anybody. A legalistic, arms-length, jerk-them-around-for-a-lower-price mentality has no place in the kind of collaborative environment you need.

Remember that the ultimate value of your organization is the composite of the cutting-edge knowledge and initiative that you and your partners together bring to the table. This is why Boeing is working collaboratively with very selected partners all over the world in next-generation aircraft (even the hitherto sacred wings), why Eli Lilly is teaming up with top-end Asian biotech firms to radically reduce time to market, and why Proctor & Gamble has declared its intention that, by 2010, 50 percent of its new products will be generated by partners outside the company.

Break-from-the-pack companies are always seeking teammates who provide fair pricing but also great momentum in helping them build defiant pipelines. That is why Apple dumped its longstanding relationship with IBM in favor of Intel and its microprocessors. Regardless of their price, IBM microprocessors were simply too hot (literally) for the increasingly small computers and multimedia devices that Apple is developing. Intel has focused on miniaturization over the past few years, investing hundreds of millions of dollars in its Centrino chips for notebooks, while IBM has gradually gotten out of the PC business. Though many of the Apple faithful loathed the idea of getting in bed with one of the "Wintel" devils, CEO Steve Jobs had no compunction about defying their conventional wisdom because he saw Intel as a more valuable ally for next-generation products.

7. Become a Pipeline for Design

Economy, simplicity, user-friendliness, flair, fits, finishes, colors, sensuality, "feel"—why can't these design features be applied to product development from the very beginning? Companies that long ago understood the power of design are now building great design as a fundamental engine for a continuing, defiant pipeline because they recognize that design's contribution is as much to the competitiveness of their entire company as it is to a product's appearance.

Retaining wall producer Anchor Wall Systems, described in Chapter 4, views design as a strategic imperative that must underlie whatever it makes. Samsung is so obsessed with the look and ease-of-use of its products that it systematically utilizes design labs and facilities around the world. The diversified Rush Communications, headed by former hip-hop artist Russell Simmons, targets the urban youth market with signature-designed "Phat Fashions," credit cards, mobile phones, and energy sodas—to the extent that the entire Rush brand constitutes a pipeline of cool design applied to familiar products.

8. Target New Terrain—Carefully

Let's go back to Gore's guitar strings. What did the $1.5-billion W.L. Gore and Associates—the makers of products as disparate as Gore-Tex fabric, heart patches, air filters, bicycle cables, and lots more—know about guitars? Not much. But because Gore constantly seeks new markets for its company's skills and then attacks those markets mercilessly, one Gore engineer felt free to draw from the technologies and materials that his team was using in developing new plastic heart implants. He applied them as a new performance-enhancing coating for his mountain-bike gear cables, which led to Gore's Ride-On line of bike cables. Eventually, he and a guitar-playing fellow engineer applied that coating to guitar strings, and Elixir was born: a high-priced yet wildly popular string that provides top-notch clarity five times as long as an ordinary string does.

Companies like Gore are boldly venturing into any terrain where its expertise and resources can yield dominance, growth, and profit. Such enterprises don't stay stuck in one business, fighting the same rivals, whining about the same industry constraints. Instead, they charge into a wide variety of businesses, but not in the conventional way. They don't acquire diverse businesses just to "be" in them, or to be a big provider of scale in a one-stop-shopping venue. Instead, their culture and business models encourage employees to carefully apply their expertise to develop products in new terrain, to achieve dominance, not simply sales or market share. The best companies know that their biggest asset is their bundle of skills, competencies, networks, and other resources, which can be aimed at dominance and growth in any arena.

That is why different divisions of Toyota are now applying their expertise and innovations in serving the lucrative aging population and the families and businesses that care for the elderly. New kinds of wheelchairs and orthopedic mattresses made from car technologies are only two of the products in the emerging Toyota pipeline. After the products take off in Japan, they'll be ready for export to the even larger U.S. market.

On an even larger scale, there's 3M. On paper, the company appears to be a hopeless conglomerate. Not at all. The company continually and selectively applies its talents to new terrain. One hundred years ago, 3M's products, including sandpaper and masking tape, were based on three technologies: abrasives, adhesives, and coatings. Gradually, the adhesives skills led to the development of the Scotch-Tape and Post-It mini-empires, as well as to entries in medical and dental fields with products like medical tapes and disposable surgical drapes. Adhesives and coatings skills led to an entry into transportation, with products like Scotchlite reflective sheeting on road signs and clothing fabrics to increase pedestrian visibility. The new skills and technologies acquired in the medical, dental, and transportation fields have, in turn, led to new core competencies in nonwoven technologies, synthetic materials, fiber optics, and electronic display.

At 3M, this constant reapplication of skills and organic morphing has led to literally thousands of diverse product families sold in more than 60 countries. But like Gore and Toyota, it has been done quietly, under the radar—very little pomp, very little fanfare and flash, very little megamerger hype. Like Gore, 3M isn't just "in" a bunch of markets. 3M enters carefully selected market segments with the goal of dominating them via its breakthroughs. New 3M market entries are small businesses focused on specific niches. Although they are backed by a $20-billion corporate "venture capitalist" called 3M, they function and are held accountable as start-ups. That's very different than the conventional mergers-and-acquisitions diversification route, and that's precisely why 3M is a recognized leader in most of its product lines.

You have to be very careful about this principle. It's not an excuse for unbridled expansion at any cost. Targeting new terrain is not about buying and acquiring your way into it because the deal looks good. Nor is this effort about violating your higher cause and jumping into any market just for presence, or for quickie boosts in revenues, or for the naïve hope of easy cross-selling. Any of these steps will indeed dilute your quest for dominance and will also blur your higher cause. Instead, the principle of targeting new terrain involves mobilizing select parts of your company's expertise and resources to initially dominate a small niche via a "start-up" division, and then continually growing that niche and further developing your expertise. You build a defiant pipeline by carefully creating defiant breakthroughs in niche after niche, segment after segment, division after division. Imagine a parent tree seeding untouched terrain, where the seeds slowly grow a sapling into a tree, which seeds again, and so on.

One last important point: You certainly don't have to expand indefinitely into hundreds or thousands of products the way Gore and 3M have. You can be as selective as you want. You can carefully define and limit your ventures, like Toyota has—or like Diebold has. Diebold began as a bank vault and ATM market leader, and even as it radically improved and expanded its ATM business, it applied its technological and security systems knowledge to become a leader in certain segments of electronic security systems for government and the private sector, card systems for education and corporations, and the electronic voting machine business. And, for the time being, no more.

9. Think Broadly, Act Narrowly

Building a defiant pipeline requires that you define your agenda broadly and then enact it with the tightest possible focus.

Start with the big questions. You can't run any organization with uncontrolled innovation. There's got to be some overarching framework. It might be your company's higher cause or the priorities necessary for dominance. It might be certain financial, ethical, legal, and market niche boundaries. Whatever the framework is, it must be made explicit so that people understand the goal lines and side lines of their playing field. I like the questions that GE Global Research senior vice president Scott Donnelly asks his managers and scientists: What are the "big areas" and "important technologies" that we ought to look at, and how do they fit into our business or market? How can these big areas and important technologies transform a specific business? Do these new areas represent a growth industry we ought to get into, *and* are they areas in which we have the capabilities to succeed and excel? These are "think broadly" questions at GE. You can develop your own.

"Act narrowly" is best described by Bill Joy, the former co-founder and chief scientist at Sun Microsystems, and the principle author of the UNIX language. "The problem with large companies isn't that they fail to do large and seemingly ambitious projects," he says. "It's that they fail to do small, quirky, controversial projects—truly innovative projects that wouldn't be accepted by the organization at large but that have the potential to grow. (If everyone thinks an idea is okay, how can it be innovative?)"

To develop defiant pipelines, therefore, you don't need to make big mega-investments in huge complex "projects of the future," nor do you need to make mega-acquisitions to enter markets because they're "hotter" than the markets you're in. Instead, you should seek to keep your organization brimming with many small teams tackling many small, quirky, controversial projects—projects defying industry norms and your current product suites—that plausibly promise dominance.

Some skeptics point out, quite rightly, that to make an impact in a multibillion-dollar corporation, a project must generate hundreds of millions of dollars. For example, adding in all of Google's revenues to Microsoft's top line would raise it by only 4 percent. Ah, but what about the huge rise in market cap Google has received? What if one little bitty project blossoms into an eBay? What if Google search ultimately becomes the next generation's central computing platform, replacing Windows? And what if you've got a whole bunch of these kinds of small projects in your pipeline?

Companies like Google and Gore that act narrowly find their success by using teams with these characteristics:

- The teams are truly small. They can gather at a restaurant table and easily communicate with their fellow members. Teams as small as three are far better than teams as large as 30.

- They are neither permanent committees nor official task forces. Instead, they consist of lunatics from any corporate level who come together with a shared passion. These groups grow and shrink as the work progresses, grabbing or deleting fellow maniacs as appropriate, taking responsibility for results, and they disband when milestones are reached.

- The teams are cross-disciplinary and cross-functional. Scientists, engineers, marketers, salespeople, administrative people, and finance people do not function in isolated fiefdoms, but work together as a regular part of their jobs, not as workers who attend to one element of a job and then throw it over to someone else to pick up. This is so important that the cultures of Google and Gore (and for that matter, 3M and Toyota) emphasize cross-disciplinary teamwork as the rule, not the exception. At 3M, scientists and engineers are bundled with marketers and potential customers from the beginning. 3M people say that this process alone has helped shrink product-development cycles from an average of four years to two and a half, while boosting operating profits by 23 percent and shrinking R&D spending as a percentage of sales down to 5.7 percent.

10. One More Time: Dominate or Leave

The "dominate or leave" theme described in Chapter 5 is so important that it must be reiterated here yet again because it applies to the very products you'll want to have in your defiant pipeline. Concentrate your imagination and perseverance on developing products that will dominate their markets. Don't let your pipeline get stopped up with products that don't distinguish you from competitors. When you see mediocre products congesting the pipeline, get rid of them, even if they're currently bringing in some revenues.

In 1996, Danone, as a "diversified food company," had a presence in a wide array of food markets, including baby food, soups, pasta, beer, biscuits, water, and dairy products. As noted in Chapter 5, Franck Riboud got rid of everything except biscuits, water, and dairy. The reason for his decision? He knew that beer is an entirely different product and market than baby food, which is an entirely different product and market than yogurt, and so on. Franck did not believe that Danone could dominate every diverse market it had entered, so he chose the ones that he believed he had the potential to command. That decision freed the company to concentrate its expertise and resources on creating vibrant, defiant pipelines in dairy products (where it is a clear number one), biscuits (where it is a close second to Nabisco in revenues, but with superior bottom-line metrics), and water (where it is running a close second to the much larger Nestle).

Here's the rule: As long as you focus on product lines that you can dominate—like Toyota, Danone, Gore, and Google do—your diverse pipelines remain defiant, and sustainable. But if not, then it's time to "leave." Holly Etlin, the president of the Turnaround Management Association, makes this point about Ford's efforts to revive itself: "If you are Ford, and you are a great truck company but not great at something else, like certain cars, or your mini-van isn't competitive, will you act on that, will you make the painful choice to get out of a business, even if it hurts shareholders and the bottom line for a while?" She knows, and we know, that the answer should be yes.

These "10 Commitments"—easy to understand, hard to execute— will let you meet the challenge of building your own defiant pipeline. If you manage it, you'll find your company consistently brimming with exciting, breakthrough products that lead you into fresh and promising territory. You'll discover not just unprecedented and enduring success, but the genuine satisfaction of providing the market with worthy and delightful products beyond its expectations. Oh, yes, one other thing: You'll definitely spurt to the head of the pack.

8

TAKE YOUR CUSTOMER TO AN IMPOSSIBLE PLACE

To achieve the kind of customer relationships that separate you from the pack, you must understand the power of taking your customers to an impossible place.

To help you do this, I will tell you a number of stories over the next few pages. The reason is that if I expect you to take your customer to an impossible place, I must take you, the reader (no doubt an analytically astute intellect), to a place you might consider impossible: a place of images, feelings, and impressions. Stories are often the best way to do this. So let's begin with two unorthodox tales.

Organization Bob

My home is 35 miles away from San Francisco International Airport, and I travel frequently. One day several years ago, I called the local taxi company and requested a cab. The company sent me a fellow named Bob because he happened to be in the neighborhood—and there my story begins.

Is there any service that is more commodity-like than taxi service? We crawl into a cab, we go from point A to point Z, we pay, and thus ends a purely economic transaction. We don't expect the experience to be anything other than bland and forgettable.

But there came Bob, wheeling into the driveway. He took my bags from me and carefully placed them in the trunk. He courteously held the door open for me, standing next to it in dignified, chauffeur-style until I got in, then offered me the daily paper. Once I became one of his regular clients, I began to understand that, whether we are part of a one-person start-up or a $2-billion enterprise, we can all learn important lessons from Organization Bob.

Woody Allen once remarked that 80 percent of success in life is showing up. Whenever Bob picked me up, he arrived, on time, at my home or at the airport, regardless of traffic or weather conditions. (A couple times his cab broke down; he still managed to show up on time.) When you're dealing with airports, such dependability is priceless. More often than not, Bob would be the one on time and I would keep him waiting. Sometimes, after completing an exhausting itinerary, when I would see Bob patiently waiting in "our" cab right outside the airport building late at night in our designated spot, even when I'd suffered unforeseen delays, I experienced a heart-warming "high" second only to reuniting with my family.

Bob was always available to his select corps of clients, whether it be 6 a.m. on Saturday or midnight on Tuesday. Unlike other drivers who worked a set schedule, he adjusted his work hours around the needs of each customer. After the company got him a new vehicle (which he was quite proud of), I complained that the back seat was so stiff that my head (I'm 6-foot-6) brushed the ceiling. Bob promptly drove the cab back to the shop and had the technicians install an older, more comfortable back seat. His reasoning was simple: I was a valued customer, he wanted to keep my business, and, from his perspective, my complaint probably represented the concerns of other, less vocal clients. He recognized a valued customer's "complaint" as a strategic opportunity, and he adjusted the vehicle (part of his "organization") accordingly.

Bob consistently impressed me with his business savvy. As a "retired" individual who had held a number of managerial and start-up positions during his career, he could talk intelligently about finance, investment, and marketing. In fact, he occasionally helped broker business deals by introducing certain of his customers to each other. For example, he once connected two of his clients—one a consultant to a major Russian bank, the other an executive in the telecommunications field—because he thought their business goals were a natural fit. As a well-read Renaissance man, he could intelligently discuss current events, art, politics, history, and travel. In all cases, I learned something from our conversations (sometimes I took notes in the cab), and the one-hour ride to the airport often zoomed by. There were times I simply wanted to nod out, use the cellphone, or look out the window. Bob's "customer antennae" were acute. He shut up. He adapted to the environment that I, the customer, chose, rather than asking me to adapt to his.

Bob viewed himself as a businessman, not a "cab driver." He did not slip into the role of powerless, oppressed employee of the cab company. Bob regarded himself as the head of a private business that happened to lease a means of production called a vehicle. As far as he was concerned, he was part of the fast-growing outsourcing marketplace. He "outsourced" to the cab company the mundane work of administration, maintenance, insurance, accounting, and licenses and fees. As he pointed out, "My fixed expenses are $30,000 annually. Everything beyond that is what I make of it."

As the CEO of Organization Bob, Bob was an active niche-creator rather than a passive recipient of orders. Early on, he targeted the airport-bound business traveler as his preferred customer base. He then slowly and carefully selected the customers he wanted to work with. A week after my first ride with Bob, my wife came back from our home mailbox wearing a curious frown. Somebody had sent us a box of See's chocolates. Yes, it was a gift from Bob, with a signed note that read, "Thank you for your business. I appreciate it." I was amazed. When was the last time you received a gift from a cab driver?

Bob has been known to shock customers by "firing" them if their behaviors and values do not mesh with his. One such individual—a hard-driving, arrogant CEO—literally begged not to be fired and promised he would do better. In fact, I have to confess that Bob ultimately fired *me*. Once too often I absentmindedly left debris and food in his cab. I was stunned, and angry, but I had to grudgingly respect the dedication Bob brought to his business.

By providing his chosen customers a seemingly impossible level of service, Bob built an enduring business for himself. Even as other drivers tried to get into the lucrative airport business by lowering their fees, Bob charged a premium price and still cornered much of the business. He rarely does local runs because his appointment book contains from five to eight airport runs per day, around which he leisurely runs his personal life.

You do the math. He leases the cab at about $100 daily. Each one-way run, depending on point of origin, yields a $70–100 fee including tips (which tend to be generous). This man makes a nice six-figure annual income doing what he likes. "At the end of the day, I've made money driving with friends," Bob says.

Last year I gave him a call. "Why haven't other drivers copied you?" I asked. "Many have tried," he replied, "but they lack the dedication." (I suspect many of them also lack his Renaissance expertise.) When I asked if it had become an issue that his fees were nearly the same as those of limos and town cars, Bob told me that several of his newer clients had defected from limo companies. He said that the wife of one of his clients told her husband that for what he's paying Bob, he ought to hire a town car. The client told her, "I could take a limo, but then I couldn't take Bob." There it is: Bob not only drives his customers back and forth from the airport with absolute attentiveness to their needs; he also drives them to an experience that the average person who hails a cab would consider impossible.

Schooling for Success

In the late 1990s, something provocative was emerging in Guatemala. Like any entrepreneur, Maria Elisa Alvarado, a practicing clinical and school psychologist in Guatemala City, saw a gap in the marketplace that she could fill. She believed that her country's middle- and upper-class parents would be willing to pay for a private school that systematically developed critical skills in their children's very formative years. With three fellow psychologists, she took the lead in launching Colegio Pequenitos. I've been to the central Guatemala City campus of Pequenitos (there are two other campuses), and I can say I would have sent my own kids there without a second's hesitation.

The grounds and facilities are extraordinary, with immaculate gardens, plenty of space for outside activities and play, large classrooms, big stocks of papers and crayons, boards and games everywhere, and a very impressive computer facility. Alvarado makes sure that Pequenitos selects and cultivates its teachers with equal care and attention. Nearly half the faculty have advanced degrees in psychology or education; the goal is 100 percent. Alvarado tells me, "We put so much emphasis on the quality of the supervision and on the amount of *weekly* training hours. We must ensure that all of the teachers continue updating their knowledge and skills." This is necessary because the mission and activities of the school include systematically building students' cognitive skills, socioemotional skills, interpersonal skills, hygiene skills, sensory-perception skills, physical and motor skills, computer skills, and—let's not forget the basics—potty-training skills. The teachers regularly research the available literature on these subjects, discuss possible interventions (sometimes in cross-campus open forums), and decide on fresh, meaningful programs. I saw one such program in session: a basic computer-interactive mathematics skills program for 3- to 4-year-olds that has been developed in Israel.

Pequenitos also offers many special features, including events such as a Physical Fitness Olympics on all three campuses, a fathering skills course for interested dads, and constant programs like Technology Week, Scientific Week, Wild Animal Week, and so on.

I was particularly intrigued by the introduction of webcams linked to the home computers of parents so they can tune in and observe their kids at play and watch their kids making presentations if they can't be there in person. Alvarado's next step is to beta-test two-way webcam communications so that kids can view their parents and the parents can make presentations to the classrooms. Why do this, I asked, when none of your rivals is doing webcams? She replied, "I have to assume they'll copy me one day, so I always want to stay ahead." Survey scores show parents are extremely happy with the program, and the word-of-mouth buzz in the Guatemala City area is now huge.

Alvarado's evolvement of the business as a whole is proceeding in an aggressive yet systematic way. The key is the careful growth of the Pequenitos franchise, a plan launched in 2002. She and her staff perform constant quality reviews of the franchises, provide training, assess performance, ensure compliance to the Pequenitos mission and values, and take a small slice of the revenues. Alvarado's vision is for franchises throughout Guatemala, then throughout Central America, and she is exploring options in the U.S. as well.

Like Bob's story, Pequenitos is not simply an "aw-shucks" feel-good tale. Its net income after taxes went from –15.2 percent in 2003 to +16.5 percent by the end of 2005. Every day, the schools document visits and inquiries from "potential customer" parents. Enrollment over the past three years has more than doubled, and the two franchises are building additional classrooms because their current enrollment is expected to double by next year. All this despite charging a premium fee in the range of $142 to $235 a month, depending on the campus and the programs requested.

All the Way to "Wow!"

What can we learn from Organization Bob and Colegio Pequenitos? One critical lesson is that neither enterprise attempts to "satisfy" customers with "good customer service." "Satisfaction" and "good service" are what their competitors strive for. Bob and Colegio Pequenitos travel a different road. Both Bob and Alvarado take their customers to a place where the customers wind up shaking their heads and saying that what they experience is simply impossible. When you hear customers make statements like "I can't believe it" or (telling a friend) "You won't believe this," or "This is amazing!" or just plain "Wow!", you're looking at a vendor that is breaking from the pack.

Any organization can transport its customers all the way to "Wow!" Barbara Bisgaier, a partner at Public Financial Management, told me about her recent PFM client, a water district "whose CFO has been doing things his way—which he believes strongly is the most correct, conservative, and risk-free—for thousands of years." When PFM was hired to build a quantitative model for helping the financial people at the district do operating budgeting and capital planning, the CFO's specific instruction to PFM was to build on the model he had already engineered and "make your numbers match our numbers." But the PFM consultants determined that the CFO's model and numbers were inappropriate for the goals he was seeking. What Bisgaier and PFM senior consultant Kevin Phillips did—without asking for clearance from either PFM or the client—-was to unilaterally create a different model, one that organized the district's relevant data in a cleaner, more flexible way that gives the CFO a new ability to measure the impact of various "what-if" scenarios as he undertakes the planning and implementation of a fairly extensive capital program.

Bisgaier and Phillips didn't just respond in a commodity-like fashion to their customers' request. Instead, without asking permission, they *led* the customer to a new place: a customized, and first-of-a-kind model that they believed served his ultimate interests better.

According to Bisgaier, after Phillips presented the new model, its implications, and its rationale, "the guy pushed back in his chair, looked at Kevin, and said, 'Wow!'"

"Wow!" is the kind of emotional reaction you should seek to inspire in your customers. The CFO, in fact, said that the input from PFM was a "career-significant" experience for him. Based on his expectations, what he heard was as impossible; he couldn't believe it. His reaction yielded follow-up business for PFM, including training staff to use the new model, writing a procedures manual for future usage, and executing spin-off work, such as helping the district with dividend allocation and arbitrage rebate. The "Wow!" PFM elicited also makes it hard for any competitor to approach the CFO and steal PFM's business by simply whispering, "Psst, I do financial advisory cheaper." That "Wow!" is no commodity.[1]

Vendors like Organization Bob and Colegio Pequenitos deliver an implicit invitation to their individual customers. "Join with me," they say, "and I'll lead you to a place you couldn't imagine, a place that will make your life distinctly better, easier, more effective, more fun, and happier. You think it's impossible? Let me lead you to that place." To institutional customers, the message is similar, as PFM has shown: "Together, you and I will make your business distinctly more efficient, productive, and profitable; more capable of reinventing itself; better able to service your own customers; or more likely to break from your pack. Impossible, you say? Then come with me…." Ultimately, as you ponder the precepts of this chapter, you'll see the difference between vendors who say to customers, "Please don't leave me," and vendors whose actions compel their customers to say, "Please don't let me go."

Beyond the Commodity Response

It's essential to recognize that "Wow!" is an emotional reaction, of a kind that is especially vital in the Copycat Economy. Today customers expect "good products" and "good service." Customer satisfaction itself has become a low-impact response; it is a commodity transaction that stirs no emotion. A few years ago, after speaking to an audience of Fidelity Investment executives, I joined a panel that included a senior member of Yankelovich Partners, a consumer attitude survey firm. He echoed my thoughts by declaring, "Our research indicates that customer satisfaction is no longer a useful goal for companies.

For customers we've surveyed, 'customer satisfaction' is simply the difference between feeling pissed off and feeling nothing!"

If you're taken aback, let me give a mundane example to demonstrate how true that quote is. Suppose you drop off a shirt or skirt to a dry-cleaner, who tells you it'll be ready on Tuesday afternoon. On Tuesday afternoon, you arrive at the cleaners, you pick up your package, and you pay. Do you do cartwheels with delight? No, you feel nothing. You've just completed a commodity transaction.

But suppose you need the shirt or skirt for a business meeting early the following morning, and when you arrive at the cleaners on Tuesday afternoon, he tells you that it's not ready. Or you discover a couple buttons ripped off. How do you feel then? Merely "dissatisfied"? Or something a little stronger?

If you were given a customer evaluation form to fill out in the first scenario, you'd probably write that you were "satisfied" with the "service" of the dry cleaner. But because there's no emotion, there's no particular attachment, commitment, or loyalty to the dry cleaner. (Small wonder that a Booz-Allen & Hamilton report concludes that "the myth that a satisfied customer will become a loyal customer is just that—a myth.")

That is exactly why companies are often shocked when customers who say they're satisfied today leave for a competitor tomorrow. I recently worked with a large industrial company that would regularly poll its corporate customers with attitude surveys filled with scales of 1 to 5, where 5 was very satisfied, 4 was satisfied, 3 was neutral, and so on. For years, the company viewed 3s as "acceptable" and lumped the 4s and 5s together as "desired" responses, until one staffer broke down the data and was distressed to find that the only decent predictor of customer loyalty and repeat business were the 5s. Indeed, those customers who marked 5s were six times as likely to be repeat customers as those who marked 4s.

Many vendors stuck in the pack are skeptical about this vital necessity of the "Wow!" response because they generally believe in one of two fallacies:

1. Fallacy #1 is that simply doing "zero defects" work will help an organization break from the pack. But as I've pointed out, customers expect the products to work, they expect you to meet specifications and the terms of the contract, they expect you to be available when you say you will, and so on. That's commodity stuff. If you deliver zero defects, you get a "satisfied" response, and you get to survive inside the pack.

2. Fallacy #2 is that customers will not pay for anything more than "zero defects." Rubbish. As customers, we do it all the time, whether we give a generous tip to a golf caddy whose advice helps us play better, or when we patronize a hotel with amenities and staff that pamper us. A McKinsey study, appropriately titled "Shedding the Commodity Mind-Set," found that many manufacturers that sell ostensibly mundane products, like industrial resin or bulk chemicals, to other companies were initially certain that the only differentiator in their offerings was price. But in careful follow-up research, McKinsey discovered that in reality, only 30 percent of those customers made their buying decisions solely on price. The other 70 percent of companies indicated that they would pay more for greater product selection, frequency of contact with vendor representatives, higher levels of technical support, and so on.

If customers will pay more for helpful caddies, and buy from vendors who provide a little more value, then how would customers respond if you took them to the place that Bob, Pequenitos, and PFM strive for—the place that customers believe to be "impossible"? That's the lesson for you. Let your competitors strive for "customer satisfaction." You're going to lead your customers to a place they can't yet even comprehend. That place might be physical, like Selfridge's department stores in England, with its flamboyant "bull ring" building design, and featuring exotic areas for events like body piercing and customer-participatory art exhibits. The place might be a seemingly impossible value proposition, like the guarantee offered by Cemex, the world's most profitable cement company. Cemex, based in Monterrey, Mexico, has somehow been able to integrate data networks within its own mix plants, its own trucks, and its customers' plants to guarantee on-time delivery of its products—regardless of road conditions, weather conditions, or the number of changes by the customer to the original order—in contrast to the industry-standard four-hour window. Or the place may be psychological, such as the one provided by Harley-Davidson, with its patented, 80-decibel "potato-potato-potato" rumble that suggests "badness." In the words of one Harley-Davidson executive, "What we sell is not the world's best motorcycle. What we sell is the ability for a 43-year-old accountant to wear black leather, ride through small towns, and scare people."

Five Steps Toward an Impossible Place

How do you take your customers to an impossible place?

Fortunately for you, there's no quick-fix answer to that question—If there were, it would be copied instantly, sending you right back to Commodity Hell. No linear, sequential map to that impossible place exists for your organization. Nor does that map exist in the minds of your customers, and the most foolish thing you could do is to ask them where that place is and what they want from you. You and your team must believe that an impossible place exists for your customers, no matter what conventional wisdom states, and that you will commit your attention and resources to creating it. The issue for you and your team is to transcend your focus on the discrete products or services you sell (or think you ought to sell) and concentrate instead on the experience you provide your customers. You'll make the map yourself, based on your knowledge and love of your customers, and your imagination and courage in forging new paths.

With those criteria in mind, here are five steps that will help you lead your customers to an impossible place.

1. Lead Institutionally

Every organization, no matter how bureaucratic or unfriendly, has a few individuals who with their own sweat and fortitude periodically do wonderful things for customers. At the same time, as customers we've all experienced the awkwardness of dealing with well-intentioned, good-hearted front-line people whose wonderful efforts to help us are frustrated and thwarted by the counterproductive systems and processes in their organizations. The first challenge for any organization that wants to break from the pack is to make those sorts of wonderful behaviors and mindsets part of the structural fabric of how the business is run.

In other words, if you want your *organization* to break from the pack, don't rely on episodic or idiosyncratic acts of heroism from individuals. Institutionalize the process so that everyone, every process, and every job contributes to leading customers to an impossible place.

GE Healthcare helped launch The Indiana Heart Hospital as the first all-digital heart hospital in the U.S. in 2003. GE Healthcare's people, systems, expertise, networks, knowledge, technologies, and capital—in short, the entire institution—took Indiana Heart to a place that many in the health-care field thought was impossible. GE Healthcare helped CEO David Veillette build a 210,000-square-foot facility capable of delivering a new level of care for cardiovascular disease, with the most advanced monitoring, diagnostic, and imaging technologies, all within a paperless, filmless, and wireless environment. GE Healthcare didn't simply "respond" to an RFP (request for proposal) to "satisfy" a customer. Instead, the entire institution—people, products, processes—provided the kind of customized technologies and expertise to create an environment that Indiana Heart could not have imagined. According to Veillette, "physicians can have life-saving information about patients in a keystroke rather than having to wait hours, even days for critical medical records and results from previous tests or treatment." There are no patient charts and folders, no record rooms, no nurses' stations—just digital data available at every bedside and at any of a thousand wireless notebook computers. All processes are integrated, from lab to X-ray to physician order entry. Physicians' homes are wired so they can be connected to the hospital network.

As a result of GE Healthcare's integrated effort, the hospital's operational and staffing costs are down. So are medical errors. Because caregivers are armed with immediate information, appropriate treatments are administered faster, and infections and adverse reactions are recognized sooner. In 2004, the hospital earned $2.6 million in profits on $38 million in revenues. One financial review suggests that as of mid-2005, after only two years, the total investment has already paid for itself. Meanwhile, GE continues to earn a healthy annual fee from Indiana Heart for upgrades to its systems, maintenance, and consultative work.

In any organization, it is difficult to institutionalize what are typically isolated and idiosyncratic outbreaks of good intentions. In 2004, I gave a presentation to the top 20 marketing professionals of a multibillion-dollar company. The company's prior successes had not translated into excitement about the future, and there was a distinct whiff of ennui in the corporate culture. I suggested that part of the problem was that the stated mission of the company was to provide "customer satisfaction." To illustrate what they could seek instead, I presented a PowerPoint slide I'd used when I was with the Tom Peters Group 15 years ago. The slide presented a list of verbs representing reactions that some of our clients (including manufacturers in supposedly "mundane" businesses) strove to stir in their customers. The verbs included *bewitch, dazzle,* and *thrill.*

The group loved the idea of bewitching, dazzling, and thrilling their customers, but shook their heads over the feasibility of such an effort in their company. "We work in a thrill-free environment," one confessed. "Yeah," said another. "We'd have to run these words by the legal and HR departments, and they'd write them up as policy manuals." And these were senior people talking!

To institutionalize a crusade to that impossible place, you must lead your people with compelling conversations about new possibilities, new directions, and new value propositions. As a leader, you must also define and raise a *collective* set of new expectations and aspirations for customer care, and build organizational processes to support them. Simultaneously, you must canvass and critique every *current* element of your business—products, processes, networks, partnerships, systems, technologies, jobs, and people—with one question in mind: Can this element—really and truly, no b.s.—help us as an organization in our quest to take our customers to a place they didn't believe was possible? Whenever the answer is no, you must initiate change.

2. Lead with Profound Authenticity

We discussed authenticity in the last chapter, and here it comes again. If you choose to take your customers to an impossible place, whatever that place might be, you must genuinely believe in what you're doing—and show it. You must commit to it with your entire heart, or you shouldn't try it at all. Unfortunately, many customers see vendor authenticity as a rare phenomenon. The glittering promises from vendors too often reveal themselves as hollow, and customers are left disappointed and angry. According to Harvard University professor Shoshana Zuboff, "People have come to accept that their consumption experiences have been largely adversarial."

Because it's rare, customers *know* when they experience deep authenticity, and it affects them profoundly. Several years ago, my wife, Leslie, had one such experience with PowerBar, the ubiquitous athletic energy bar: "While at the supermarket, I decided, for the first time, to buy a big box of PowerBars, which I stored in the kitchen. A few days later, I grabbed a PowerBar on my way to an aerobics workout. I unwrapped it while driving, and as I went to take a bite of it, I saw something white and shiny. It was a protein source moving on my protein source. A worm!"

Now that she'd lost her appetite, my wife pondered her response. Just forget it, I advised, and don't ever buy a box of PowerBars again. Leslie wanted to call the toll-free number on the wrapper. I snorted with derision. She'd only get a bureaucratic runaround or a form letter six months from now, I told her. It would be a waste of time. There are a zillion competitors to PowerBar. Buy them instead.

PowerBar is currently a division of Nestle, but at the time it was still an independent, $100-million company headed by founder Brian Maxwell. As Leslie reported: "Sophie, the woman who answered the phone, was incredibly nice, extremely apologetic, and very informative about what happened to me." What had happened was the work of the Indian Meal Moth, a harmless pantry pest that feeds on grain-based products and lays its eggs there, which eventually hatch into tiny worms.

I was impressed by the niceness of Sophie, but Leslie and I were bewitched, dazzled, and thrilled by what happened next. Leslie received a personal note from CEO Maxwell postmarked the same day as her call, apologizing for what she had experienced. The note detailed the science of the Meal Moth, averred that the worm problem was rare, and acknowledged it was "disgusting." It was personally signed by Maxwell and included a handwritten note of apology from Sophie. Although Leslie hadn't asked for a refund, enclosed was a check reimbursing her for her purchase, along with paraphernalia she could use to mail the culprit PowerBar to the company for analysis. When she sent the PowerBar back, she got another handwritten note of thanks.

Intrigued, I called the company myself, told them of my wife's experience, and asked to speak to Maxwell. I was connected with him right away. I learned that the worm might not have even originated at the PowerBar facilities. "We've cleaned up our own facilities, but we can't control what happens at the packers, the retailers, or even the customer's kitchen. But that doesn't matter," he went on to say. "*We take full responsibility for the customer's experience.*"

What? No hiding behind legalisms? No blaming a supplier? No lip service to "the customer is king"? Maxwell told me that he values customer complaints because they help PowerBar grow. A few years earlier, a customer complaint had first alerted the company to the meal moth problem and led to a revamping of manufacturing and quality processes. Then, without a hint of hype, he told me, "We *treasure* Leslie's complaint." When was the last time you heard a CEO say anything like that?

Even though the PowerBar CEO was instrumental in setting the tone of the culture, this story is not about Brian Maxwell. It was the deep authenticity throughout his company that took my wife to an impossible place. A loathsome worm led her to a wonderful complaint process that she could never have imagined, which, in turn, led her to conclude, "I now want them [the PowerBar company] to succeed. I feel happy to support them." Vendors can't fake this stuff. Are you surprised that, since then, we've both stayed loyal to PowerBar? (And we haven't seen another moth!)

3. Lead with Genuine Caring

In February 2002, an improbable cover story appeared in the edgy *Fast Company* magazine. Written by an ex-Yahoo executive named Tim Sanders, it was called "Love Is the Killer App." Sanders argued that love, compassion, and empathy are key drivers of business success and leadership. The article generated an enormous positive response from readers—4,800 messages in the first week after publication alone, and many more in the years that followed. Sanders had touched a nerve. But love, unfortunately, is seldom developed by organizations as a killer app for customers. Sure, we always hear pap like "We love our customers," but we know it's a con. That's why if your concern and caring is genuine, that alone might lead customers to an impossible place.

One way to show caring is to be physically and emotionally available when your customer is in trouble, regardless of the immediate payoff to you and your company. While doing research for a speech I was to give at a national meeting of Mutual of Omaha insurance people, I was touched by letters that customers had written to the company about their agents. One man who had suffered a work accident that left him disabled wrote about how his agent, "Mike," comforted him after his accident and remained available long afterward. A woman whose husband died wrote about how another agent, "Brad," came over right away and was a steadfast support. The impact of these acts of concern had nothing to do with the size or image of Mutual of Omaha, nor did they relate to the commodity payout of the insurance policy. They had everything to do with the true caring shown by the company's agents, which, of course, yielded loyalty and support for the company.

I've reviewed several research studies examining what helps insurance companies sell more policies, and the data repeatedly points to the power of caring. As one report noted, "Our customers do not necessarily place great value on specific product attributes; instead, they emphasize the nature of the relationships they have with the company through the agent and the agent's staff." Another report showed that even though "I got a better price elsewhere" is the most frequent reason customers leave their insurance provider, the reality is that "price is often simply the event that brings other issues to a rolling boil." In fact, reasons for leaving that applied to insurance agents—such as "nobody cared about me," "nobody knows who I am," "nobody contacted me," and "nobody called me with suggestions that would help me"—were much more powerful determinants of customer disloyalty than price. The best agents venture past the commodity mentality. They demonstrate that they think about the customer's welfare, truly understand the customer, empathize with the customer, initiate ideas for the customer, and are always there for the customer, regardless of whether there's a sale to be made. Their caring transcends their companies' "products" and leads to more sales.[2]

I have personally witnessed the power of genuine caring and how it has made me adhere to a particular service provider in one of the most commoditized of markets: travel planning. My travel agent, Milo Shneeman, works across the continent from me in Washington, D.C. Of course, if she was only a "travel agent," I'd be working with someone closer to me in the San Francisco Bay Area, or else I'd use the Web exclusively. But Milo is my savior. She takes me to impossible places, no pun intended. Even though she is now the manager of two MacNair Travel offices, I have her phone numbers 24/7, and I can't tell you how often she has gone out of her way to recheck a supposedly full flight every day to plug me into it when an opening occurs, or how often she has negotiated with the airlines for the seat that best suits my height, or how often she has walked me through airports via my cellphone when the unexpected crisis has occurred. But telling those stories wouldn't do her justice.

One anecdote will suffice: A couple years ago, I was getting ready to go to Beijing, and six days before my departure, Milo called. After reminding me to take my passport (thanks, Mom!), she inquired if I had procured my visa. Silence. Uh-oh. I experienced feelings of embarrassment and then, recognizing that due to the

Chinese bureaucracy, obtaining a work visa can take weeks, the beginning of panic. Milo and her team to the rescue. "Okay, today is Monday," she said briskly. "I'll e-mail you a link to download the application. Fill it out, and FedEx it to me along with your passport. I'll send one of my people to the Chinese embassy to stand in line and be insistent. We'll get this done and I'll FedEx it back to you for Friday delivery so you can be on your way Saturday." And so it was. Once again, Milo took me to a place I didn't think was possible. Once again, she provided a genuinely caring gesture that made my life much easier than it would have been if she wasn't in my life. And because this is one of many anecdotes I could tell, Milo makes it impossible for me to use someone else as a travel agent, or even to use the Web except for the most mundane transaction. Because manager Milo is working to institutionalize this type of caring in both of her MacNair offices, my assistant, Lauren Swalberg, feels comfortable in dealing with a couple other agents when Milo is not available. I'm more pigheaded because I feel safer when Milo takes care of me personally, so I try to talk to her directly. In a world where the entire travel agency business has become thoroughly commoditized, my only concern is that one day Milo might leave me. Do you think your customers say that about you?

4. Lead with Turbo Speed

As I've described throughout this book, speed is a great differentiator in a Copycat Economy. Especially when a customer has a crisis, speed itself becomes an impossible place.

If your company can eliminate customers' waiting time, you open up a huge opportunity for breaking from the pack. It's astonishing how many corporate leaders build huge empires via big acquisitions and slick marketing campaigns, but fail to understand the importance of this speed principle—or, worse, do understand its importance but, because of their organizations' size and complexity, are utterly incapable of delivering on it. Sometimes they make matters worse by becoming slower and more bureaucratic in dealing with customers.

Customers hate waiting, whether it involves standing in line, being relegated to phone hell, experiencing slowness and delay in getting help, or experiencing slowness and delay in receiving something—a service, a message, a document, or a product. If you can configure your business's systems, cultures, and employees to reduce radically the amount of time customers have to wait, then you're on your way to taking them to an impossible place—building their loyalty. For example, one client told me that because the Tennessee-based furniture company England, Inc., reduced the industry-standard waiting period from six to eight weeks to a mere three weeks, it got his business, even though he had to pay more for their speed. Another, less creative furniture company might have accepted protests from everyone in its supply chain saying a three-week delivery is next to impossible, but England has reconfigured its culture, technologies, and supply chains to make speed happen. That's why England can charge more for the speed it offers, even as its alacrity lowers its operational costs.

On a personal note, I remember vividly how Kinko's took me to an impossible place with its turbo-speed a couple years ago. My colleague Ben McCleary and I were preparing a major strategic and financial report for the top 50 managers of a national firm. On a Tuesday afternoon, after numerous discussions and alterations to our findings, I suddenly realized that we were to present our report on Thursday morning, yet my half of the report was still in my laptop in San Francisco, and Ben's half was in his laptop in New York, and we would both be in transit the next day, Wednesday. How would we ever have time to put together 50 hard-copy 60-page binders for each of the managers to be ready by the 8 a.m. Thursday meeting?

I felt a ripple of anxiety, but Ben remained remarkably calm. "Just send your part of the report to me. I'll take care of everything," he intoned. I was prepared to be his slave for a year in gratitude, but as it turns out, what he did was pretty simple. Once he received my e-mail, he pasted my document as the second half of the report, did some minor editing to integrate his part and mine, and then logged on to the Kinko's website. With a few easy clicks, he was able to customize the look and design of the binder, as well as the appearance of the text and graphics. After he tapped in the location of our meeting site, all the bits and bytes of our project were zapped to the Kinko's location nearest to the hotel where we were to be meeting, and Kinko's only remaining question for Ben was whether, for an extra $9, we would like them to deliver the 50 binders to the hotel. (Duh, yeah!) And so, those binders were happily waiting for us at the hotel before we even got there. That's turbo-speed in action.

Having had nightmarish visions of all-night design and photocopy sessions, I was dumbfounded and delighted by this perfectly mundane but "impossible" place that Kinko's took us. Note that this is not an aw-shucks story of a good-hearted front-line Kinko's staffer who toiled all night at the copy machine and then drove across the country in his own car to deliver the documents to us at 7:59 a.m. Thursday. Instead, per principle #1 above, the entire process was fully digitalized and institutionalized for maximum turbo-speed responsiveness. The results thrilled us, and Kinko's has gotten a big increase of our business workload since then.

Wherever the place you take your customer, do it with turbo-speed if you want it to matter. You can start by responding to every customer comment, query, or complaint on the same day you receive it, the way PowerBar did. Then start running your entire business with the same turbo approach that Kinko's and England do. Ultimately, you can start shooting for the goal that one of my clients is now striving for: "We want to become so fast and efficient that we provide each customer with 'resources on demand.'"

5. Lead with the Individual Customer in Mind

Because "mass" (as in mass production, mass marketing, and mass distribution) is no longer a predictor of value-add, the more an organization is capable of treating each customer as an individual market unit of one, the more likely it is to break from the pack.

Even as more gaming casinos spring up in Nevada and on Indian reservations, Harrah's Entertainment (with 26 casinos in 13 states) has built an unsurpassed record of same-store sales growth and what is perhaps the top sustained financial performance in the industry. Harrah's has also performed an exceptional job of raising customer retention and "share of wallet." It has accomplished this feat not by building gargantuan palaces the way Kirk Kirkorian and Steve Wynne have done in Las Vegas, but by effectively mining its vast databases to provide customized incentives and rewards to people who have utilized its services. More than 25 million customers use Harrah's "Total Reward" card to earn redeemable prize points, which also allows the company to track the kinds of meals eaten, merchandise bought, and games played by each one of those millions of customers. Harrah's then creates customized incentives and rewards to match those customer preferences. I am often amazed at how many vendors today do not capitalize on data-mining technologies to develop a rich comprehensive database on each and every one of their customers, to individualize the services they provide. If Harrah's can do it with 25 million customers, so can you.

Individualization is not just about marketing to specific people; it's about the products themselves. In a world of uniformity, customization and built-to-order products make a big difference in customer attitudes. Until it adopted this perspective, Bally Refrigerated Boxes was a flat-earnings, commodity provider of walk-in coolers and freezers, refrigerated buildings, and blast freezers. Since the time it began to provide customers with literally thousands of built-to-order choices and modular options, the company has commanded a 5 to 8 percent price premium, along with a steady growth in market share and customer loyalty. At the other end of the consumer spectrum, Mars, Inc., has discovered that people are willing to pay literally triple the going price for a bag of M&M's if they can choose the colors in it. Mars' online stores now offer us 21 different colors from which we can draw to create our own personalized bag of candies. Despite the candy's price tag, it's one of the company's hottest sellers. Go figure.

Notwithstanding this data, most companies are still built for mass and standardization. Sure, their leaders give big lip service to the notion of customization. They do some minor tweaking of their standard products and services to fit individual customers' needs a little better. Naturally, they trot out the tired "We sell solutions" sales line even though cynical customers know that by some remarkable coincidence, the solutions that the company peddles today happen to be the products it has been selling for years—products that don't offer solutions tailor-made to their needs.

Start investing in flexible business systems, data-mining capabilities, and intimate customer collaborations. If you don't take the lead on individualization, your customers will. With all the choices at their disposal, they'll gravitate toward the vendor who deals with them as individual entities. This is absolutely true because, in the future, you can bet that customers will *expect* individuation. I recently saw evidence of this trend at a meeting hosted by a Fortune 500 company for its top 100 corporate customers. The host company had just completed a major acquisition, and its representatives made multiple presentations about how wonderful this acquisition would be for everyone. When the customer representatives took the floor, however, their reactions were more guarded. They made comments like, "Don't try to sell us what we don't need just because you now have more products in your portfolio." "Don't use this acquisition to cross-sell so that you can reduce your debt." "Focus on our needs, not yours." "Understand each of our businesses, what we need, and we'll be receptive."

These customers made it clear they did not intend to be pawns to be moved around to satisfy the host company's strategic plans. *If you view us as your meal ticket to pay for this acquisition, we're outta here,* their comments implied. *But if this acquisition helps you to really understand our individual businesses and help us improve them, we'll be on board.*

Over the past few years, I've learned that the key to taking individual customers to an impossible place is *not* to throw umpteen million choices at them in the name of "customization." Customers feel overwhelmed by market choices as it is. They need help in feeling less overwhelmed. The key is to assist them in solving their unique problems and making their unique lives better. That means not just providing them a slew of options, but helping them navigate through those options—or, even better, taking a lead in creating new options just for each of them alone. That's precisely what GE did with Indiana Heart Hospital. That's also what industrial and medical gas producer Air Liquide did. The company occasionally unveiled a product innovation, like the October 2005 launch of a new anesthesia drug in Germany. But the company was not able to build a sufficiently large and defiant pipeline around all its gas, chemical, and welding products. So it took a different tack. Air Liquide consolidated its resources (expertise, technologies, systems, and so on) to help corporate customers optimally manage their unique energy needs, be they higher process yields, or simpler gas supply management, or better safety standards, and so on. Once again, note that Air Liquide didn't point customers to a huge mish-mosh menu of services. It offered a truly customized service component which has made customers feel "taken care of," and has created far more value and growth for the company than its traditional product line on its own.

Even websites can do it. The Lands' End virtual fitting room at the company's website doesn't throw a gazillion links, windows, and options at the customer. Instead, the website is very focused on assisting each customer to buy the clothing that is best for him or her. Through the instructions and visuals of My Virtual Model, you can create a 3-D model of your body shape and size, and then try on the catalog company's clothes for optimal style and fit. In fact, the "My Fit" link shows you how snug or loose the garment is on different parts of your body. As you assess the fit on your particular body, you can ask questions and seek advice by using Lands' End Live to chat live via instant messaging, or make a phone call to a customer rep— both available 24/7. Furthermore, you can use the Shop with a Friend online option to invite someone to browse clothing options together with you from two different computer locations. And if you want professional help, you can use an online My Personal Shopper preference engine expert (a.k.a. a virtual "personal wardrobe consultant") to help you make decisions. Note how the process itself reduces the hassle factor and makes customers feel taken care of, even while online. That process, coupled with a 100 percent no-hassle return policy, has taken so many customers to an impossible place that the virtual-shopping business is one of the company's fastest growers, at a 34 percent conversion rate, with higher margins and customer satisfaction, to boot.

Rafael Pastor, the CEO of Vistage International, an organization that provides professional development services to its CEO members, has the perfect take on this issue: "The one thing that is not commoditizable is the integrity of the individual." If you can build your organization with the agility, competence, and commitment to take each individual customer to an impossible place, you will never fear the twin scourges of commoditization and imitation.

Seven Quick Impossible Questions

To conclude this chapter, here are seven quick, simple questions you should be continually asking yourself and your team. These questions transcend "products" and "services" and are, appropriately, presented from the perspective of the customer. If on a regular basis you and your team literally approach your work from the point of view of your customers, then you'll be taking significant steps to lead them to an impossible place.

1. How *easy, hassle-free, fast, and fun* is it to work with this vendor—before *and* after the sale?

2. Does the vendor really, truly *listen* to me? *Seek my input? Understand me* and the challenges and opportunities in my life (or my business)?

3. On a *personal* level, how *responsive, caring, empathetic, and concerned* is the vendor toward me? Do I feel taken care of when I deal with this vendor?

4. Does the vendor know me (or my business) so well that he or she can *anticipate* what I might want and need before I do?

5. How effective is the vendor in devising a *fast, creative solution* to my *real* problems and *unique* needs?

6. Can I *trust and count on this vendor* to continually come up with great ideas for me (or my business)?

7. When I get involved with this vendor as a corporate customer, is my *work distinctly better*? Is my *business distinctly better*? Or, if I'm an individual customer, is my *life distinctly better*?

When your customers answer these questions ultra-affirmatively about your organization, you'll know you've taken them to an impossible place.

A Quick Postscript on Branding the Impossible

Your organization's brand is its identity in the marketplace. If you want to reap full and sustained benefit from taking your customer to an impossible place, or, for that matter, from building a defiant pipeline, from carrying out your higher cause, or from dominating a market space, you must ensure that those factors define your company's brand. The way to do that is not to simply rely on public relations campaigns, ad rollouts, logos, slogans, color schemes, online sales tools, and such. The way to build your break-from-the-pack brand is to demonstrate to the market that your organization *will consistently, reliably, efficiently, authentically, and quickly deliver on the great things it says it will deliver.* As Atlanticare CEO George Lynn puts it, the unique value your organization provides must be "pervasive, relevant, and credible."

When customers and investors can count on you and your organization to deliver the extraordinary, through thick and thin, you've branded yourself in their psyches, and you've identified yourself as a lead dog in the pack. The real reason Bob the cab driver has his fanatically loyal customer base is that those customers can count on him to consistently provide them with a special experience that they would not get with another driver. It's not a one-shot or haphazard event. It's not even a 90 percent event. It's as close to 100 percent as is humanly possible. The real reason 30 million customers make their multiple journeys to Starbucks every month is that they can also count on a special experience—that unique refuge from the chaos and pressures of the world that defines the Starbucks higher cause. Millions of people are wedded to buying Toyotas because they can count on having a uniquely positive experience regarding quality, design, innovative technology, fair price, comfort, "feel," and after-sale service. Millions of people are devoted to Pixar films because they can count on having a uniquely delightful movie experience with cutting-edge 3D computer technology and a great story line with brand-new characters that has separate but equal joy-appeal to adults and kids. And when customers can confidently count on these things, so will investors. That's the power of branding in a Copycat Economy.

In a Copycat Economy, hype will not sustain a brand. In 2005, car manufacturer Fiat rolled out a huge smorgasbord of marketing activities aimed at making "the brand" more visible and exciting. The company sponsored the 2006 Winter Olympic Games in Turin, placed its Panda car as James Bond's car in the film *Casino Royale*, put its logos on the most hip and upscale clothing, signed big entertainers for avante garde television commercials, produced gala extravaganzas to feature its products—and it all worked. Fiat's image was resuscitated. The only trouble was that people still didn't buy the Fiat cars. After all the sound and fury and expense, the company's survival remains in question.

The lesson is simple. Don't equate branding with marketing. Equate branding with the consistency, reliability, and integrity of the extraordinary things you will provide and *do* on behalf of your customers. To be sure, there's a strong supportive role for good marketing in any branding strategy, but the real payoffs come when the organization is so sincere, genuine, pervasive, relevant, and credible that the market can fully trust that the exceptional outcomes that are implicitly promised will really happen—time after time after time.

Endnotes

[1] Several months later, Barbara Bisgaier emailed me: "I thought you'd be interested that our 'wow' water client just got their credit rating upgraded from AA to AA+ by Standard & Poor." Remember, shooting for "Wow!" is not an excuse for dressing up mediocre performance with fancy bells and whistles. You can't sustain a customer's "Wow!" without simultaneously delivering exceptional performance.

9

TAKE INNOVATION UNDERGROUND

You might call it your company's back-end operation, or the backstage exertions that make your company's onstage efforts possible. I call it your organization's underground.

I borrowed the concept of "underground" from the old Disney theme parks. Back in the 1950s, '60s, and '70s, Disney theme parks were an arresting new concept, and customers were entranced by the magic and the fantasy that they enjoyed "above ground." For Disney, the revenues were huge. But a good part of Disney's financial success was due to the magic that went on literally "underground," where a massive inventory of costumes, props, materials, equipment, and back-office services (like laundry, personnel, and maintenance) were managed with exceptional efficiency, yielding lower costs "below" and a better customer experience "above." Back then, the creative attention that Disney bestowed into its underground was unique. We can learn a lot from it today.

The hidden underground is the root system that sustains the mighty oak of your organization and, when nurtured, allows it to flourish. From sales support and procurement to cost accounting and inventory management, the underground has huge impact on the health of your company and its capacity to deliver value to customers.[1] If your company is to break from the pack, the under-ground demands not just attention, but innovation. Just ask the mak-ers of Two-Buck Chuck.

Learn from "Two-Buck Chuck"

Fred Franzia's tractors pick their way through moonlit vines near the foothills of California's Sierra Mountains, harvesting grapes at their coolest and most delicious temperature. By dawn, up to 120 truck-loads of crisp, clean fruit have been collected for crushing, their work completed even before the hand-pickers at other farms start their day. The trucks will eventually make their way to Napa Valley, where the grapes will be bottled into the fastest-growing wines in the industry.

Welcome to Bronco Wine Company, at $350 million now the fourth-largest wine producer in the U.S. It is the scourge of the industry that it leads in growth. CEO Fred Franzia has committed an unpardonable sacrilege: Since 2002, he has profitably marketed a $2 bottle of wine. It has become the fastest-growing wine by volume in the history of the industry. As a result, Bronco has assaulted the industry's entire production, marketing, and pricing structure.

Thirty thousand carefully engineered acres and even more care-fully engineered plant facilities guarantee Franzia the low-cost lever-age to beat any competitor on price—and then some. His $1.99 Charles Shaw label has become famous as "Two-Buck Chuck," an affectionate nickname that originated with incredulous-but-grateful customers of the upscale Trader Joe's grocery chain, where it is sold exclusively and where a new shipment has been known to cause a stampede on the shopping floor.[2] While $2 bottles of wine have long existed (such as Boone's Farm and myriad box wines), Two-Buck Chuck is a different concoction altogether. So is Napa Ridge, Glen Ellen, Salmon Creek, and the other fast-selling, low-priced Bronco brands that appeal to upscale consumers.

Setting aside for the moment the question of whether Two-Buck Chuck is drinkable, how can a winemaker make a profit on a $2 bottle of wine?

The answer begins with corks. "I probably spend more time buy-ing corks than anything else," Franzia says. His commitment to shav-ing a penny off the cost of each specially designed cork used in the

Charles Shaw label saves the company nearly three-quarters of a million dollars a year. As a nephew of the world-famous Gallo brothers, Franzia knows not just wine intimately, but, more important, from his perspective, he knows the business of wine intimately. He knows the precise cost of juice, glass, cork, and label, and every production step in between. Those are the details that obsess him. Fred Franzia points out that his wines are not "cheap," but "inexpensively made." When he says "There's not a wine made anywhere worth more than $10 a bottle," he's speaking as a businessman, not a gourmet.

Franzia's obsession translates into every facet of Bronco's wine operations. To begin with, the efficiencies of the 35,000 (and growing) Bronco acreages allow the company to plant and pick at lower costs. Then there's the fact that the Charles Shaw wine is filled with 70 percent grape juice from the Central Valley and coastal regions, at a cost of $100 a ton, instead of solely Napa juice at $2,000 a ton. The vineyards themselves are laid out in 3-mile-long segments to minimize the need for workers to frequently turn their tractors around. Compared to the typical farm where workers turn their tractors every quarter-mile, Bronco's layout yields big savings on fuel and tire maintenance.

During the harvest season, trucks filled with Bronco field grapes arrive around the clock at the headquarters in Ceres, California, in the central California valley. The locations of the fields, and the logistics of truck movements, are all carefully planned, timed, and staggered so that the actual picking prolongs the ripening of the grapes and the deliveries avoid any slowdown or congestion—all steps that ensure every ounce of efficiency from facilities and work processes. Deviating from the industry norm, Bronco facilities themselves are built for efficiencies, not show. Don Russell, writing in *SF Weekly*, noted that "Bronco's sprawling operation on the edge of Ceres has all of the charm of an oil refinery." Huge white storage tanks hold up to 80 million gallons. The Titan ICBM missile fuel tanks, bought on the cheap from military surplus, will soon be used to produce Bronco champagne. Even the Bronco offices are unpretentious and low cost. Fred Franzia's presidential suite is a brown-paneled trailer containing little more than a desk, a phone, and a couple of chairs.

From Bronco headquarters, the wine is off to Napa facilities for bottling—at a rate of 250 bottles a minute. Two hundred and sixteen million bottles a year will be produced, twice the annual average produced by all Napa-based wineries combined. And this is just the beginning. Bronco purchases at least 1 square mile of land per year for more planting volume and efficiencies. The company recently introduced a "high-end" Merlot and Chardonnay under its Napa Creek label for a whopping $3.99 a bottle. The wines already have a nickname: "Four-Buck Fred." New ventures include a Salmon Creek label that restaurants can sell by the bottle at $10, and a series of specialty wines for chains like Wal-Mart and Costco.

But we're talking wine here, not cable wire or sheetrock. What kind of wine does $1.99 buy? Even though a rock-bottom price generally dooms a label to the ignobility of the bargain bin, Two-Buck Chuck has gained the reputation—some say notoriety—as the cheap wine that doesn't taste at all cheap. At the 2004 International Eastern Wine Competition, the 2002 Shiraz from Charles Shaw not only advanced to the finals from a field of 2,300 entries, but as the stunned audience looked on, it snagged the coveted double-gold medal. In other words, four out of five judges in blind tastings had awarded their highest rating to a bottle that retails for $1.99. And when a prominent industry analyst declared Bronco Wine Company his pick for winery of the year during another gala awards ceremony, the crowd of a thousand industry types were shocked into silence. Many hissed. Meanwhile, in the restaurant world, restaurants are losing their reluctance about selling Bronco's $10 Salmon Creek as a premium wine. Customers like it.

Winemakers haven't exactly embraced the prospect of quality wines being sold at obscenely low prices. More than a few have openly wondered whether Franzia somehow repackages excess inventory from financially troubled wineries. Because Bronco does not own any vineyards in Napa, The Napa Valley Vintners Association went so far as to lobby for a new state law that would prevent Franzia from printing labels with his Napa bottling address (the law passed but was struck down on appeal, and the battle is still progressing in the courts).

I think the antagonism toward Bronco springs from something deeper than a fear of unorthodox competition. After all, Bronco-induced sales cleaned out a lot of excess inventory in the industry and helped boost sales of wine to 280 million cases, which means that the U.S. is on track to overtake France and Italy as world's top wine-consuming nation within a decade. The tide is lifting the entire industry. Something else is going on that drives a deeper, more pervasive anxiety. In industry after industry, innovation is going underground, and break-from-the-pack companies are leading the charge. While Bronco is unprecedented in the world of wine, parallels can be found throughout the marketplace, from the low-cost, low-price formula of

IKEA and Dell, to the ease with which JetBlue has overtaken the industry leaders, to the constant ratcheting up of better and cheaper choices in everything from groceries to cellular phones. Savvy wine-makers know big change is coming, and I'll bet what makes them squirm most is the fact that they have no idea what it means or what to do about it. In this, they are not alone.

Venture into the Underground

Just as Disney once engineered a unique and efficient underground, literally and metaphorically, today there is a group of companies whose executives devote their *primary* attention to their corporate undergrounds. The secret to success of companies like Bronco, Emerson, IKEA, Wal-Mart, CostCo, Target, JetBlue, Southwest Airlines, Ryan Air, Gol Airlines, indiOne Hotels, Dell, ExxonMobil, and the entire EasyGroup empire is that they are ruthlessly hyperef-ficient in their underground operations and supplier relationships. That means they can afford to sell commodities as a profitable growth business. These companies' efficiencies are not static; there's a con-stant innovation in their processes and systems that allow them to continually and creatively shrink their costs and cycle times. Because the innovation occurs underground, far from the eyes of customers, it's not directly experienced by customers except at the end point: lower prices, convenience, reliability, and fast service.

Companies like Bronco, Dell, and the others just listed owe their break-from-the-pack status to their ability to dominate on cost-reduction, operational efficiency, and, ultimately, price. By dominat-ing on cost-reduction and operational efficiency first, they can then skillfully lower their prices to squeeze out competitors while main-taining their own margins and growth. Indeed, their underground dominance is so powerful that they not only capitalize on commoditi-zation, they seek it out. They may initiate it, even to the point of proactively turning noncommodities into commodities. In Europe, EasyGroup has applied its successful no-frills "yield-management" model from its EasyJet company to commoditize (and make money from) other businesses, like discount movies, Internet-based pizza delivery, cut-rate toiletries, low-budget lodging, and low-price cruise tours. In Asia, the Bangalore, India-based indiOne Hotel is so suc-cessful at profitably assembling a lean, high-tech, "smart basic" hotel room for $22 a night that management expert C.K. Prahalad believes that similar strategies could one day lower the price of many U.S. hotels to $40 a night.

When Dell enters a particular market, everyone knows that market's product is now officially a commodity. Dell will make it an even cheaper commodity and will make money off of it at everyone else's expense. That means the entire competitive landscape shifts. Competitors will have to match Dell's cost structures (which nobody in the tech sector has been able to do yet). Or they'll have to match Dell's prices, often with ruinous consequences (the way HP did in its PC wars with Dell). Or they'll have to decommoditize their products with nonprice designs and features that Dell can't or won't match (witness what Apple has done with its PCs and iPods).

Yet, when asked if he was worried about copycats, Michael Dell laughed and replied, "All these companies that are copying me are losing money!" He's right. Many companies want to copy Dell, and why wouldn't they? Dell turns its inventory 107 times a year, compared to HP's 8.5 and IBM's 17.5. Dell's cost advantage through close-to-zero inventory is as high as 8 points, a remarkable metric in commodity business. Five years ago, it took two Dell workers 14 minutes to build a PC. Today it takes a single worker roughly five minutes. That labor efficiency translates into roughly 2 percent of the average PC's total cost. And because of its direct-to-customer model in which the company receives payment right away, Dell has *negative* cash-conversion cycle of 36 days (that is, they receive payment of goods 36 days *before* they pay for parts).

Michael Dell knows that dominating the underground requires a staggering amount of discipline and passion to make cost-efficiency his first priority. It's a ferocious commitment few leaders are prepared to make, and that's why so many do a lousy job at copying him.

To break from the pack, you don't need to have the all-consuming obsession with the underground of a Michael Dell or a Fred Franzia, but you still must learn something vital from them: the amazing competitive opportunities of the underground. Like Disney during its theme park heydays in the '60s, you can—and probably will—concentrate on building above-ground, front-end strength relating to products, services, and customer care. Like the old Disney, if you choose to innovate above ground *and* underground, you're much more likely to break from the pack. I set the stage for this concept with my discussion of "passion for precision" way back in Chapter 4, but in this chapter I want to up the ante. You need a passion for precision, yes, but to get your best shot to break from the pack, you must demonstrate as much *obsessive innovation for the underground* as you do for the above-ground product development, design, marketing, and customer service.

Before I get into some how-to specifics, I emphasize that you must not confuse this message with the obvious and constant business necessity to keep a lid on costs. Anyone can cut costs, however compulsively. You can always order department and division heads to reduce their budget or payroll by 5 percent, even though that might be woefully superficial and insufficient. You can always dump assets to reduce out-of-control debt or to quickly raise cash, even if some of those assets might have big upside potential. You can always hire accountants and efficiency experts to carve away at corporate fat, even though more drastic surgery might be needed. You can always go into a frenzy of downsizing and make huge reductions in capital improvement, R&D, and employee training to meet your quarterlies, even though your actions will be slicing long-term muscle as well as immediate fat.

The biggest problem with these actions is that there's not a drop of imagination or creative judgment in any of them. What's missing is strategically focused, sustained, and disciplined innovation. The message of this chapter is not "Reduce costs." It's "*Innovatively* reduce costs" in your underground. It's "Do curious, cool, and crazy things underground" even as you do cool, curious, and crazy things above ground.

GE chairman Jeff Immelt told one interviewer that 40 percent of his company's cost structure revolved around administration, finance, and back-room functions. He followed that statement by declaring, "Over the next three years I want to shrink that by 75 percent." Immelt knows that the only conceivable way he can reduce his back-office cost structure by 75 percent over three years is through radical, well-planned underground innovations in automation, digitalization, re-engineering, outsourcing, partnering, restructuring, and outright elimination of steps and functions. Conventional cost-cutting solutions will simply not suffice. The big, bold target Immelt set for GE, and the obsessive innovations in cost-cutting it will require, will be an object lesson in taking innovation underground.

When leaders fully appreciate the power of the underground, they understand that even small wins down there can have substantial impact above ground. In the waste management business, for example, the $400 million Wastequip is the largest manufacturer of products like compactors, dumpsters, and trash containers. At the company's annual meeting in spring, 2006, CEO Bob Rasmussen celebrated the company's record sales in 2005. But he also described several important underground innovations, like the ones that saved the company $130,000 in 2005 UPS costs. That $130,000 alone, Rasmussen emphasized, equaled the operating profit generated by the sale of *three thousand* two-yard containers.

When leaders fully appreciate the power of the underground, they can widen a company's distance from the pack, regardless of whether they sell high-priced or low-priced goods. Specialty furniture maker Herman Miller worked for four years with German design firm Studio 7.5 to perfect a new Mirra desk chair. At $500, the Mirra chair is not cheap. But to build margin while keeping the price lower than its own flagship Aeron chairs (which are in the $600–$800 range), Herman Miller delved underground. It overhauled its supply chain, keeping a tight network of 500 suppliers fully integrated with real-time information flow about product demand and inventory. It researched and purchased new high-quality, low-cost materials. It worked closely with suppliers to reduce the time it takes to ship a customized order to the customer to less than 20 days. Herman Miller executives understood that by imaginatively reinventing supply chains, information systems, and materials management, they were able to drive down the actual cost of doing business, sharpen their operation, clean up their fundamentals, and better deliver a high-quality, high-design, lower-priced product while simultaneously strengthening gross margins. Like their counterparts at Toyota and Zara, leaders at Herman Miller understand that innovation in the basement is as important as innovation in the living room.

Note the power of this philosophy. If your product becomes commoditized, or if you yourself accelerate the commoditization of your product, taking innovation underground will still let you reap the benefits of margin and cash flow. And if your product is so cool that you can charge the premium price, taking innovation underground will let you enjoy a much fatter windfall in these financials. You win either way.

To take innovation underground in your own organization, you must consider six precepts of leadership, which we explore in the rest of this chapter.

1. Adopt a Genuine Underground Mindset

To take innovation underground, you must approach your business with an underground mindset. Here are the personal attributes you need to demonstrate to do so:

A Personal Commitment to Lead the Charge

If you want innovation to happen underground, you must take fundamental command of the effort yourself. Jeff Immelt understands that to be able to cut his underground costs by 75 percent in three years, he cannot blithely "delegate" that goal to the "finance and efficiency people" while he concentrates on the business above ground. He's got to be actively involved.

I'm not suggesting that you become an efficiency expert if that's not your proclivity. But leaders such as Immelt understand the importance of making the underground a strategic priority. That requires hiring great people to initiate innovation underground and holding them accountable for extraordinary results. Most important, the leader must *personally* care and lead the charge "down under" as well as "up there." The worst leaders are those who focus entirely on "vision" and deal making, and leave all the details of implementation to others. Great leaders delegate and empower others, to be sure, but they are actively involved in both strategy and execution. As part of their commitment to the underground, they stay "in the know," ask the tough questions, and work with others as partners to overcome hurdles.

"I've not seen an effective manager or leader who can't spend time down in the trenches," says Amazon CEO Jeff Bezos. "If they don't do that, they get out of touch with reality, and their whole thought and management process becomes abstract and disconnected." But when Bezos spends his time in the trenches, as he does frequently, he doesn't play the role of the pompous CEO making a regal visit. He gets down and dirty—on his knees with the warehouse equipment, for example. He asks a lot of "what if?" and "why not?" questions—not to intimidate, but to foster a vigorous problem-solving conversation. He peppers people with questions about operations speed, the number of customer contacts per order, the average time spent per customer contact, the breakdown of e-mail vs. phone contacts, and the total cost of each. He wants to know how the system can get better, and what he as a CEO needs to do to help the process.

Finally, if you're serious about personally living the message, you need to be somewhat literal about the term *living*. The crummy but low-cost office of Fred Franzia parallels the barebones, nondescript corporate offices of Wal-Mart in Bentonville, Arkansas. When Franzia visits the bottling facilities in Napa, he stays at a cheap motel or spends the night in the factory itself. Wal-Mart CEO Lee Scott has been known to share a $49 hotel room with whatever executive he's traveling with. Both CEOs are rich, but they understand the power of role modeling. Don't worry, you don't have to emulate the hostelry habits of Franzia and Scott, but remember that it's really tough to demonstrate a personal commitment to the underground if you're living a lavish lifestyle as the leader

A Drive to Cut Costs and Boost Efficiency Anywhere, Everywhere

JetBlue CEO David Neeleman is adamant about above-ground issues like passenger comfort and hassle-free service, but he also says, "What I think about incessantly—incessantly—is building the most efficient business." That urge to foster efficiency and cut unnecessary spending is practically a compulsion for leaders intent on making their companies' root systems sturdy and sustaining for the entire organizational organism.

At Amazon, it was only when founder Jeff Bezos demonstrated that he, too, was serious about the underground that the company began to turn profits and pique investors' interest. Amazon's cool above-ground features have always been well known and admired, but what's less well known is that the company turns inventory over 19 times a year, nearly double that of Costco and triple Wal-Mart's, with no loss in asset efficiency. The company's concentration on underground efficiencies has helped yield a 25 percent gross margin that is nearly double Costco's and three points higher than Wal-Mart's. This kind of success always starts with a sense of urgency.

For that same reason, JetBlue continues to prosper in a brutally difficult business. As of 2004, United's unit cost (the cost of flying one airline seat 1 mile) was 10.2¢ a mile, while JetBlue's was 6¢ a mile. Even after the company's recent purchase of a hundred 100-passenger Brazilian ERJ 190 aircraft for short hauls, Neeleman's obsession persists. The ERJs are set to operate at a cost of 1¢ more per mile than JetBlue's larger-capacity planes, but still 3¢ to 4¢ per mile lower than competitors' (while still offering the personalized

TVs). Obviously, David Neeleman's "incessant thinking" about costs is paying dividends.

A Commitment to Run the Company Not Just for Sales, but for Sales and Profit

A leader has to believe that profit is the key definer of corporate health, and act accordingly by enhancing revenues *and* reducing costs. This is why Wal-Mart's latest big initiative is to innovatively revamp its enormous U.S. distribution system. Doing so will not only further improve internal efficiencies and drop costs, but it will also boost sales by keeping shelves perpetually replenished with fast-moving merchandise.

As a leader, you cannot divorce profit from discussions of sales growth and performance reviews, and you must insist that none of your people does, either. Toyota executives are maniacs for this commitment. In 2003, the company articulated two goals in the same announcement: a 15 percent global market share *and* a 50 percent cost reduction. Toyota consistently averages more than $1,000 profit per car, in no small part because its obsessive managers see to it that production and distribution efficiencies continue to get better than industry standards. Even as Dell expects to grow to an $80-billion company by 2008, it plans to cut another $2 billion from its manufacturing and supply chain in 2005–2006.

When companies trumpet sales and market share but gloss over profitability, you know there's something amiss underground. Art Schuller, a national account executive at Sterling Trucks (a division of DaimlerChrysler), told me that in his career, he has found that too often "profit is considered a dirty word." He has seen leaders focus on growing sales and market share, while hoping, in his words, that their "green visor people will somehow figure out ways to lower costs and make the final profit numbers work out." That approach, he says, is grossly inefficient, if successful at all, and it excuses too many corporate leaders from accountability around profit making.

The Recognition That Lowering Costs Can Mean Lowering Prices for Customers

There's no mystery to the huge value of lowering your costs while keeping your prices intact, especially if they're premium, plump-margin prices to begin with. If your pipeline products and "impossible" services are so "must have" cool that you can do that, then you're *way* ahead of the pack! But a great payoff of taking innovation underground occurs when you realize—as executives at Bronco, Wal-Mart, JetBlue, Toyota, Dell, and Amazon have—that you can build profitable growth and customer loyalty by proactively lowering your prices *before* the market forces you to do it. As Fred Franzia puts it, "There's no reason for people to be embarrassed about buying wines for $5 and under. We believe the wine-consuming public needs wine at a price they can afford to drink every day with their meals."

When you understand this principle, you can understand why Wal-Mart refuses to add a dollar, or 10¢, or even a penny to the cost of every one of the umpteen million items it sells, even though one can only imagine the boosts to its top line if it did. On the contrary, Wal-Mart's obsession is with continually lowering prices for its customers while maintaining healthy margins. Likewise, IKEA is committed to *profitably* lowering its prices by 2–3 percent annually.

JetBlue's David Neeleman understands. In 2002, he said, "In second quarter, we did 18.6 percent operating margin. If we did 22 percent, I would have said, that's too much. We don't want to be above 20 percent. That's fair to our customers. Anything above that would spoil the formula we have with them."

Too many companies operate on a different formula. They sock customers with huge prices on high-demand goods and services to pay for cost overruns or debt-ridden acquisitions, at least until customers get tired of feeling ripped off and either revolt or leave. Then the company's frenetic search for fresh sources of income begins anew. Disney under recently departed Michael Eisner was a master at this destructive stratagem. United Airlines, even as it faced bankruptcy, has been notorious for charging obscenely expensive domestic round-trip fares—as high as $2,200 for coach and more than $3,000 for first class—in destinations that have no viable JetBlue or Southwest Air competition.

In contrast, the rationale for the pursuit of low prices at companies like JetBlue, Dell, Amazon, Wal-Mart, and Bronco is straightforward. Because you know that in a Copycat Economy, prices will fall eventually, you can take the initiative by steadily lowering them before commodity copycats enter the arena, even if you bring new higher-priced products to market. You manage this by continually improving efficiencies underground. What you get in return is steady profitable income from loyal customers. That's the formula that Intel uses by improving its underground and dropping the prices on its current microprocessors, even as it swiftly develops next-generation ones for which it will initially charge more.

2. Get Passionate About Supply Chains

Leaders who are passionate about supply chains view them not as routine operations, but as revenue and margin drivers. For these leaders, supply chains are not a set of contractual commodity transactions, but creative partnerships in the effort to reduce costs and raise sales for all parties.

Wal-Mart chooses suppliers that can reliably provide necessary product and who themselves can get more cost-efficient every year. In October 2002, Levi Strauss began to supply Wal-Mart with jeans. Before that time, Levi Strauss had a 65 percent on-time delivery rate to retailers. That was unacceptable to Wal-Mart. As a Levi Strauss manager explained, "Being a supplier to Wal-Mart demands a certain level of performance—and cost control. Wal-Mart drives you to work with your supply chain to put the same requirements on your suppliers that Wal-Mart puts on you. If you can't make your supply chain work, you won't benefit from being a supplier."

To win the Wal-Mart business, Levi Strauss overhauled its antiquated internal technologies and information systems so that it was able to track product in real time. The company revamped its distribution system to allow quicker regional response. It implemented technologies to exchange with Wal-Mart the EDI transactions that support collaborative demand forecasting, product modification, and orders planning. Cross-functional teams modified everything from logistics to data warehousing.

The result? A 95 percent on-time delivery rate, which not only reduced costs but also boosted sales and revived a seriously ailing apparel company. Wal-Mart, of course, was the catalyst for the changes at Levi Strauss and gained by having a reliable, low-priced brand name supplier. One can argue whether Levi Strauss risks cheapening its brand by supplying Wal-Mart with low-priced "Signature" line clothing, but one can also argue that Levi Strauss is a stronger, more competitive company by virtue of its ability to hurdle the bar that Wal-Mart raised.

Even though effective underground companies like Wal-Mart and Dell constantly drive down their own prices, they don't automatically choose suppliers whose sole saving grace is lowest prices. Quality and reliability are also critical selection criteria, and suppliers also must demonstrate a good fit with Dell's and Wal-Mart's unique technologies, structure, and performance goals. Dell, in fact, rates all vendors on cost, technology fit, reliability, and service—and posts comparative scores daily on a password-protected website. Quarterly performance reviews allocate percentage of future business based on these metrics.

Even as the kings of the underground demand non-negotiable results from their suppliers, they are surprisingly integrated with them. When you're in the fold, you get help. Wal-Mart's 21,000 suppliers gain access to Wal-Mart's databases; they harness Wal-Mart technology to monitor inventory flows of their products every day as well as the inch-by-inch movement of their goods in stores and warehouses, and they do so in an atmosphere of mutual trust. Toyota sponsors regular joint programs between its own employees and those of suppliers to figure out ways to help both parties radically cut the number of steps needed to make cars and parts. (This step alone, according to Toyota, has generated multibillion-dollar savings.)

How can you and your suppliers jointly achieve the payoff of significant, sustained, and imaginative cost reduction? Here are some suggestions.

- Find good-fit suppliers that can help you spread risk and further reduce cost; look for suppliers with a commitment to these goals and a unique and relevant expertise to help achieve those goals.

- Choose suppliers that are trustworthy and have a belief in collaboration. That is, choose suppliers with whom you can share databases, sensitive information, training, and personnel. Avoid suppliers you don't feel confident about having that sort of relationship with, even if they offer the lowest prices. You want to get close enough to suppliers that the relationship is more transparent and collaborative than a conventional arm's-length, hyperlegalistic, opaque commodity relationship.

- Link up with great suppliers in a seamless, friction-free context so that their input becomes indistinguishable to the ultimate customer. To your customers, your suppliers are you anyway. Customers don't make the distinction of whose fault it is when your supplier screws up and you don't deliver on time. From your customers' perspective, it's your fault, period. So create a tight, efficient network that operates as "you." You'll save money and make your customers happier. At Dell, as at Cisco Systems, the supply chain is so well integrated and seamless that corporate and individual customers think they're dealing with Dell people when they're really dealing with suppliers.

Wal-Mart notwithstanding, an increasing number of manufacturing and service companies are reducing the number of their suppliers and seeking reliable partners for collaborative innovation rather than continually jerking around a large number of suppliers to get the lowest cost available today, damn the consequences for tomorrow. As of 2005, for example, Ford cut by more than 50 percent its number of parts suppliers and health-care suppliers, and allocated a larger chunk of work to the survivors. The idea is to involve a smaller, more manageable set of elite suppliers early on in efforts toward underground cost reduction and above-ground product development. (Johnson Controls, the proactive, higher-priced "defiant pipeline" auto parts company described in Chapter 7, is, unsurprisingly, one of the seven ultra-elite suppliers that Ford has chosen for its core team.)

3. Get Real About Outsourcing and Offshoring

Technically, outsourcing (domestically) and offshoring (abroad) should be part of the earlier supply chain management discussion in this chapter, but because they've become such political lightning rods, it's worth examining them independently. I've written articles about these issues from a public policy perspective, but here all I want to state is the obvious: Whatever your personal beliefs are about outsourcing and offshoring, the fact is that they are both *fait accomplis*. More companies are outsourcing and offshoring pieces of their underground, and they will continue to do so at accelerated rates. Outsourcing and offshoring can remove costly underground fat, cut capital requirements, enlist outside talent to boost underground innovation, and free up resources for innovations above-ground—all of which ultimately spur company growth and further job creation.

More companies are finding out how beneficial it is to outsource many relatively small aspects of their underground operations that cost money and divert attention from real value-adding activities. Let's examine one example. Many companies that own and use trucks hire Bandag, Inc., to monitor and service their tires. Bandag is a world leader in truck tire retreading, offering more than 275 customized tread designs and sizes to customers on five continents. From working with Bandag, I've learned that there are sizable differences in fleet costs and efficiencies when tires are well maintained.

But still, why outsource this seemingly minor function? One Bandag customer with a fleet of trucks explains his rationale. His company used to handle all road calls about tire failures, constantly check air pressure and tread depth, remove tires and get them retreaded, "and do virtually any other functions associated with keeping our fleet on good, dependable rubber." By outsourcing these functions to Bandag, the company has outsourced excessive costs, distractions, and headaches as well. Another Bandag customer said, "I can still get involved in the minutia of the day-to-day tire operation if I so desire. But why would I want to when I can rely on tire experts who are there to let me focus more on my core business?"

Savvy leaders know that no organization can truly innovate underground if the underground is full of distractions. They also know that outsourcing to experts who direct their innovative expertise toward those functions spreads that innovation to the outsourcer's underground.

The same can be said for offshoring. If outsourcing occasionally stirs controversy, then offshoring can make people hysterical. When organizations scan the globe for talent and resources that can help them do something better and cheaper, they incite a whole new set of economic anxieties and angers when jobs get farmed out abroad. We've already seen how in today's market environment, borders, distance, time, and space become increasingly irrelevant. We accept that reality when it comes to products and information, but we resist it when it comes to jobs. We are bothered when we hear about American companies manufacturing x-ray imaging equipment abroad, designing and programming that equipment abroad, and servicing it abroad—all at one-tenth the cost in the U.S. When we hear about American hospitals digitally zapping x-ray images to reputable radiologists in India, who make their diagnoses and zap their conclusions back, at one-sixth the salary of their American counterparts, we are even more disturbed. For many, it doesn't matter that offshoring reduces the cost of health care or frees corporate resources to compete better with new products and services, which, in turn, will mean new waves of hiring at higher levels. Somehow we feel it's *today's* jobs that are sacred, even if those jobs themselves are becoming commodities that can be imitated abroad for a much cheaper price tag.

Without a doubt, the suffering of people who lose their jobs is tragic, especially those who find their entire job categories eliminated and must find new places for themselves in the American economy. I've written articles calling for corporate and federal investment in skills training and career development that will help people retool their abilities and find jobs further up the economic ladder. But in the broader scheme, even more jobs will be lost if companies fail to judiciously offshore when they can. They will find it increasingly difficult to take innovation underground, or even to survive. Before its partnership with Wal-Mart bought a little stabilization, Levi Strauss's decline was due to a number of factors, including the company's above-ground failure to come up with cool clothing that captured the imagination of non–baby boomer generations. But another primary source of decline was Levi Strauss's corporate value of maintaining high-cost manufacturing plants and assembly jobs within the U.S. The value was noble, and it almost killed the company—and, thus, nearly destroyed everybody's jobs. Today, like most American apparel manufacturers, Levi Strauss is making its products abroad. That alone won't save the company, but without offshoring, the corporate underground would have continued to be a budget-sucking beast.

Outsourcing and offshoring must definitely be parts of your underground innovation initiative, but you must undertake them thoughtfully, keeping in mind these three premises:

- Use outsourcing and offshoring to liberate value-creating resources in your organization from subsidizing commodity work that can be done much cheaper, and often better, elsewhere. Too many organizations bestow in-house monopoly status on cost-draining tasks and functions that do not directly contribute to the company's growth or core mission. Outsourcing and offshoring should challenge these sacred cows in a thoughtful, disciplined way.

- Don't view outsourcing and offshoring as a quick-fix panacea for your company's competitive woes. Delegating elements of your underground outside will not compensate for lousy products, rotten service, poor leadership, or cost overruns everywhere else in your company. Likewise, if outsourcing/offshoring adversely impacts your "above ground" activities, take immediate corrective action. Concern about service is one reason why Dell brought back some—not all—of its offshore call centers in

Asia; American customers were complaining that they couldn't understand the service people abroad.

• Make sure that your offshoring and outsourcing initiatives are strategically and operationally integrated with each other, as well as aligned with your growth plan. Nike shrewdly builds shoe soles in one country, cuts cloth uppers in another country, and stitches everything in a third country. Toyota factories in Thailand make light pickup trucks and SUVs, drawing components from factories in surrounding Asian countries like Indonesia, Vietnam, and the Philippines. Both companies seamlessly integrate these processes with design, marketing, and distribution activities, which take place in carefully selected locales around the world.

4. Make Technology Your Lifeline

Leaders who really understand the power of the underground also understand that they have to ride the most cutting-edge technologies to fully capitalize on the underground's possibilities. For example, while Dell has occasionally been criticized for not being "innovative," in fact the company is quite innovative underground where its core strengths lie. Over the past few years the company has logged over 550 significant patents for its internally developed new business process technologies, like cellular work stations and wireless production systems. Similarly, under CEO's Sam Walton, David Glass, and now Lee Scott, Wal-Mart has become a reservoir of innovative underground technologies. Internal satellite systems and point-of-sale software track the movement of every product and allow any employee or supplier to link up to any data and anyone else. Numerous state-of-the-art technologies link suppliers to inventories, to each other, and to Wal-Mart. Wal-Mart has been a leader in adapting and promoting "smart" RFID (radio frequency identification) tags. The company made it mandatory for its top 100 suppliers to deploy RFID for tracking goods in 2005, and extended the call to all suppliers in 2006. As of 2005, RFID was arguably more expensive than the current bar code system, but ultimately, Wal-Mart executives know that it will be an easier, faster, and more accurate means of tracking and managing inventory. Stratton Sclavos, CEO of VeriSign, notes that 8 percent of manufacturers' profits are lost through poor inventory management.

Wal-Mart's leadership on RFID, therefore, will also help its suppliers boost their own profit numbers.

Technology is at the root of JetBlue's efficiencies, so I wasn't surprised to learn that instead of toting heavy manuals and paperwork, JetBlue pilots are provided with specially equipped laptops for computerized flight manuals and instruction books. Instead of accumulating and thumbing through paper, they log onto the Web for regular updates to flight manuals and any up-to-date information about upcoming flights. Nor was I surprised to learn that JetBlue's plan is to link its parts manufacturers and fuel suppliers to the company's internal systems, once again reducing unnecessary steps and costly operational friction while making people's jobs less frustrating.

Unsurprisingly, JetBlue employees tend to like their company. Neeleman, in fact, tells his colleagues at other airlines that to have agents who are nice to customers and don't quit, "the secret is furry slippers. They love their jobs because they're in furry slippers, working from home." Yes, JetBlue lets agents work from home using fast, low-cost Voice Over Internet Protocol telecom. The result is lower costs, nicer service, less attrition.

If you exploit technology to the max, the possibilities are vast. The Pacific Northwest zone region of State Farm Insurance has enjoyed a nice financial turnaround over the past year, in no small part due to its digitalized claims center, which boasts no missing files, no sending for and waiting for files, no record storage requests, and no bulk inventory of paperwork. It's not merely that internal costs and cycle times have shrunk. As evidence that the back-end advances aid front-end efforts, State Farm's faster response time on claims pleases its agents and customers, and has become one of the company's selling points.

5. Make Underground Management Cool

Until a few years ago, Nike leaders didn't consider the underground as cool. In the old days, the company operated pretty much on gut, intuition, and instinct—even when it came to forecasting demand, getting product delivered, and dealing with costs. There was little planning, few systems in place, little emphasis on financial discipline, and very little passion for precision. That's the way the company liked it because gut and intuition were cool, just the way design and marketing were cool, just the way spokesmen Michael Jordan and Tiger Woods were cool. Because executives viewed the underground as uncool, Nike's sclerotic back-end capabilities dragged down the company's financials in the late 1990s, along with its capacity to create great new product.

More recently, attitudes have changed. Nike leaders have over-hauled supply systems for better ordering, faster response, and more efficient clean-up of inventory. Twenty-seven computer systems that previously couldn't talk to each other have been transformed into one integrated system. Projected costs and returns on investments are standard discussions at Nike management meetings. The result? Both the underground and the above ground have prospered, and Nike is now turning in its highest revenues and fattest margins in years, yield-ing double-digit growth in earnings and worldwide orders.

The lessons for leaders are these:

- Treat underground management as cool (that is, vitally impor-tant and worthy of innovation) as customer service and product development. If you approach the underground as cool, so will the people who look up to you, and that's how you build a culture that takes these matters seriously. In fact, make it a bottom-up employment responsibility of everyone (managers and nonman-agement) in every function to figure out ways of reducing costs.

- Approach your business with the following Dell mantra: Time is cost, inventory is cost, pass-off is cost, management layers are cost, and unnecessary steps and activities (including paperwork and meetings) are costs. Therefore, per Dell again, try to creatively *eliminate* as much of that stuff as you can and replace it with the kinds of technologies and empowering management systems that can do the job far more effectively. In many segments of Ford and GM, the number of management layers is double that of their Toyota counterparts. The call ought to be: Don't "improve" layers, get rid of as many as you can. Remember the old Peter Drucker advice: In organizations, there is nothing as stupid as making more efficient what shouldn't be done at all. Elimination of slow-mov-ing debris that gums up progress in favor of "fast and flexible" ought to be at the top of the list of cool.

- Measure everything obsessively. Says Whole Foods CEO John Mackey, "Anything worth doing is worth measuring." That is why at Whole Foods, above-ground and underground factors like inventory turns, sales per square foot, and margins per store are all compared and publicly posted per store, across stores, and per industry average. Dell concentrates on underground factors like days in inventory, cash-conversion cycles, time to actually build a PC, and supplier performance. If it's cool, it's important, and if it's important, you measure it—and if you yourself are cool, you'll share that data with as many people in as transparent an environment as possible.

• Make cool happen by setting underground goals that simply cannot be accomplished unless some audacious innovation happens. Remember GE's Jeff Immelt calling for a 75 percent cost reduction in back-office operations? Take the approach of Dell CEO Kevin Rollins, who says, "I set irrational goals, Michael [Dell] and I together, to encourage our team so they don't think of conventional solutions…. If we asked for a 10 percent or 15 percent increase in productivity, we'd get conventional solutions. But if we ask them to double their productivity, then they have to rethink everything." Of course, you can't just demand an unreasonable goal with a crack of the whip. When you set "irrational goals," you must give people the power and support to rethink and rebuild every process, element, and feature downstairs. That's what taking innovation underground means.

• Finally, if you're serious about making the underground cool, then, for heaven's sake, hire cool people to innovate down there. Hire the iconoclasts who are burning to take charge and accomplish the impossible; give them a few non-negotiable ethical, legal, and financial boundaries; and then let them loose. If you hire grim "green visor" types, or annoying "hall monitor" types, or the loathsome "teacher, you forgot to give us our homework" types, you'll never get innovation. At the end of the day, it's not your plan or your organization that will make the difference. It's your people. If you hire cool, exciting, irreverent people for the underground, and provide them potent jobs, career opportunities, and attractive compensation, you're a lot more likely to see magic happen down there.

6. Adopt the Philosophy That a Strong Underground Exists Primarily to Build Growth and Strength Above Ground

Producers of theater, ballet, and rock concerts know that the backstage stuff of lighting, sound, design, financing, insurance, and such is vitally important. But when we customers go to these events, we don't go to see the lighting and insurance. In fact, we really don't care what happens backstage as long as it works and ultimately enhances our experience. Our experiences and perception with the product propel customer loyalty and business growth. Taking innovation underground, even for underground kings like Bronco Wine and JetBlue, is vitally necessary, but they've still got to provide wine and travel service that turn people on.

Taking innovation underground is a critical means to that end. Remember, the desired end is faster and better service, faster speed to market, greater agility to respond to fleeting opportunities, and more resources available to build the business for the long term. Taking innovation underground gives organizations the extra fitness and muscle to do that. In other words, taking innovation underground helps companies dominate their markets, execute a higher cause, deliver on their defiant pipelines, and take customers to impossible places.

In October 2005, *Fast Company* magazine bestowed on the online DVD subscription company Netflix its best "high tech" customer service award. The $700 million company dominates the online DVD rentals business so thoroughly that after a few attempts at competition, even Wal-Mart threw in the towel, choosing to partner with Netflix rather than compete against it. To its 4 million customers, Netflix already has cultlike status. The whole idea of choosing three DVDs from a massive online library, getting them overnighted to your home with a free, pre-paid return envelope enclosed, keeping them until you're ready to exchange them, without due dates or late fees—well, that alone is worth the monthly price of admission.[3] It certainly is to my family! Above-ground, Netflix rules.[4]

The magic of Netflix is that it's also innovating underground to provide even better value above ground. It's spending millions to further automate its 37 distribution centers to reduce costs (thus keeping prices low) and speed up shipping times (thus maintaining its one- to two-day mail guarantee even as the number of selections, and customers, increases). Netflix continually invests in expanding its distribution centers to try to get that two-day turnaround down to one whenever possible. The company has developed networks that detect spikes in movie demand and help avoid DVD shortages, as well as RSS feeds that automatically probe databases and send customers updates on new releases and account changes. Finally, it's worth noting the underground efficiencies at Netflix are so seamless and thorough that the questions and complaints from 4 million customers are handled by only 43 representatives.[5]

Netflix demonstrates that the ultimate value of the underground is to serve the company above ground. CEO Reed Hastings is, first and foremost, a fanatic about customer service. He pays so much attention to the underground because he knows that innovative excellence down there can help him achieve his primary goal that "once you subscribe, our interest is purely your happiness." Apparently, he's achieved his interest, because according to surveys by Foresee Results and FGI Research, Netflix has been the number-one-rated website for customer satisfaction in 2005 and 2006. He also understands something else: When the company is run like a well-produced play, customers never see what's going on in the wings; they just experience the effects.

Too often, companies forget that truth. They call for sweeping reductions in cost, and after each silo in the organization meets its goals, the net effect is to make the ultimate experience of the customer worse: fewer and less competent staff to answer questions, more phone hell, less customization, and so on. You should never improve the underground at the expense of above ground. You should improve it to enhance the above ground.

These, then, are six paths to taking innovation underground. Let me leave you with this thought: At the deepest level, the reason the underground is so important for breaking from the pack is that, ultimately, the backstage and on stage, the back end and front end, all blend to one and the same. They're two sides of the same coin. As Reed Hastings tells his troops: "Tomorrow when you come to work, if it doesn't make the customer happy, move the business forward, *and* save us money, don't do it. Anything we're doing has to meet *all three criteria*." That's good practical advice. The bottom line is this: Those organizations that can create magic both underground and above ground are by far the most likely to break from the pack. Help your people do both.

Endnotes

[1] A failure to fully appreciate this point will seriously dilute the financial and market impact of many of your above-ground activities. Airbus spent many resources on developing and promoting its super-jumbo A380, not enough on operations and execution. Accordingly, the July 11, 2006, Wizbang website noted: "Production delays have pushed back delivery dates by over a year and have cost Airbus over 4 billion dollars. And that number continues to climb as more customers demand compensation for delivery delays."

[2] Stampedes apparently generate sales, because in 2005 Bronco Wine sold six million cases of Two-Buck Chuck.

[3] Actually, there are eight subscription plans. The most popular is the one for $17.99 per month allowing three DVD's out at a time. Netflix is able to deliver any of its 55,000 titles within one business day in 90 percent of cases. The hassle factor has been reduced to near zero.

[4] Other above-ground initiatives include Web distribution of movies, special joint ventures with producers of quirky but potentially high-rental films, and investment in independent filmmakers for sole distribution rights.

[5] Given the above-ground and below-ground innovations at Netflix, it should not be surprising that in 2005, the company's revenues rose 36 percent to nearly $700 million while its profits doubled to $41 million. During the same period, competitors like Blockbuster and Movie Gallery lost a combined total of a billion dollars. With its unique business model, Netflix believes it can achieve consistent profitability, a billion dollar revenue status by 2007, and 20 million subscribers between 2010 and 2012.

10

CONSOLIDATE
FOR COOL

In 1997, I was at Dell headquarters in Round Rock, Texas, leading a seminar with Michael Dell, Kevin Rollins and other Dell managers, when rival Compaq announced its intention to acquire Tandem for $3 billion. The following year Compaq's $9.6-billion acquisition of Digital Equipment Corporation made it the world's second-largest computer company. One industry analyst at the time congratulated Compaq for moving up to the major leagues and not "screwing around with the Dells and Gateways" of the world anymore. Although analysts and observers were predicting catastrophe for Dell, I can tell you the reaction at Dell headquarters to both of Compaq's acquisitions: They cheered the news!

The Dell people expected Compaq to be consumed for several years with integrating both DEC and Tandem. They expected Compaq to be bleeding cash, focusing on its internal tribulations, and becoming distracted from growth opportunities that Dell would jump on. Dell would stay lean and profitable, and Compaq would remain a large, costly patchwork of quasi-aligned systems and corporate cultures.

The predictions came true: Compaq's performance and financials dropped after the merger and stayed that way for the next four years. But what Dell didn't anticipate was that, incredibly, Compaq would be rescued from its acquisition follies by a company willing to over-look trivial matters like Compaq's lousy performance and the com-moditization of the entire PC business. In 2002, HP paid $19 billion for Compaq, even though Compaq was still digesting Tandem and DEC. As a result of buying another company, HP did indeed become the number one seller of PCs, but the newly consolidated company had two little problems. As noted in Chapter 5, one problem was that, while Dell was posting quarterly profits on its PC business and sharp-ening its ability to create cheaper built-to-order machines, HP was bleeding red ink on its investment and struggling just to maintain its market share—not by innovating, but by reflexively cutting prices to match Dell's, thereby accelerating the bleeding because its costs were so much higher than Dell's.

The second problem went even deeper. Here's how the *Economist* critiqued HP's defense of the acquisition:

> HP is trying to be all things to all kinds of customers, and is leaving more and more of them plain confused. HP domi-nates in the market for printers, both laser and inkjet, and both for consumers and companies…[but HP's] public rela-tions minions regularly circulate long and tedious lists of obscure sub-segments of the market in which HP has the largest market share—"fault tolerant systems," "external stor-age systems," "tape drives," "virtualization technology" and so on. Being big in so many different areas, they argue, means that HP is the "leader" and vindicates the merger.

Investors didn't buy it. HP's stock and reputation continued to plummet until CEO Carly Fiorina was finally forced out in 2005. Meanwhile, with quiet and relentless momentum, Dell continued to profitably grow its PC sales until finally it toppled HP from the num-ber-one PC position in 2004. Dell maintained a growth in sales (17.1 percent), net income (6.4 percent), and return on assets (13.7 per-cent) that was significantly greater than comparable numbers for the much larger HP.

In 1997, Michael Dell told me that every week his office was inundated with intense investment bankers, corporate lawyers, and other assorted dealmakers trying to entice Dell to do deals, any deals, so that Dell could look like HP. Ignoring them was a full-time job. Michael Dell was smart. Conventional mergers and acquisitions can easily cripple your chances of breaking from the pack.

In this chapter, I want to prove to you that your company is far more likely to thrive if, like Michael Dell, you just say no to many merger and acquisitions "opportunities" and resist the usually flawed rationales for them. However, I also demonstrate that there are indeed valid acquisition opportunities that can help your company break from the pack. But in a Copycat Economy, you'll need to employ new and rigorous standards for consolidating with other companies. After I present the reasons most mergers and acquisitions fail, I reveal six criteria guaranteed to help your company pull ahead of the pack, and guaranteed to drive deal-hungry investment bankers and egoistic CEOs crazy.

Failure to Succeed: The Record on Mergers and Acquisitions

Merger and acquisition, or "M&A," has become the growth strategy of choice for a huge number of executives. Is your company stuck in Commodity Hell? Are margins shrinking and customers bolting? Do you have few prospects for growth? Are your investors and board members getting restless? There's nothing as fast and sexy as a high-profile merger to quickly inflate your numbers and show that you're a "bold, can-do" leader.

During the 1998–2000 bubble era, annual deal volume averaged $1.6 trillion, peaking at a whopping $3 trillion in 2000. By 2004, it had dropped to "only" $809 billion, still a 30 percent increase over 2003. In 2005, the number went up another 30 percent; in Europe, it went up 50 percent. The numbers are shockingly high and cut across most industries. Invariably, when I begin work with a new client, I hear the words "There's a lot of consolidation going on in our industry," as top executives cast a hungry look at a menu of other companies that they think might provide them with nutritional value.

A slew of rationales and justifications exist for all this frenetic deal-making activity. You've heard them all: Mergers are supposed to increase sales, market share, synergies, the breadth of product portfolios, and distribution channels for products, while providing cross-marketing opportunities, economies of scale and scope, leverage with suppliers, market exposure, and geographical penetration. Mergers are also supposed to spread risk, save taxes, and reduce redundancies. What could possibly be wrong with that? But the fact is, all those lovely, conventional-wisdom reasons for merger deals are like the beautiful but deadly Sirens beckoning Ulysses. They look and sound great, and too often they'll run your ship right into the rocks.

More than a decade's worth of evidence shows that the HP/Compaq acquisition debacle was actually the rule, not the exception. As early as 1995, a *BusinessWeek* cover story, "The Case Against Mergers," reviewed the available date and declared, "Over the past 35 years, mergers and acquisitions have hurt more than helped companies and shareholders." In 1997, Mark Sirower of New York University published *The Synergy Trap*, summarizing data on 168 deals and concluding that literally two-thirds of them destroyed shareholder value. The analysis in *Barron's* 1998 cover story, bluntly entitled "Why Mergers Don't Work," leads it to state that "most of the research indicates that between 60 percent and 80 percent of mergers are financial failures."

Other studies went on to find the same results. Steven Rattner, deputy chairman of Lazard Freres, reported in 1999 that his firm discovered that in the mid- to late-1990s, "the average acquirer's stock was 3.7 percent lower than its industry peer group a year later." According to Rattner, "companies that remained on the acquisition sidelines performed better in the stock market than acquirers." That same year, Harvard's Robert Eccles and his colleagues published empirical research in the *Harvard Business Review* concluding that "well over half of mergers and acquisitions failed to create their expected value" and, in fact, "in 59 percent of the deals, the total market-adjusted return of the acquiring company went down *on announcement.* That means the market thought the deal would destroy rather than create value for the shareholders...." In 2000, a KPMG study found that 83 percent of 700 large mergers failed to boost stock price, while a McKinsey study found that only 23 percent of acquisitions ever recover the costs of the marriage, and the *Wall Street Journal* ran a lead story with the headline "Big Mergers of '90s Prove Disappointing to Shareholders." A series of studies by Booz Allen & Hamilton published in 2001 showed that "fewer than half of these mergers succeed.... By whatever measure you choose—stock price, revenues, earnings, return on equity—most deals fall short of expectations."

More recently, in 2005, *BusinessWeek* reported that its own "investigations in 2002 and 2004 showed that 61 percent of big deals hurt the buying company's shareholders. Half of them also leave customers dissatisfied." *Fortune's* take on the matter in 2005 was not dissimilar: "Today's merger craze is most likely to have the same results as in the past: For shareholders, big deals typically produce about twice as many losers as winners."[1]

You would think that this evidence would have given executives pause before embarking on buying sprees. It hasn't. Moreover, once a feeding frenzy begins in an industry, all caution is abandoned. The 2000 *Wall Street Journal* article pointed out the data on the failures of M&A's "does little to slow the pace of acquisitions."

Perhaps one reason that the evidence seems to be irrelevant is that everyone can point to at least one high-profile deal that "worked"—just the way Las Vegas likes to remind all the sad-sack losers about the lucky stiff who copped a million bucks on the slot machine a couple months ago. Of course, as there are occasional big winners in Vegas, there are occasional big winners in Mergerland. I've had my MBA students research the field and deliver good news about a number of successful deals as diverse as Wells Fargo and Norwest, Anthem and Wellpoint Health, Southwest Airlines and Morris Air, Ferrari and Masserati, Nike and Converse, Yahoo and HotJobs, Grand Metropolitan and Guinness, Oracle and PeopleSoft, and Exxon and Mobil, among others.

But, as the data shows, for every one success, I could point out four stinkers. Like gambling in Las Vegas, the M&A process is a game of probabilities. In the big-media field, for example, GE's acquisition of Universal Studios seems to have worked out, but the overall success rate of media mergers is so awful that many researchers have simply concluded that they have rarely, if ever, delivered on the synergy and efficiencies that their perpetrators promise. Look at TimeWarner and Turner Broadcasting System, AOL and TimeWarner, Disney and CapMarketsABC, Viacom and CBS, Matshusita and MCA, Sony and BMG, Vivendi and Universal, and don't forget Edgar Bronfman Jr. plowing—and losing—billions of his family's Seagram shareholder funds into MCA because he was bored with booze and liked to write songs.

When it comes to serial acquirers, those whose growth path is based almost entirely on wheeling and dealing—well, on average, their returns strikingly underperform the S&P 500 and sometimes lead to outright financial disaster, as managers do whatever it takes to patch the assets together and try to make the numbers work out. That is what occurred at MCI, Vivendi, Tyco, and Cendant. In 2004, Cendant (a megamix of real estate services, car rentals, hotels, mortgage brokerage, time-share, truck leasing, and more) was crawling back from some near-death experiences from the serial M&A narcotic. To get back in Wall Street's good graces, CFO Ronald Nelson told *Investors Business Daily*, "The market viewed us as serial acquirers who couldn't shake the narcotic of growing by acquisition. We had to convince the market we were adamant about our strategy to improve transparency, buy back stock, make no acquisitions, and provide organic growth."

But, you may argue, why not examine what made deals like Wells Fargo/Norwest and Exxon/Mobil successful? My students and I did investigate them, and we found some positive recurring themes, such as shared cultural values among the parties, good communications in integration, sound strategic logic for the deal, a compelling new vision for the new integrated company, emphasis on execution, and supportive leadership. But those are the exact same themes that define failed M&A's, too, such as the HP/Compaq deal. These positive elements are not unimportant, but clearly they don't have the cause-and-effect power to predict sustained success for consolidating companies. Perhaps the periodic successes have been due more to plain good luck than to some elusive set of skills. Someone who's a good craps player will probably do better in the casinos than a rank novice will, but those same casinos will still happily fly the "experts" into town for free because even the best craps players mostly lose.

Eight Reasons Why Mergers and Acquisitions Fail

Why does the typical merger or acquisition fail? My research indicates eight reasons.

1. Fantasy Logic

Remember the joke about the guy who throws his darts on the wall and then paints a bulls-eye target around each dart? Some executives have such a bullheaded need to acquire that they put together whatever rationalizations they need to justify what they want to do anyway. Any smart person—throwing out the right words like *synergies* and *scale*, and armed with mind-numbing spreadsheets—can offer a logical justification for any potential deal, no matter how ludicrous.

Apparently, there exists a logic explaining why Nestle should make dog food and ophthalmic drugs, or why Amcol should be in cat litter and trucking services, or why Sara Lee should remain, in *Forbes*' words, "the hopeless hodgepodge which makes everything from sausages to underwear."[2]

Occasionally, the market decrees that the ludicrousness is so overwhelmingly obvious—such as Comcast's proposal to buy Disney in 2004—that the buyer's logic is simply ignored and the deal unravels. But most of the time, the executives and investment bankers' tortured reasoning wins the day and the deal gets done. That is why, back in the 1980s, the market accepted United Airlines' "synergy" rationale when it melded the airline, the Westin hotel chain, and Hertz rental car to create a one-stop-shopping travel company—which a few years later was dismantled, with the merged pieces sold off, as is so often the case after high-profile mergers.

More recently, we witnessed the steady decline of the acquisition-built Morgan Stanley Dean Witter organization, intended to be a one-stop cross-marketing mecca. By 2005 it had turned out to be what the *Economist* called "a financial conglomerate in which the original business is shackled to a lame brokerage outfit, a troubled mutual-fund unit and a credit-card division that is losing market share." Under Philip Purcell, the CEO who assembled this Rube Goldberg structure, the corporation showed little of the innovative domination of markets exhibited by the nimbler, elite-oriented investment banks like Goldman Sachs or the pure credit card companies like MBNA and Capital One. The ensuing confusion, internal dissent, and performance mediocrity drove out droves of top talent until Purcell finally resigned in June 2005.

In 2000, I was invited to sit on the board of directors of a young software company. The company had already burned through most of its limited capital, and it needed help fast. At my first meeting, I kid you not that the first item on the agenda was a proposed acquisition of another company to expand market "reach." The company I signed on with was nearing insolvency, yet instead of using its precious resources to build vitally needed product features or hire some desperately needed talent, it wanted to blow much of its remaining capital on buying another company to obtain customer lists. To me this proposal was insanity, but an impressive PowerPoint presentation by extremely smart consultants convinced most of the other board members that it was a very savvy move. Even if the numbers didn't add up, the consultants persuaded the board that the "strategy" behind the move was sound. The company folded within a year.

Smart people can always make a compelling case for literally any deal. That's a big reason why they make so many dumb decisions.

2. Delusional Projections

Leaders must be optimistic, but they also have to be somewhat grounded in reality. Too often, the projections of fabulous post-merger outcomes are outlandish. In *The Synergy Trap*, Mark Sirower concludes that the main reason for the 67 percent failure rate of mergers is the unsustainable belief that synergy will guarantee quick, compelling cost reductions and market dominance. Sirower notes that what fouls up these "synergy" projections are uncomfortable realities like the fact that competitors don't stand still while your merged company is busy integrating, that culture clashes are often ruinous, and that ROI pressures are often so enormous that they generate myopic, self-destructive decisions.

The rhetoric that accompanies merger announcement is shameless. As the *Wall Street Journal* notes, "M&A rhetoric is universally optimistic, and dressed in a dreamy gauze of post-deal cooperation. Its practitioners are by custom prevented from admitting the slightest weakness." It wasn't enough for Viacom CEO Sumner Redstone to say that Viacom's acquisition of CBS in 1999 was "highly complementary" (itself a questionable premise), but that it was also a merger "dictated by destiny." Unsurprisingly, destiny devolved into disappointment.

In 1995, after engineering the $9.4-billion acquisition of Scott Paper Co., Kimberly-Clark CEO Wayne Sanders brimmed with confidence because the merger transformed Kimberly-Clark into the world's largest tissue maker. He predicted that global growth and synergies from the deal would yield a doubling of operating profits within five years. "Prospects have never been as strong as they are today," he declared. Within 14 months, Sanders was humbled. Cost overruns, excess inventory, an inability to integrate systems and people, and customer confusion about competing brands had led to a 4.6 percent drop in sales and a 4.8 percent tumble in operating income. "We didn't anticipate this when we did the merger," he conceded.

Exactly right. In practice, things get much more complicated. A McKinsey study showed that with just a 1 percent shortfall in revenue growth, a merger's anticipated value will occur only if the company achieves cost savings that are 25 *percent higher* than those it had originally projected. Too often, executives fail to appreciate the unintended consequences that can easily emerge when attempting to glue together complex entities like corporations. That is why, says the *Economist*, when it comes to corporate marriages, "falling in love is often a triumph of hope over experience—and the history of mergers contains enough tragedy to terrify the most resilient romantic."

3. Absurd Overpaying

In one of the most egregious and common reasons for merger distress, executives become so enamored of a prospective deal that they overpay, sometimes insanely. This problem is exacerbated when the deal is fueled through inflated stock rather than through the discipline of paying cash. If there's no "real" money involved, the buyers will just lay out an overly generous stock premium, causing a secondary consequence: The buyer effectively transfers the bulk of future economic gains to the shareholders of the target company.

Examples of irrational payouts are numerous. When Bank of America paid $48 billion for FleetBoston Financial in 2003, when eBay bought $60 million Skype for $2.6 billion in 2005, and when AT&T bought BellSouth for $67 billion in stock in 2006, the markets reacted negatively to what they termed "vast overpayment" and the corollary vast pressures shouldered by the buyers. In the AT&T case, the price was so far above the real worth of BellSouth that a Sanford Bernstein analyst concluded that AT&T was basically giving away the value of any potential synergies to Bell shareholders.

4. Obsession with the Top Line

Carly Fiorina and Wayne Sanders crowed about how their deals made their companies number one in PCs and tissue paper. We know the aftermath. Consistent with recurring themes in this book, the focus on top line and market share over measures of profitability and sustained growth are among the most powerful and self-defeating biases that underlie mergers.

5. Lousy Due Diligence

In view of the huge measure of uncertainty in valuing any big transaction, one would assume that careful, obsessive due diligence would be *de rigeur* as a prerequisite to any acquisition. Yet in my own consulting work, I've sometimes been flabbergasted by the sloppy preliminary research that companies have performed before making a huge merger. I've seen superficial due diligence lead to embarrassing post-mortem reactions ("I didn't know we were taking on this debt!" or "I didn't know about all those problems in the factories!"), stupidly high purchase prices, and naïve projections on returns.

In 1998, Halliburton CEO Dick Cheney decided to combine Halliburton with Dresser Industries, a Texas-based energy company. Incredibly, Cheney and his team failed to consider the implications of a mountain of class-action asbestos claims that were about to engulf Dresser. The $4.2 billion in claims continually put a brake to the forward progress of Kellogg, Brown and Root, the Halliburton subsidiary that got shackled with the Dresser liabilities.

Likewise, in 2000, the German banking firm Dresdner Kleinwort Benson paid a jaw-dropping $1.37 billion for the boutique investment-banking firm Wasserstein Perella. What made the price astonishing was that even the most modest investigation would have unearthed that Wasserstein Perella had had only a minimal involvement with some high-profile deals listed in its public relations pieces, and that the company was getting close to failing to make payroll.

6. Crummy Customer Consequences

To justify the price they have paid, the leaders of a merged company have got to sell more products to new customers and more products to the same customers. A lot of individual and corporate customers, having graduated from the school of hard knocks, know that their overall post-merger experience with the vendor could well deteriorate as the new vendor's complexity, bureaucracy, and hyperactive need for more high-pressure sales increase.

If they don't know, they often get a rude awakening. My haircutter, Wolfgang Zech, actively and quite successfully trades stocks. In January 2006, I went to see him for my regular haircut and was puzzled to find him muttering over the speakerphone. He had already been "on hold" for 15 minutes before I arrived, he told me. Wolfgang had been a loyal online trading customer with Harrisdirect for a long time. And then, in August 2005, ETrade bought Harrisdirect as part of its effort to become a "full-service financial firm." Ever since then, he said, he had endured one frustration after the other. He told me about password hassles, procedures hassles, and most of all, waiting hassles. At night, he trades online. During the day, he occasionally trades over the phone when he's at his salon. When Harrisdirect was independent, Wolfgang said he waited an average of one to three minutes on the phone, and he could efficiently place his order between appointments with customers. After ETrade's acquisition of Harrisdirect, his waiting time increased to more than 30 minutes. And in fact, for the next 40 minutes, as Wolfgang cut my hair, he continued to wait on hold, the two of us forced to endure that hideous "we value your call" announcement that came on every two minutes. Finally, as I was leaving—after Wolfgang had been waiting 55 minutes—a real human being came on the line. This "customer-service" travesty occurred a full six months after the acquisition was completed.

Wolfgang's situation is by no means an isolated instance. Documented drops in customer satisfaction after a merger are not uncommon. Small wonder that after an acquisition, individual and corporate customers so often become wary, weary, and willing to bolt. Are you terribly surprised that Wolfgang is now with another provider? Are you surprised that he's advising his friends and customers who trade online to do the same?

Post-merger projections naively assume that customers will cooperate with the plan by sticking around—even as more innovative and customer-responsive companies beckon. Think about your good old radio. The wave of consolidation in the radio business has resulted in more automated, me-too, take-no-risks programming, with more commercial breaks per hour to pay for the deals. That's hardly an improved customer experience. Unsurprisingly, the industry is feeling a lot of heat as waves of customers bolt for other entertainment sources.

7. A Naïve Belief in Easy Integration

Trying to meld two distinctly different cultures is daunting, at best. Recounting to me the abject failure of a failed merger in which he was involved, one businessman described the core problem. "One culture was 'Ready, aim, fire!' The other culture was 'Ready, aim, aim, aim, aim, aim....'"

The people who traditionally cut deals are financial and legal experts who often have little interest in these integration matters. When pressed, their responses often reflect a naïve assumption that somehow the acquiring company's overworked staff will make it all happen. Even if the two company cultures have similar values, it's still a formidable challenge to synthesize two complex sets of systems, people, and attitudes. Some companies, like Cisco Systems and Washington Mutual, have a good reputation on this kind of integration. But the Daimler-Chrysler merger, which has destroyed more than 50 percent of shareholder value since 1998, is a classic example of horrible integration of disparate products, cultures, systems, supply chains, and employee functions.

In 2004, eight full years after the Morgan Stanley and Dean Witter merger, a Morgan Stanley manager wrote me to say that "Heritage Morgan Stanley employees often do not want to share access to resources with the heritage Dean Witter employees. This might be in the form of denying a certain internal specialist access to a meeting or a specific product offering…. [Also] to date the firms still work off of separate broker dealer platforms."

Integrating disparate cultures is essential, but I must disagree with those who argue that this is the biggest factor in whether a merger will succeed. Like *Mergers & Acquisitions* editor Martin Sikora, I believe that the impact of culture integration is "vastly overblown." As he further notes, "Culture integration…is always the excuse when something doesn't work out." Remember, HP and Compaq people did a stellar job in integrating the two firms' cultures. The deal still collapsed because the other seven factors weren't in place.

8. The Dinosaurs Mating Syndrome

Perhaps the greatest delusion executives have about mergers is the belief that that somehow two bureaucratic, backward-looking corporations will join forces and spawn an impregnable giant. The underlying assumption is that two companies that have individually managed to generate flat earnings and declining share will be able to magically continue their comfort-zone strategies by jumping into bed together. But companies that merge primarily to protect faltering product lines and business models are doomed to failure in a Copycat Economy.

You don't need to be an econometrics genius to figure out that many rosy post-merger scenarios are built on today's realities, ignoring or discounting the entry of new technologies, products, and vendors that will inevitably render those realities obsolete. In the early 2000s, the talk in the music industry was about mergers that could somehow offset steep declines in sales of compact discs. The *Economist's* commentary back in 2003 was right on target: "Mergers would allow music companies to cut their costs further, cushioning their profits against falling revenues for a while..... But consolidation will do little to solve their biggest problem, which is that their customers are deserting them for free music downloads on the Internet and for other forms of entertainment.... At worst, merger deals will tie up management's time resolving anti-trust issues and clashes of corporate culture at a moment when a much more urgent issue must be addressed: how should the recorded music industry change in order to survive?"

Ultimately, a merger might temporarily prop up any two beasts by providing them better scale and better marketing, but the end result is still extreme vulnerability, if not extinction.

The Motives Behind Bad Mergers

Despite all the evidence, M&A remains the number-one "go-to" growth strategy for many executives. How strange. I am convinced that the reason has little to do with the obvious and overwhelming economic evidence against rampant consolidation. I'm not a psychiatrist, but I suspect the promiscuous reflex toward making mergers arises from some deeper, unexamined motives. Here are some labels for executives' flawed logic, and some unspoken words describing their reasoning:

- **No vision, no alternative**—"The analysts are screaming and the board is on my back to *do something* about the lousy financials (or the excess cash). Since I have no breakthrough vision, a nice acquisition will prove I'm a can-do leader."

- **Easy pickin's**—"It's easier to try to buy success than to do the grubby work that might lead to it. And if I use stock as currency, I don't even have to pay with real money. And if I use borrowed money, well, it's not my money, anyway."

- **Opportunism and expediency**—"I love quick fixes, and there's nothing quicker than being able to literally double our size and press exposure by—poof!—putting my signature on a contract and then delegating the post-deal implementation trauma to underlings."

- **Herd instinct**—"Everyone else is doing it—and getting good headlines, to boot. Count me in."

- **Megalomania**—"Forget this 'being the best' nonsense. I want to be the biggest."

- **Megapayoff**—"The merger may be a dog, but since I'm the top dog, my net worth will soar no matter what happens."

- **Megafear**—"We're getting killed. What do I do? I haven't a clue. Merger? Fine, I'll do whatever it takes."

- **A Twentieth-Century Mindset**—"Our numbers are good. Since our last-century business model is obviously a keeper, let's bulk it up so it'll last for the rest of this twenty-first century."

Are all reasons behind M&A's bad ones? Not at all. You don't want to foreswear mergers and acquisitions entirely. There do exist some good, unorthodox acquisition opportunities out there, based on sound reasoning, that will help you break from the pack. We explore them next.

How to Consolidate for Cool: Accessing the Intangibles

When you deconstruct nearly all conventional mergers and acquisitions, you realize that they're all about building the three S's: *size, scale,* and *scope,* as noted in Chapter 2. But if you want to break from the pack, your company's acquisitions ought to help build an enterprise that embodies the three C's: *curious, cool, and crazy,* as we discovered in Chapter 4. In a Copycat Economy, consolidating for cool trumps consolidating for size.

Leaders with conventional approaches to M&A view the three S's as salvation. Accordingly, they focus on how consolidating will bulk up tangible factors like balance sheets, existing product lines, the number of customers, the range of territories, and the volume of sales dollars. In contrast, break-from-pack companies have learned that in a Copycat Economy, a deal creates value when it augments their capacity to bulk up on intangible factors like knowledge, innovation, agility, audacity, speed, and collaboration.

To those who say you can have it all—a mixed formula of S's and C's—well, that tortuous equation logic might look good on paper but frequently doesn't translate into reality. Certainly, there are companies that are both innovative and big, and this book has applauded many of them. But keep in mind that a far larger crop of stagnant and declining big companies suffer from what could be called "dis-economies of scale," like hyperbureaucracy, slowness, risk aversion, and a cultural lock-in to the sunk costs and legacies that represent the past. After a merger that quickly inflates the size of a company, the dis-economies often take front-and-center stage. Such companies become all S and no C.

If you're contemplating helping your company merge with or acquire another company, are you consolidating for cool or are you stuck in conventionality? Assess your situation by asking these questions:

• Would this acquisition make us a cooler company, or just a bigger one?

• Would we be increasing our capacity to create new markets, or would we just be buying old ones?

• Will we be faster, more imaginative, and more customer-centric after the acquisition than we were before it?

• Does this merger increase the values of our *intangibles*?

Let's use these questions to evaluate the Adidas-Reebok merger. In 2005 Adidas bought Reebok for $3.8 billion in cash. The new, consolidated $12-billion Adidas has more clout with suppliers that will help it garner lower prices from retailers, and it will capture more shelf space. The new Adidas announced that it intends to lop off $120 million in duplicate costs over the next three years (no sure thing, by the way). It will combine the global Adidas presence with the Reebok base in the U.S. Finally, the new $12-billion Adidas will rival the $14-billion Nike in revenues, though the newly consolidated company will lag significantly in the more important metrics, like net income and market cap.

But the real question for Adidas and Reebok—and for any merger—is how much the consolidation will expand the company's *intangible* assets, the kind of assets that, according to the Brookings Institute's research, account for 80 percent of the value of the S&P

500. In the fickle world of sports gear, will this merger jack up the new intangibles to a level *higher* than that of the new tangibles? Will the new company be cooler—faster, hungrier, more agile, more audacious, more innovative, more talented, more efficient, and more forward-looking than it was *before* the merger? Will there be more breakthroughs, like hot-selling $250 chip-embedded Adidas "intelligent shoe"—or will there merely be more advertising dollars spent on existing lines? Regardless of the answers that corporate leaders give, customers will cast the final vote on this merger. They have a ton of choices about their shoes and clothing, and they'll exercise those choices primarily on the basis of perceived intangibles. Investors will follow soon afterward.

Therefore, here are the kinds of intangible elements that your prospective merger or acquisition needs to aggrandize if it is to help propel the new company in front of the pack:

- **Knowledge**—Intellectual property, great ideas in the pipeline, cutting-edge science and technology, great databases, being best-of-breed in everything from design to assembly

- **Talent**—Top-notch people and the ability to attract and retain them, as well as the capacity to attract external partners who are world class in breakthrough knowledge and innovation

- **Imagination**—The ability to leapfrog over conventional wisdom with creativity and innovation, and to quickly translate that ability into very cool products

- **Speed and agility**—The capacity to react, make decisions, spread information, do follow-up, and go to market before any competitor

- **Foresight**—The capacity to look ahead and capitalize on fleeting opportunities, while being willing to let go of what no longer works

- **The desire to be a renegade**—The company-wide contrarian, rebellious hunger to set the agenda of the industry and go where nobody else has gone

- **Inspirational leadership**—Businesspeople who combine bold vision with operational excellence, inspiring and mobilizing their teams to strive for extraordinary goals

If you're committed to breaking from the pack, and the prospective consolidation won't jack up the combined companies' intangibles, then stop. Don't do it! If it truly does augment the intangibles, then you're ready to evaluate the merger based on the six principles of cool consolidation.

The "6-T" Merger and Acquisition Blueprint

Regardless of the kind of suitor you are—a publicly traded or privately held corporation, a hedge fund, a private equity firm—if you are serious about building intangibles and consolidating for cool, here is a set of principles to guide you. If a proposed consolidation meets the "T1" through "T6" criteria below, that acquisition is significantly more likely to be successful in helping you break from the pack.

T1 = Tomorrow

Value creation lies in anticipating and capitalizing on tomorrow's playing field. Does your potential acquisition prepare your company for leadership in emerging, fast-growth businesses that will define tomorrow's markets?

If an acquisition primarily improves scale of current processes, or cross-marketing opportunities of current products, or your share of a current market, it's of questionable long-term value. GE chairman Jeff Immelt approaches M&A with this principle in mind. What Immelt seeks to buy is not "bigness" today, but *the ability to grow*, even if that means buying a company that's not big today. Some of GE's recent small-to-medium acquisitions have included a Spanish-language cable channel, several water-treatment companies, and several security-technology firms. These acquisitions promise to reach big markets tomorrow. In 2002, GE acquired Enron Wind. GE had studied the wind power business for more than three years and saw an acquisition opportunity when bankrupt Enron was ready to sell its wind turbine–manufacturing subsidiary for a paltry $250 million. GE was responding to the 20 percent growth rate in the business, the increasing global interest in renewable energy sources, and the opportunities to accelerate the company's growth rate with the help of other GE technologies.

Criterion T1 is also why GE bought Great Britain's Amersham PLC for $10.3 billion in 2004: to enter and accelerate the emerging, next-big-thing "personalized medicine" market, where new technologies can predict an individual's diseases before symptoms emerge and doctors can tailor therapies to fit his or her genetic profile. Note that neither Enron Wind nor Amersham represented unfamiliar markets to GE, which, after all, has substantial energy and health-care businesses. What these acquisitions did was to help GE dislodge stagnant elements of its mature business position today (rather than "improving" them), and point itself for success in a fast-growth market tomorrow.

The same mindset—to position for tomorrow's markets, not to have a bigger stake in today's—spurred Dean Foods' acquisition of Horizon Organic Holding Corporation, and FedEx's acquisition of the Asia-based Flying Tigers. None of these deals was a 2 + 2 = 5 merger made for today's market. They were all aimed at what Jeff Immelt calls the 2 + 2 = 7 potentials for tomorrow and the day after.

T2 = Top Technology

Acquiring a company to obtain a specialized or new technology that offers measurably quantum improvements in customer care, response time, and penetration into tomorrow's market might well help propel the acquirer ahead of the pack. Cisco Systems' purchase of companies like Komodo Technologies, IP Cell, and Vovida in the early 2000s was based on its desire to capitalize quickly on the emerging Voice Over Internet Protocol market, to build it into its product suites, and to accelerate its R&D efforts in this arena.

Apple's capacity to pursue digital media innovations was sharply accelerated by its acquisitions of such companies as Key Grip from Macromedia to enhance QuickTime Software, which it then used as an essential component for its new Final Cut Pro and iMovie digital video applications on the iMac and iPod Video. Apple later acquired Astarte for its DVD-authorizing software, and used that software to create DVD Studio Pro, a software package that caters to the company's professional multimedia base. The original iPod was developed as rapidly as it was in large part because in 2002 Apple bought Emagic, a German company that owned the specialized music software that was needed to make iPod a reality. In all cases, Apple's acquisitions were geared to procure the breakthrough technologies that could be used to spur innovations for breakthrough products with breakthrough applications.

T3 = Top Talent

Your potential purchase should bring with it an abundance of top talent who possess genuinely state-of-the-art, cutting-edge expertise and experiences—not just "good people" with usable commodity skill sets. Does the company you want to acquire possess an abundance of top talent? If it's only a few exceptional people you want, then make them an offer they can't refuse rather than buying the whole company.

Break-from-the-pack players understand that some employees will lose their jobs after an acquisition as duplication is eliminated and operations are streamlined. But the most savvy businesspeople view the real value of acquisitions as *expanding* the head count—of top talent. They see acquisitions as a targeted opportunity to acquire new and extraordinary minds, and then to create a liberating environment so as to retain and unleash them to carry out a radical strategic vision.

When Proctor & Gamble bought Dr. John's Products, the little startup that created the technology for the SpinBrush, it deliberately bought the talent of its developers. The mandate for founder John Osher and his partner entrepreneurs—a mandate visibly supported and protected by senior P&G leaders—was to shepherd the SpinBrush prototype through a P&G development system traditionally hostile to a "not invented here" product. Said Osher, "My job was to not allow P&G to screw things up." Their mandate was also to coach P&G employees to be more entrepreneurial: to develop new technologies and designs faster and on a shoestring budget, to distribute product without heavy inventory, and to market in ways hitherto inimical to the company's practices—such as having no mass ads, or adding a Try Me button on the packaged brush so that consumers in stores could test the product before buying it. For P&G, acquiring and effectively utilizing the disruptive talent was as important as obtaining the technology.

Polycom, the maker of the SoundStation conference phone system that is the staple in many board rooms, requires that any prospective target for acquisition *must* be chock full of technical talent. This philosophy, one that is well worth adopting when considering an acquisition, holds that, whatever the rationale for the deal, the merger should leave you engulfed in top talent in design, distribution, marketing, engineering, or whatever critical functions you designate.

T4 = Turbo-Time

When considering a consolidation deal, ask, "Will this acquisition make us a *faster* company?" Purchasing a new company should turbocharge your company's product development and execution, speed to market, alacrity in dumping technologies and processes that no longer add value, and quickness to cannibalize existing products. Break-from-the-pack leaders naturally see turbospeed as a competitive advantage and strategic priority. If an acquisition doesn't make the companies faster and more agile than they were, the deal is suspect. This criterion alone would eliminate a lot of conventional deals from the table. The Apple acquisitions cited earlier helped make Apple a much faster company in the emerging digital media market. Apple got into it faster and, since then, has fully exploited those deals to maintain its leadership role because of the speed that it brings the next wave of new breakthrough products to market.

Speed can also be considered from another perspective. Your potential acquisition should be one that can be *absorbed* quickly, without trauma or creaking machinery, so that you can actually benefit from your purchase quickly, to demonstrate the value-add. If the logic of the consolidation is 2 + 2 = 7, how fast can you get to 7?

When one is trying to break out of a fast-moving pack, the key to successful acquisitions is putting the cultural, systems, and financial pieces together fast, and creating fresh, new deliverables fast. Speed of execution and delivery is often even more important than the logic of the deal itself. At Cisco, a key preliminary question in any due diligence is: How compatible is the new company's culture with ours, and how quickly and efficiently can we fully integrate the new company? Cisco doesn't even consider the deal if there are serious doubts on this matter. Polycom goes even further. It will not consider an acquisition unless it can increase the company's bottom line within two quarters. With the bar raised that high, a high probability for fast integration becomes an imperative, or the deal doesn't get done.

T5 = *Titillation*

The result of a merger or acquisition should titillate your customers and make them say, "Wow!" The effect of consolidation should be to make your customers' lives distinctly better, easier, more productive, more profitable, and more fun. After the deal is done, will customers benefit with "knock-your-socks-off" products or faster, easier, more customized, more innovative services? Or will they experience the obverse? We've seen that customers have learned to regard consolidations with a beady, jaundiced eye. The job of your newly reconstituted company is to make their eyes sparkle, and if you don't believe that will happen, think twice about the acquisition.

In 2002, eBay purchased PayPal for $1.5 billion, an acquisition that met the titillation test. While credit cards worked well for online purchases made at established firms like Amazon or Orbitz, eBay's business model revolved primarily around person-to-person payments. From 1995 to 1998, individuals on eBay who agreed online on a purchase price were forced to complete the payment portion of the transaction offline; many individual sellers did not have merchant credit accounts allowing them to process credit card transactions via e-mail or phone. Sellers would thus ship the goods with the invoice and pray that they would receive a legitimate wire transfer, money order, or check in the mail. Check fraud was a big problem. Even in legitimate deals, the "paper methods" took a long time to process—with international sales, they sometimes took weeks. To address this daunting problem, eBay installed an online payment service called Billpoint.com, a partnership with Wells Fargo that relied on customers using credit cards to back up their payments.

However, in 1998 an independent company called PayPal.com captured the fancy of many eBay customers with its titillating features. The beauty of PayPal was its simplicity, reliability, and safety. Users opened accounts with their e-mail address and deposited money in that account backed up by a legitimate bank account. When making purchases, they sent money by simply typing in their e-mail address and drawing an amount. The system provided assurance that the funds were available, and the buyers and sellers could also remain anonymous. For a small fee per each transaction, the system reduced the customer's hassle, waiting, and anxiety factors immeasurably. By early 2002, 40 percent of eBay payments were transacted through electronic payment services, and 70 percent of those payments were transacted through PayPal.com (the others were from providers like

Citi, Yahoo!, AOL, and others). That translated into 15.4 million PayPal users. That's a lot of titillation, and clearly the plan of eBay CEO Meg Whitman and her team was to integrate the PayPal technology more seamlessly into eBay platform to make it even easier and more attractive to use, and then market it so effectively that more customers would use PayPal rather than other independent providers. After the deal was consummated, not only did corporate net revenues and net income rise sharply into double digits, but PayPal has become its own successful standalone business. It is now the dominant provider of online electronic payments for auctions and smaller online merchants on any site, and it contributed mightily to eBay's 40 percent surge in revenues in 2005.

T6 = Tininess

You may have noticed that the examples I cite in the second part of this chapter are mostly pretty small, below-radar acquisitions. That's not coincidental. For Wall Street "Masters of the Universe" deal-makers and CEOs addicted to big deals, here's the *piece de resistance* of the 6T blueprint: Keep your acquisitions small. The more "mega" the merger and the more the merger dominates national headlines, the less likely it's going to help the buyer break from the pack. Certainly, as noted in the first part of this chapter, one can point to the occasional great megamerger, but the cold reality is that the larger the deal, the more likely it's being done for the wrong reasons rather than the right ones. Likewise, the smaller the deal, the more likely that it will be easier to comprehend and execute, and the more likely it won't slow down the company, won't lock it into a fixed position that might not be viable tomorrow, and won't devour the company's financial resources.

Even more important, leaders who focus on tiny deals understand that there are no magic bullets that come from acquisition. They understand that, by definition, sustainable, break-from-the-pack competitive advantage can occur only when the core of the innovative products and customer loyalty comes organically. The value of carefully planned small acquisitions is to fan healthy organic flames in very specific directions.

"Tiny" acquisitions can add adrenaline to the race you're running. They help you negotiate the bumps faster, vault the ditches, and discover better detours. But they can't replace the pieces described in

Chapters 5–9. The bottom line is this: *Organic* growth companies that do periodic, judicious, prudent, *small* acquisitions to fill carefully defined strategic holes are more likely to find competitive success than those companies that rely on megadeals to totally alter the soul, scope, and size of the firm.

Now, of course, "small" is relative to the buyer's size. For a $157 billion company like GE, a $10 billion investment in Amersham is a relatively modest acquisition, and the $250 million price for Enron Wind doesn't even register. For a smaller buyer, these price tags might be prohibitive. But the principle remains. Keep it small.

Taking the "tiny" perspective will surely ruffle the feathers of traditionalists, but consider the alternative. Over the past few years, Nestle considered buying General Mills, and Microsoft considered buying SAP. Both mega-acquisitions would probably have been disasters, saddling the buyers with enormous costs, complexities, integration issues, too large a menu of yesterday's products and systems, and a reputation of no longer having the wherewithal to grow and compete on their own. Fortunately, cooler heads prevailed. The deals died. Instead, Nestle has been buying tiny companies like PowerBar to help it capitalize on the emerging health foods market, and Microsoft has been buying tiny companies like Great Plains Software to help it capitalize on the emerging midsize business software market.

You Don't Have to Buy or Own

Leaders of companies who have learned to appreciate the value of Tininess gain another great insight. They not only realize that big acquisitions are not "the" answers to competitive dilemmas, but they also understand that acquisitions, per se, are not necessarily "the" panacea for their problems. They recognize that in a global knowledge economy, no company—regardless of its size, regardless of how many acquisitions it makes—can possibly own all the finest talent, best technologies, and preeminent products. Increasingly, savvy leaders are realizing that they don't have to own the resources; they can borrow them. They can ally with curious, cool, and crazy partners rather than seeking to consume them. Focusing on strategic alliances, they can continually scour the planet to access the best minds, networks, and technologies for specific ventures while staying lean, agile, and unencumbered. If they themselves are already break-from-the-pack players, they are more likely to attract the same as allies.

Granted, managing alliances is itself an art. It demands genuine commitment and collaborative candor, but when done right, the pay-offs are exceptional. When Dell got into the printer business, it did so with a lean-and-fast mindset of using strategic alliances to help get to market quickly and efficiently without having to do major acquisitions. Accordingly, Dell scanned the globe for top-level expertise in selected areas, and thereby hooked up with Lexmark for inkjet printers, Fuji Xerox and Samsung for laser printers, and Kodak for digital photo-printing technology.

The reasoning behind the Samsung-Mitsubishi alliance begun in 2001 was to accelerate and blend both companies' R&D expertise. The goal was to co-develop LSI camera chips for mobile applications like cellular phones, PDAs, and mobile PCs. This process allowed both companies to co-mingle their expertise, learn from each other, continually evaluate their "dating" relationship, and retain their independence with separate product releases. They didn't need to blow their financial resources and brand identity in buying each other out. Neither did Pepsi and Starbucks. Since 1994 they have had joint-venture arrangements to create new coffee-related products like the fabulously successful Frappuccino for mass distribution through Pepsi channels, including retail groceries. Pepsi didn't need to suddenly become an expert in coffee and coffee bar amenities, and Starbucks didn't need to bone up on mass distribution of food and drink. Both companies can concentrate their financial and intellectual energies on dominating their areas of expertise rather than diluting them, which would certainly have occurred had they merged.

Putting Consolidating for Cool into Perspective

Building your prowess to break from the pack has been the theme of this book. To do so, you can accelerate your organic development with small acquisitions that have fiscal and logical integrity, propel you to tomorrow's markets, give you critical access to top technology and talent, allow you to become even faster than you are now, and provide you with additional capacity to titillate your customers. But at the same time, keep in mind a comment that appeared in, of all places, *Mergers and Acquisitions Journal:* "In today's markets... business leaders increasingly are opting for joint ventures, strategic alliances, and other partnerships over costly acquisitions and internal development in order to pursue new growth opportunities."

One last thought: I'm not naïve enough to expect the transaction-driven M&A industry to embrace the 6T Blueprint, but I do hope that *you* will seriously consider it when the subject of acquisition comes up in your management meetings. Ben McCleary, a former lead invest-ment banker at Lehman Brothers and currently a partner at Seaview Capital, has some useful advice for you. The 6T Blueprint is hard to quantify, he says, which can open it up to potential abuse or disregard. But, he continues, if you read the 6T Blueprint in the privacy of your office or home, think carefully about your motives and options, look in the mirror, and *then* ask yourself "Is this deal the right thing to do?", then you just might make the right decision that will truly help your organization break from the pack.[3]

Endnotes

[1] Even Martin Sikora, the editor of *Mergers & Acquisitions: The Dealmaker's Journal*, readily agrees that "the accepted data say that most mergers and acquisitions don't work out."

[2] Sara Lee CEO Brenda Barnes is currently in the process of slashing the company's revenues by 40 percent by divesting and spinning off unrelated businesses, leaving the company with three divisions: food, beverages, and household and body products. I predict the company will be doing a lot more slashing in the near future. As is so often the case, businesses that were acquired yesterday are divested tomorrow.

[3] I have presented the six break-from-the-pack strategic directions in Chapters 5-10 to numerous clients and corporate audiences, who have embraced them enthusiastically. But I find it interesting that not once have I been asked whether an organization has to successfully embark in all six directions to break from the pack. The research sug-gests that no organization can be great in everything. For example, it would be extremely difficult for an organization to be best of breed in cost efficiency, product innovation, *and* customer care.

The break-from-pack exemplars I've cited in this book are usually pretty strong in most or all of the six areas, and particularly strong in one or two. For example, based on the earlier presentations, one could argue that Dell is particularly strong in both Domination and

Innovation Underground, and strong in the remaining areas with the possible exception of Defiant Pipeline, which doesn't seem to apply to its business model. Apple, of course, is outstanding in Defiant Pipeline, Domination, and perhaps Impossible Place, while being a little questionable on Innovation Underground. It seems that in order to truly break from the pack, an organization might be able to survive a slight softness in one area, but it must be strong in the remaining areas, and outstanding in one or two. It's also reasonable to suggest that the more directions a company excels in, the further it can break from the pack, and the more likely it is to stay ahead.

These are empirical questions, worthy of future research efforts that will one day present some definitive answers. However, these questions are apparently not a significant concern to practicing leaders, who quickly grasp the special value of each one of the six strategic paths, and who understand that by selectively committing to the paths they can best accomplish, they are significantly improving their organizations' odds of breaking from the pack. They're right.

PART III

HOW *YOU* CAN LEAD
THE PACK

11

You, the Leader
of the Pack:
A 12-Step Recovery
Program

Why have a chapter on leadership when the last eight chapters in this book have been loaded with proactive steps for leaders? The answer is that each of the previous chapters has focused on one particular element of strategic leadership. This chapter presents an overarching perspective on the kinds of *personal* leadership that you will need to demonstrate to inspire people to do the extraordinary, break-from-the-pack things that have been described throughout this book.

I'm pleased to say that oh-so-common admonitions like "have a vision," "empower people," "build teams," and "communicate" are absent from this chapter. Such nostrums do have value, but they do not ignite and sustain the kind of leadership you need to effect transformation in your organization. Moreover, terms like these have been corrupted. I've seen so many bland, uninspiring, and me-too "vision statements" that I could swear I've seen the same words in other companies' vision statements. (Is there a factory somewhere that mass-produces vision statements?) I've observed earnest leaders trying to "empower" their people by loosening their chains a little bit and giving them slightly more freedom to improve (but not transcend) their commodity products and services. I've looked in on training sessions in which participants dutifully learn communication and teamwork skills, and then return to their places in top-down structures with fiefdoms and closed doors. In such cases, the payoff was negligible.

To add some serious value to both your organization and your career prospects, you will need to move beyond nostrums. You will need to get down to the bare-knuckles basics of leadership. If you've read this far, you're pumped up to help your organization break from the pack. You're willing to take on the blueprints for change outlined in the prior chapters. Most important, as a leader, you're ready to commit to some new and rigorous behaviors, and leave some low-value habits behind. For you, I've developed a "12-Step Program" to put you on the path to success. If you take it seriously, you'll spur your organization and your career to the head of the pack.

Step 1: First, Admit You're a Commodity

This admonition pertains to your organization's products, your organization's value proposition, and your own career. They're all impacted by the ravages of the Copycat Economy. The first step to salvation is to admit it.

Your Career as a Commodity

Before we look at your company and your business, let's take a look at something even more fundamental: your career.

In this Copycat Economy, the skills and competencies that have brought you career success so far are themselves becoming imitated and commoditized. The entire outsourcing and offshoring phenomena are based on the proposition that our jobs can be performed as well and often more cheaply by people who are outside the company and maybe even abroad. Automation and digitalization mean that the skills we thought gave us added-value are, well, not even worth doing by a human. The characteristics that do make us human—our expertise, experiences, enthusiasm, creativity, and leadership abilities—require constant revision and renewal to remain relevant. Amid the intense competitive pressures of the Copycat Economy, we get either updated or outdated.

Even if your job and leadership position don't appear to be on the block, it is to your advantage to proactively seek to enhance your abilities before they become commodities in the eyes of the market—and your bosses. Don't cling to habits that are becoming irrelevant. Don't cling to skills that are becoming commonplace. Don't simply wait for your company to offer you "training." Seek learning and new knowledge from anywhere and anyone—continuously. Make it *your* responsibility to decommoditize your competencies and unimitate your capabilities.

Your Business as a Commodity

Even as you seek to break from the pack as an individual, you will be wise to admit that in a Copycat Economy, whatever your organization is doing and providing today—no matter how lucrative and "hot" it is—is right now becoming imitated and commoditized, and, therefore, will inevitably require significant change. You cannot wait until the need for change sends your organization into a death spiral. Dave Dorman, the outgoing CEO of a collapsed AT&T at the time it was bought by SBC in 2005, learned this the hard way. "If you don't shape the future by making changes, it will happen anyway," he said. This is where leadership comes in, and the first step in leadership is to "come clean."

Here's what I mean by coming clean: If you join Alcoholics Anonymous (AA) or a similar group, the first step in its 12-step program is to admit your real problem. If you don't cop to it, you won't do the hard work of change. You'll rationalize your current behaviors. You might go through the motions, but in reality you'll stay close to the familiar. You'll continue doing what you've done in the past.

Of course, I'm not equating management with addiction, and I'm not suggesting that a manager who fails to challenge a withering product line, supply chain, or corporate culture is the same as an alcoholic who fails to challenge his or her own self-destructive behaviors. But the metaphor is useful because if you want your organization to lead the pack, your first step as a leader is to acknowledge the cold, hard reality that nothing escapes commoditization and imitation, including whatever you and your organization are currently doing.

To acknowledge the need for significant change is a courageous step. Florida State University football coach Bobby Bowden defines courage as "something you need to do that might get you hurt." The path of changes is pockmarked with periodic pain, setbacks, frustration, and disappointment. This is fortunate because if those changes weren't filled with pain, setbacks, frustration, and disappointment, everybody would do them and you'd be stuck right back in the pack.

Back in the 1990s, after examining the realities of softening financials, drop-off in customer renewals, and impending disruptive technologies, Unisys senior vice president Jim McGuirk courageously confessed that his Federal System division's business model was becoming a commodity, with a three-year window before it reached what he labeled "dinosaur status." That acknowledgment spurred him to transform a transaction-driven, product-oriented hardware and software business into one that sold customized expertise and tailored IT solutions to government agencies, and then raced to the head of the pack. "I decided we could work on managing a dying business and squeezing whatever we could out of it," he told me, "or we could change the business. I didn't want to get stuck in trying to revitalize a dying horse."

In a Copycat Economy, all horses eventually die. If your horse is dying now, dismount the way McGuirk did. If you're lucky enough to be sitting atop a Triple Crown winner, then ride like the wind, but don't get complacent and arrogant enough to assume your steed will gallop indefinitely. Even as you're riding your winner today, anticipate he'll gradually fall back in the pack, and start preparing the winner for tomorrow. Admit your organization's output is becoming a commodity before it actually does become one, and commit to initiating appropriate changes today. That's the first rule.

Step 2: Take a Risk on Risk

Strategy guru Gary Hamel has dryly noted that strategy appears "easy" only if you copy someone else's. But as we've seen throughout this book, that's potentially the riskiest strategy of all. Despite all our affection for concepts like innovation and entrepreneurship, however, we are often strikingly risk averse, even when we're dissatisfied with the status quo. We fear the negative consequences of risk, even as we ignore the even more negative consequences of staying the course. Instead, the second rule posits that we need to reassess risk and then take a prudent risk on risk.

As leaders, we should always undertake due diligence before taking action, but there's no way to cut all risk if you're breaking new ground in products, service, marketing, or distribution. What all this means, says Ralph Shrader, CEO of the consultancy Booz-Allen & Hamilton, is that "leaders need to become comfortable with imperfect data" when making decisions about which markets to enter, which projects to support, which suppliers to enlist, which acquisitions to make, which assets to unload, and so on. Why? Says Shrader, "Time was, when faced with a decision, the chief executive officer and board of directors could set up a task force to look at the options for a matter of months. Today failure to decide and act quickly can pre-empt options altogether."

Once your preparation provides you with basic intelligence, then trust your instincts! Colin Powell suggests that leaders should postpone decisions and seek more information only if they believe they have less than 40 percent probability of making the right decision with the amount of information they currently have. But, he says, "Once the information is in the 40 to 70 percent range, go with your gut." When leaders insist on studying a problem until they have amassed sufficient information to be absolutely "sure" of making the "right" decision (the 70 to 100 percent range), they increase the probability of making the *wrong* decision—wrong not in terms of intellectual truth, but wrong in terms of competitive success. That's because even while the organization is doggedly accumulating yet more data and information, the market battlefield changes. New competitors, new technologies, new value propositions, and new products emerge from elsewhere. Or a fleeting, wonderful market opportunity is lost, and a nimbler competitor capitalizes on it.

As Air Force Col. "Hoot" Gibson argues, you might think that you're in great shape if you operate in a zone of rosy 100 percent certainty. But in real life there's no such zone; if you believe you're in it, then you're probably in a perilous state of routine and complacency. Says Gibson, "Ninety percent is inside most people's comfort level, and 80 percent doesn't induce much sweat." That means that the closer you try to operate in a near–100 percent certainty zone, the less breakthrough action you'll be motivated to take. Rapid response, imagination, and entrepreneurial initiative happen when leaders sweat a bit as they deliberately go beyond their comfort level.

I want to add one more ingredient to this discussion: love. Billionaire Mark Cuban, the owner of the Dallas Mavericks basketball team, cut his chops on start-up ventures like MicroSolutions, Broadcast.com, and HDNet. Cuban's philosophy on risk begins with an interesting ingredient. "First, I ask myself if this is something that I would enjoy doing." It's important, he says, to "find something you love to do." If you love what you do, you're more likely to make it successful, and if you fail, then, as Cuban says, "at least you love going to work."

Step 3: Set "The Way"

Many a company is drowning in plans, spreadsheets, mission statements, and values credos, and yet its stakeholders (including employees) are still not clear about where the organization is going and why they should care. That's a big opportunity for you to establish a concise, urgent, and inspiring direction for your company. I call it "The Way," in deference to "The HP Way" that defined the credo and values of Hewlett-Packard during its most lucrative decades.

To lead the pack, you must define The Way for *your* organization. The Way has two components: path and tone.

Your Path

As you pull together the strategic concept for your organization, you can begin with some basic questions that will help you define the process and reach a conclusion:

- Where are we heading, what are our priorities, and how will we conduct business to break from the pack?

- What will we do that will set us apart as distinct, exciting, and special?

- Why do we need to do this?

- What are our individual roles in making this quest successful?

- Why should it matter to our employees and customers if we succeed?

I've alluded to these kinds of questions throughout the book. As a leader, if you can't articulate the answers, then initiate dialogs about the questions to bring a precise arresting focus to your organization.

Ultimately, your strategic priorities and rationales should be succinct, lucid, unmistakable, easily understood, and easily communicated. They should be free of ambiguity, fuzziness, professional obfuscation,

psychobabble, vague generalities, excessive verbiage, and thick docu-
mentation. (No 100-slide PowerPoint presentations allowed.)

Keep in mind that your path must buck some conventional wisdom and strive to rewrite some industry rules. Seamus O'Connor's
fast-growing young company Airtricity bypasses utilities and supplies
wind power directly to retail customers in Ireland and England. By
pocketing the middleman's markup and thus boosting margins to
nearly 20 percent, O'Connor says with justifiable pride, "We totally
rewrote the rules." His is the kind of path you want to pursue so that
you can ultimately speak with his kind of pride.

Your Tone

Tone is the climate, the "vibe," the mood, the atmosphere that
expresses your organization's values and soul. New York City Mayor
Michael Bloomberg, explaining how he established his dominating
Bloomberg LP financial-data empire, states that one of the most
important things done by a CEO or mayor is to "set a tone." Here are
some elements of strong, break-from-the-pack tones in other organizations that I'm pretty sure Bloomberg would approve of.

- **Boldness**—Organizations with strong tones strive for breakthroughs. They avoid reactiveness and mimicry. When Stephen
  Privett came on board as the new president of the University of
  San Francisco in 2000, the local press asked him about "the
  competition." His response: "We compete against our own
  standards. Nobody imitates their way to greatness." The tone
  he set has helped galvanize USF to develop distinctive new
  programs in its professional schools and fresh new approaches
  to liberal arts pedagogy. These initiatives helped propel the
  university to several national "top 100" lists in both undergrad-
  uate and graduate education for the first time.

- **Aggressiveness**—On-the-offense tones are powerful because
  they concentrate people's attention on creating new products
  and markets, and attracting new kinds of customers. Defensive
  tones focus people's attention primarily on protecting the company's product line and defending its market share from competitors. That's fine, to an extent, but remember former HUD
  secretary Henry Cisneros's observation earlier in this book, that
  managers can no longer be content "managing for steady state"

because the incessantly changing market will no longer allow steady-state success. *Forbes* publisher Rich Karlgaard defined the difference between offensive and defensive tones when he explained why talent and buzz are flowing toward Google at the expense of Microsoft. "At Google one works to change the world," he said. "At Microsoft one works to protect the Windows and Office profit margins. Which mission do you think (the most talented) people prefer?"

- **Collective impatience and urgency**—Before Pixar was bought by Disney in 2006, President Ed Catmull constantly warned his people about the dangers of complacency. Even today, as head of Disney animation, he's quite candid that "the success of *Toy Story* can make you think that you're good at everything.... It's easy to fool yourself." The tone at Pixar was marked by a constant hum of dissatisfaction with current results and a visceral resolve to make quantum improvements. "Every single one of our films has been the worst thing you've ever seen," said Pixar executive vice president John Lasseter—until brutally honest working sessions catapulted the product to new heights.

- **Hope and optimism**—If people are to strive for extraordinary goals, they must feel confident that they can hurdle barriers. As a leader, the tone of optimism and hope you set is essential. As motivational speaker Keith Harrell notes, "A dead battery can't charge another battery." When Katharine Graham ran the Washington Post Co., she was well known not only for her personal, can-do optimism, but also for urging her staff to get on with it and "don't tell me 'never.'" Hope and optimism are vital parts of a healthy organizational tone because there are so many forces of resistance to anything that violates conventional wisdom. Ex-GE chief Jack Welch says that one of the most important things a leader must do is to constantly resist "the gravitational pull of negativity." I believe that people aren't just "born" leaders; they can learn to be leaders. But my research suggests that some people come to the table with certain attributes that make it easier for them to learn. One of those attributes is optimism. Frankly, if you're not an optimistic person yourself, it is very difficult to create the collective tone of hope and confidence that is so necessary to achieving break-from-the-pack outcomes.

- **Clear parameters defining appropriate and inappropriate behaviors**—If a leader doesn't set clear parameters about what's acceptable and what's unacceptable, says Public Financial Management CEO John White, then "all actions are acceptable," which is unacceptable. White encourages—indeed, expects—proactive and daring decisions from all PFM consultants, but at the same time, their judgments have to be aligned with the company's core values of client protection, ethics, transparency, collaboration, and talent development. These parameters shape PFM's tone. Tone imposes discipline, control, and stability in an ambiguous, chaotic business environment—even when the leader is not in the room.

Step 4: Believe That Customers Are More Important Than Investors and Employees

As a leader, you'd be foolish to ignore the needs of your employees and the concerns of your shareholders, but as you seek the break-from-the-pack competitive advantage, you must be able to convey to people that the prime purpose of their jobs and investments is to help make today's customers, and tomorrow's customers, very, very happy. A March 13, 2006 *BusinessWeek* story on new Boeing CEO Jim McNerny describes how he asked a technology executive to explain the benefits of the composite technology used in the new 787 aircraft. When the executive began to describe the numerous technical advantages of the material, McNerny stopped him. What he wanted to know was the benefit of the technology to the *customers*—the airlines and their customers, the passengers. That is an excellent example of a leader who has the priorities right.

Peter Drucker always said that the only reason for a company's existence is to create and serve customers. Many businesspeople, including employees and investors, seem startled by this notion. However, no matter how much resistance you receive, you must lead with the premise that all else follows from your success with the people for whom your company exists.

Customers More Than Investors

Investors are quite properly very attentive to metrics such as a company's market capitalization and stock value. Sensibly, the company's leaders should be, too. But smart investors—and good leaders—increasingly recognize that financial and stock metrics are scorecard consequences strongly influenced by the perceptions and reactions of customers. When customers react to a company and its offerings with enthusiasm and excitement, investors follow. When customers leave in droves, investors are also sure to follow. Businesspeople who pander to distant investors and nearby owners, while putting customers second, lower their probability of truly mobilizing their companies to break from the pack.

When corporate leaders view escalating shareholder value not as the consequence of a customer-alluring strategy, but as the *raison d'être* of the business itself, double trouble begins. Managers become obsessed with short-term financials and "meeting their numbers" any way they can—customers be damned. Most of the innovation and entrepreneurship goes into "creative accounting," earnings gaming, and financial sleight-of-hand, not toward products, services, and experiences that delight customers. And, of course, the heroes inside the company become those people who count things rather than those who make and sell things. Unless you're shorting or spinning stocks, is this the kind of company you'd want to invest in?

Ron Baron, whose Baron Partners Fund was the best-performing diversified stock fund of 2004, says, "You can cut all kinds of corners to make your company look good in the near term. But your people are going to leave, and customers are going to find alternatives." That, in turn, will lead to lower returns, which means that, paradoxically, the more that leaders focus on investors as opposed to customers, the more likely the returns to investors will suffer.

Customers More Than Employees

Organizations are not built for employees and managers. They're built for customers who are willing to pay for goods and services. As I noted earlier, one of the best predictors of organizational decline is a bloated payroll of "happy" employees and managers who are content with the status quo and mediocre performance.

Should a company prize its employees? Absolutely. Hal Rosenbluth built the great Rosenbluth International (a $3-billion global travel agency that was bought by American Express in late 2003), and Howard Schultz created the great Starbucks empire, both using the catchy credo that "the customer comes second," and employees first. What they meant, quite correctly, is that companies need to concentrate on making sure that their employees have the best possible skills, technologies, power, compensation, and morale. Why? Because that's the best way to serve customers! As it turns out, some of the most innovative customer-pleasing interventions at Starbucks—like the CD-mixing and the Frappuccinos—were developed by store personnel in the field, not by staffers at corporate headquarters. Furthermore, the front-line people are essential to making the Starbucks' "refuge" vision a genuine experience and a coherent, reliable brand for customers. In other words, the corporate value of the people is ultimately about the value they provide for customers.

Very simply, what this all means is: Run your business with the premise that the most important people are paying customers. Period.

Step 5: Unleash Talented Maniacs

Break-from-the-pack leadership requires you to seek people with maniacal goals and missions because they tend to accomplish things that "reasonable" people will not. Break-from-the-pack leaders continually scour the landscape not for people who can "do the job," but for maniacs who, without being asked to, will transform their jobs on behalf of the team, not their own egos. University of Michigan management expert Noel Tichy says that "getting the right people on the team is far more important than team building itself." Great leaders begin the process of breaking from the pack by deliberately selecting, developing, and promoting the kinds of people who are committed to doing what conventional wisdom says is ridiculous or impossible.

Back in the 1990s, I was on the editorial board of Tom Peters's monthly newsletter, *On Achieving Excellence*. The last page was always devoted to a question-and-answer dialogue between readers and Tom. In one issue, a reader wrote the following: "How do you rein in an employee who has taken ownership, but has crossed the line into a job you didn't hire him or her to do?" Tom's reply was priceless: "It's a lot more fun trying to cool off hot people than it is to try to hot up cold people. You've got the better of the two problems. I would rather be working with a group of maniacs whom I was trying to keep under vague control than a group of dead souls whom I was trying to wake up to the need to deal with the latter part of the century."

Mania, however, is just chaotic energy unless it is paired with *talent.* Talent is partially about "smarts," both intellectual prowess and street savvy, but more important, it's about the ability to learn, innovate, grow, contribute, collaborate, and assume responsibility. Once again, those are the kinds of people you look for. In other words, to lead your organization to the front of the pack, you don't simply hire someone for a job. Gone are the days you built a static box called a job description and looked for a person to squeeze into it. In today's marketplace, you hire for talent. You set a bold course of action, and then you snare talent wherever you can find it—the kind of talent that during performance reviews will tell you not how well they did a job but how well they *changed* it to add new value to customers and investors.

Finding and unleashing that maniacal talent—liberating those people to achieve the extraordinary goals you've set—doesn't mean walking away and hoping for the best. Noel Tichy points out that after you choose the best people for a team, "you have to invest like crazy to support them." That means, from my experiences, that you must provide those talented people with the training, development, information technology, and other resources so *they* can figure out how to best reconfigure their jobs to achieve your organization's objectives.

Finally, great leaders create a culture in which people know that if they go for those higher bars and make a mistake, they do not face career suicide. Explaining the phenomenal wealth creation in the Silicon Valley, successful entrepreneur Randy Komisar notes, "Silicon Valley does not punish failure. It punishes stupidity, laziness, and dishonesty." Strive to create a similar mindset and climate in your organization; that might represent the most potent support of all.

Step 6: Rev Up Your Base

For any break-from-the-pack initiative to succeed, everyone in an organization must be involved, enthusiastic, and committed. Recruiting and unleashing talented maniacs will help a lot, but most leaders inherit an installed base of employees, which they must also rev up. Here are three courses of action to guarantee that your people—maniacs and otherwise—will get on board with your break-through goals. But be forewarned: You have to embrace all three paths; you can't pick and choose.

Open the Windows

Too often, only a select few leaders in a group or organization have the opportunity to examine the reality outside their jobs. They are aware of the detailed metrics of the entire organization's performance and the shifting sands of market realities: the new competitors, tech-nologies, customer expectations, demographics, and the outside analysts' and investors' appraisals of their company.

The select few who can look out the windows see the reasons for change. But for everyone else, whose windows are closed and the blinds drawn, it's business as usual. Because they're not exposed to the same data that generates anxiety or enthusiasm among leaders, they don't see any particular need to join in when their leaders call for a new way of doing things. Why fix it if it ain't broke?

To get people on board, help them open their windows and look at the world outside their jobs. Expose them to the same eye-opening information you have, and discuss it candidly. Share your interpreta-tions and reactions to the data. If they don't have the skills to analyze and interpret the data, then provide them with coaching and education. You don't need to have a Ph.D. to appraise a balance sheet, a competi-tive analysis, or a market research study. People get on board when they see for themselves the reasons that are inspiring *you* to change.

Open the Doors

To rouse others to feel confident in forging forward, open as many doors as you can so that you can openly and effectively interact with everyone on your team. Keep your planning and decision-making processes as transparent and inclusive as possible—even when the sub-ject matter is unpleasant. As a leader, you must take the lead not only in setting "The Way," but also in including others in business analyses, strategic conversations, and operational problem solving thereafter.

Closed doors create barriers and friction that are completely coun-terproductive. Leaders who work behind closed doors—literally or fig-uratively—pretty much ensure that they'll have problems in getting others on board on behalf of change. When people wonder what's being discussed and decided behind closed doors, you can bet there's a hefty dose of anxiety, uncertainty, insecurity, powerlessness, ignorance, and skepticism in the air. That's hardly an encouragement for the people you need to rally to your cause. Therefore, make it a point to challenge any vestiges of closed-door cultures such as hierarchical power trips, turfism, information hoarding, and the like. Nothing gets people on board faster than a belief that "we're all in this together."

Transparent cultures and open dialogues will also help you determine why some people resist your calls for change, or why they don't have the fire in the belly to go forth and make great things happen. Perhaps your plan and its rationale are unclear. Perhaps they are so bland and mundane as to not be worth getting excited over. Perhaps people feel that there's no payoff for them Perhaps they believe a plan is simply being imposed on them. Perhaps they're scared or bewildered. Perhaps you have the wrong people on your staff. Doggedly pursue the truth on this issue, even if you don't like what you find. It will be a lot easier to unearth that truth when people can interact with you authentically.

Start Driving

In his book *Good to Great*, Jim Collins says the strength of an organization's new strategic and cultural direction is highly dependent on how many people are "on the bus." I want to take this metaphor a little further. Once leaders have clearly articulated The Way and have opened windows and doors, it's time to challenge people to get on or off the bus because it's time to put the operation in gear and step on the gas.

At State Farm Insurance, senior vice president Harold Gray thought a bus was too clunky and slow an image for the turnaround plans he had for his Pacific Northwest territory. His metaphor for enacting his strategy was a faster, sleeker bullet train, a more appropriate vehicle for a one-year journey in 2005 in which he expected his region to reach some very ambitious goals. Gray's message to the troops in the first few months of 2005 was frequent and unequivocal. The bullet train has left the station, he said, and for anyone still debating whether to board, "Remember that the remaining stops will be fewer and farther between."

Getting people on the bullet train is the first step. When the journey begins, the leader must ensure that the people on the train are more satisfied than those who have chosen to stay behind. Those on board must get the most appealing career-development opportunities, job and project assignments, promotional opportunities, and pay increases. If the leader doesn't differentiate properly between those who have chosen to board and those who haven't, he or she will wind up ensuring that the ones on the train (often the best and the brightest) become the most dissatisfied and cynical—and they will be the ones most likely to disembark and leave the organization entirely.

By unapologetically rewarding the critical mass of people on the bullet train more than those who aren't on the train, leaders bolster team spirit and team focus. They also send an unmistakable message to those who chose to stay behind: One, this train is bound for glory, and two, you can still board if you want. But as the train continues to gain velocity, it will be harder to slow down to let you on, and if you can't be with us as we hurtle forward, then we might all want to consider whether you'll be happier in another organization.

Step 7: Get Personally Engaged

Impressed by the financial record of Canadian oil giant Syncrude, I asked CEO Charles Ruigrok his leadership secret. His response was very simple: "Stay engaged."

Personal engagement is an abstract concept for any CEO who takes a separate elevator to the executive suite or surrounds himself with suck-up gatekeepers. In their book *Execution: The Discipline of Getting Things Done*, former Honeywell CEO Larry Bossidy and executive consultant Ram Charan point out, "People think of execution as the tactical side of business, something leaders delegate while they focus on the perceived 'bigger' issues. This idea is completely wrong.... The leader of the organization must be deeply engaged in it." When leaders are disengaged, the impact on morale and performance can be horrendous—even though the disengaged leader won't be aware of it until it's too late. I am always struck by the lack of "personal-ity" among leaders who don't quite fathom the importance of engagement.

Great leaders delegate liberally, but they stay engaged: They *personally* remain in touch with employees to learn their perspectives. They *personally* stay involved with critical issues like product movement, staffing, reward incentives, operational planning, productivity, and financial metrics—not only so their decisions aren't made in a vacuum, but also to use their power to help their people achieve big goals. They *personally* immerse themselves in seeking the truth. I saw Charles Ruigrok spend nearly two days going over employee responses to work attitude surveys and, with his executive team, planning human resource policy changes and future dialogues with workers. Is it any wonder that in heavily unionized Canada, in a largely unionized oil industry, Syncrude has remained union-free and enjoys exceptional productivity and profitability?

Engaged leaders do not micromanage and second-guess their people, but they constantly stay involved and in-the-know, to help accelerate that process within the framework of The Way. Political writer Bob Woodward told a group of us that when Katharine Graham was the CEO of the Washington Post Co., she was the best manager he'd ever experienced because "she managed with the principle of 'minds on, hands off.'"

Truly engaged leaders want to smell and feel the business, not simply attend to it from afar. Describing his job as CEO of Jet Blue, David Neeleman said, "I fly at least one flight a week. I serve the customers snacks. I pick up trash, and when the plane lands, I help clean the airplane. I go out on the ramp and I throw bags." Neeleman's actions go well beyond enhancing employee and customer morale. They also help him stay viscerally in touch with the entire business without the filters. His decisions about which routes to acquire, which planes to buy, which services to implement, and which technologies to employ are better as a result. Bill George, the CEO of Medtronics whose 1,200 observational visits to the operating room I described in Chapter 7, would certainly agree.

Step 8: Lead from a Glass House

Everyone in an organization is a boss-watcher. "Whether in the Army or in civilian life," says Colin Powell, "the other people in the organization take their cue from the leader—not from what the leader says, but what the leader does."

Leaders always function from a glass house, where their actions and attitudes are visible to everyone around them. Good leaders know it and operate accordingly. They recognize that although people listen to the noble words that a leader might pronounce, what really affects them is what the leader pays attention to. They carefully track what questions their leader asks daily, what reports she asks for and actually reads, what meeting agenda priorities he sets, what kind of resources she allocates to which part of the enterprise, who he criticizes and for what, what visibly thrills or angers her, who he lauds and for what, who she promotes, who he assigns to which project, which people she visits and hangs out with, and so on.

People observe these behaviors, and then—regardless of the leader's words—they draw conclusions about what's truly urgent and what they should consider top priorities. This is such a powerful and predictable process that Jackie Osborne, a human resources executive at Hewitt Associates, has concluded, "Leaders have no neutral actions." All their choices have great symbolic impact. Good leaders consciously leverage that awareness daily when they schedule meetings, make budgetary decisions, converse with employees, and the like.

The glass house effect is so pervasive that it makes people draw conclusions about the leaders themselves. When the leader's words and deeds match, the leader's credibility and influence go up. When they don't, they go down. Many leaders think nothing about promising something and not delivering, or declaring a priority and not "living" it. When that occurs, trust plummets. In his book *Trust in the Balance*, Robert Shaw defines trust as "the belief that those on whom we depend will meet our expectations of them." Trust is the glue that holds together any team that strives to lead the pack, and the leader is the ultimate role model for organizational trust, or distrust.

To engender that kind of trust, you must conscientiously monitor what you say and do. Deliberately behave the way you want your colleagues to behave. Go on record and make it clear that The Way will drive every one of your management decisions—and then follow through on that avowal. Be busy with a clear and bold purpose in mind, and make sure everyone sees and understands what you're doing. Peter Drucker once noted that too many managers "are magnificent at getting the unimportant things done. They have an impressive record of achievement on trivial matters." If you visibly and authentically adhere to a clear path of *nontrivial* priorities, you will build your own credibility and your organization's integrity. You will reduce people's fear of the future, and you will inspire their hope and confidence as they pursue uncharted paths.

Step 9: Honor a Minimal Number of Priorities

There's a clear limit to the amount of resources, attention, and energy that people can allocate for genuine commitment and breakthrough performance. The fewer priorities you have, the more likely you'll be able to honor them, and the more likely you can achieve the breakthrough results necessary to lead the pack. When I see a corporate plan with numerous "mission-critical" priorities, I know that the leader's focus will become diffused and that little of importance will get accomplished. Any plan with more than five "priorities" usually winds up prioritizing nothing. The result is mediocrity.

During the 20 years that Jack Welch transformed GE into one of the most valuable corporations on earth, he put forth only a small sequential set of simple strategic priorities: boundarilessness, debureaucratization, Six Sigma quality, globalization, and e-commerce. None of these initiatives was revolutionary. What made them distinctive is that Welch honored them. He demonstrated a fanatic obsession with driving each of those initiatives throughout the organization and holding his managers accountable for achieving results consistent with them. His success was made possible because he put on the table only a few major corporate initiatives. It would have been impossible for him to have shown the kind of passionate commitment and follow-through if he had listed dozens of major corporate priorities.

Colin Powell's leadership credo has always been, "Figure out what is crucial, then stay focused on that. Never allow side issues to knock you off track." During his tenure as Secretary of State from 2000 to 2004, that's how he operated. After examining the multiple reports documenting the myriad operational, personnel, and budgetary problems in the huge, sprawling global bureaucracy called the Department of State, he told me and the other members of his Leadership Advisory Committee that one of his first decisions as "CEO" of State was, "No more reports. We know the challenges. It's time to act." The second decision he made was to limit core strategic priorities to no more than five:

1. **The Diplomatic Readiness initiative**—In the wake of the radical downsizing of the 1990s and the needs of the post-9/11 environment, Powell aimed to fill the foreign service talent shortfall and drastically overhaul human resource policies to ensure a steady flow of the "best and brightest" employees to diplomatic posts.

2. **The Information Technology initiative**—Powell made the overhaul and modernization of State's global information technology a top goal, with the objective of having a state-of-the-art, "enterprise-wide knowledge-management system."

3. **The Security initiative**—In the wake of 9/11, Powell aimed to streamline the visa-application process to ensure speed and national security, and to use the data to network effectively with anti-terrorist organizations, while simultaneously upgrading personal security for all State personnel abroad.

4. **The Facilities initiative**—The goal, said Powell, was to "completely revamp the way we construct our embassies and other overseas buildings; they must be better places to work and they must be more secure."

5. **The Management Reform initiative**—Powell's focus was on overhauling budgeting and resource allocation, and doing "right-sizing" to streamline the entire department. He sought to employ the minimum resources necessary to attain the President's top priority objectives.

The Foreign Affairs Council's November 2004 independent assessment of the State Department confirmed a number of extraordinary achievements during Powell's four-year tenure. Here are just a few:

• "State has redressed in three years almost the entire personnel deficit of the 1990s (some 2,000 employees hired above attrition)."

• "State has completely replaced and modernized its hardware infrastructure…. Overseas, IT has been used to create 15 "virtual" Foreign Service posts…."

• "The new Consular Consolidated Database is refreshed every seven minutes, contains 75 million files (including photos and applicants' total visa histories), and is immediately accessible to all visa officers and to immigration inspectors at U.S. ports of entry."

• "State's Bureau of Overseas Building has completed 13 major capital construction projects, all within two years and $63 million under budget."

Is it any wonder that another set of measurements showed that morale within State around the world shot upward during Powell's tenure?

At State Farm Insurance, Harold Gray took Powell's philosophy and applied it with even more simplicity to his seven-state Pacific Northwest zone. He wanted to propel the Pacific Northwest zone's revenue and cost performance from the bottom third in the State Farm internal rankings to the top third within one year. After careful scrutiny and analysis, Gray and his team calculated that the entire zone's performance could catapult toward this goal if it could meet just three objectives from December 2004 to December 2005:

1. Each independent agent sells a net increase of three auto policies per month.

2. Each independent agent sells a net increase of one home-owner policy per month.

3. Despite new investments to help agents meet those above two goals, the zone incurs no change in total expenses.

To be sure, Gray and his team addressed a myriad of diverse management issues throughout the year, including accelerating the sales of other products, like life insurance and mutual funds. But the "0-3-1" credo (zero expenses, three auto policies, one homeowner policy) propelled the zone's efforts. Gray applied the credo to budgeting, training, meeting agendas, sales conferences, leadership retreats, performance reviews, information systems, and, of course, his regular communications with his troops and agents. Throughout the year, all the zone's activities were evaluated in terms of how well they advanced the 0-3-1 credo. Gray often said that an employee's commitment to "0-3-1" was the figurative "door key" combination to board the bullet train.

Gray argued that by focusing on just three big, laser-beam goals, people would experience the urgency and wherewithal to achieve them. He told me that asking people to make big changes to the status quo in the absence of 0-3-1 would be far less efficient than having them come to their own realization that the only way to achieve 0-3-1 would be to make big changes. He was right. Within one year, the Pacific Northwest zone reached 127 percent of its target and leapfrogged to the top third in the internal State Farm performance rankings. Gray's team is now in the process of enacting a three-year plan that will target a few specific markets that will spur the next wave of growth. However the plan for the new bullet train "combination" materializes, Gray will make sure it will honor a minimal number of priorities. That's a good combination for you, too.

Step 10: Team Up with Aliens

If you want to break from the pack, doesn't it make sense to seek compelling ideas and energies from outside the pack? Doesn't it make sense to learn from people and organizations that have thrived beyond your industry, particularly those that are doing things that people in your field consider unthinkable and insane?

The Power of Outside Observation

If you want to improve assembly-line conversion in your factories, for example, you could benchmark fellow manufacturers in your industry and come up with conventional and marginal improvements. Or, you could do what leaders at General Mills did. They sent a number of factory teams to NASCAR races to benchmark the pit crews in action. The General Mills teams came back and ultimately reduced the time to switch an assembly line from 5 hours to 25 minutes.

If you want to show quantum improvement in speed and on-time delivery in the cement business, you could benchmark other cement companies for a taste of conventional wisdom. Or, you could do what Cemex, the most profitable cement company in the world, did a few years ago to turbo-charge speed and delivery. CEO Lorenzo Zambrano sent a number of teams to Houston, to figure out how Houston's emergency 911 crews deliver care. They also went to Memphis, to figure out how FedEx delivers packages.

When 3M was seeking breakthroughs in low-priced infection-preventing surgical drapes, it got some truly innovative advice from Hollywood make-up artists and veterinary surgeons. The point is: If you want breakthrough knowledge, leap outside the walls of your industry whenever possible.

The Power of Outside Partnering

You'll gain even more insight and power when you go beyond observing and partner closely with talented aliens outside your industry who don't come to the table with the mindset and history that's considered conventional in your business.

Partnering provides you with two big payoffs. First, you'll be able to expose your people to state-of-the-art talent and expertise that is unavailable among the players in your current value chain. More than a decade ago, Atlanticare CEO George Lynn allied his organization with 3M to raise the quality metrics in Atlanticare's two hospitals. 3M, as a medical supplier to the hospitals, participated in quality projects on site in Atlantic City and hosted hospital personnel in training workshops in St. Paul. Today Atlanticare's quality and resultant cost savings and patient satisfaction are well ahead of the pack. Atlanticare's new Epidemic of Health initiative, described in Chapter 6, is so revolutionary that Lynn once again is seeking partners outside the health-care industry because, as he says, "what we're trying to do is unfathomable to most players in health care."

The second payoff is subtler but just as important. The best partners from the outside wind up questioning the very way you do business. They suggest new approaches to everything, even things that aren't part of your original alliance with them. Ford Canada has partnered with Dell to overhaul its enterprise information systems, to help its dealers manage leads, cross-sell insurance and financing, and document service faster and more cheaply. Such an alliance makes for sensible outsourcing and partnering, but the real payoff comes from how Dell outsiders point to certain Ford organizational practices and business assumptions that simply make no sense. Partners from Dell have suggested changes in operations, design, people management, customer care, and corporate culture that violate conventional wisdom in the auto industry.

Of course, the aliens benefit, too. Working with Ford, Dell gains deeper sales entry into a huge company, gets more exposure to the massive global auto industry, and expands opportunity to refine its low-cost enterprise IT strategy. 3M gains more intimate ties with a valued hospital customer and more understanding of the entire health-care industry. It's a win-win situation all around, but only when the relationship is approached more in terms of collaborative learning than transactional commodity.

As a leader, you can't limit your quest to the spuriously "safe" and familiar zone of your industry. Don't ignore the breakthroughs that are occurring elsewhere just because nobody in your industry has embraced them—yet. Expand your search for superb teammates in alien industries, as well as in universities, art and design studios, think tanks, research institutes, nonprofit advocacy groups, nongovernmental organizations—any source that can help you look at your business differently and lead to unconventional choices. Send your people to NASCAR. Send them to the Rocky Mountain Institute. Send them to Interaction Design Institute Ivrea, send them to Harley-Davidson HOG (Harley Owner Group) events. Go there yourself and expand your mind. Whatever you do, encourage as many of your people as possible to see the value in alien knowledge and partnership.

Step 11: Lead From the Middle

"How can I do this stuff without getting fired?" That is a question I periodically hear when I chat with managers who are somewhere in the "middle" of the organization. Sometimes after I deliver a speech, someone will come up to me and say, "That was great stuff, but you don't know my company"—or boss, or business. "We need to shake things up in this company, but I'm not the CEO. How can I do all this great stuff without approval—or without getting canned?"

Peter Standish, Senior Vice President of Marketing at Warner Bros. Records, has little patience with the constraints that midlevel leaders feel as they contemplate effecting change in their organizations. "Unless you're CEO of the entire corporation," he says, "you're always in the middle of something. I am. I honestly don't know how many levels are above me or below me because it changes all the time. And I don't care. At the end of the day, whatever your level, you gotta make shit happen. You can lead and be a hero wherever you are."

I believe that you have a lot more power than you think you do. If your first name isn't "CEO," and you're somewhere in the middle of the hierarchy, here are a few points to show how you can make break-from-the-pack change happen.

Don't Wait for Orders—Initiate Solutions

I meet with a lot of CEOs and senior executives, and I can absolutely assure you that with rare exceptions, they understand the realities of the Copycat Economy. They see huge payoffs in breaking from the pack, and they know they can't do it by sticking to the status quo.

To a person, executives tell me that they desperately need fresh ideas and initiatives from everyone. The big caveat is that they don't want people just to come up with a great idea (or a great complaint) and then toss it upstairs. They want their midlevel leaders to create solutions. They want people who will initiate due diligence to show that their great idea has economic and operational logic. They want people who will create a rough plan of action, form a team to get some preliminary data, fight for resources, and demonstrate that their ideas have merit. If you do these things as a middle manager, not only will you create value for your organization, but I can assure you that your career will zoom past that of your colleagues who simply wait for orders.

Focus on the Customer's Needs

One of your safest bets is to let the customer drive your imagination. Concentrate your creative juices on figuring out ways to make customers more delighted and more loyal. To demonstrate that your ideas, however radical, are good for the customer and thus for your company, find allies and sketch out some plans, projects, and pilots. Develop some rough standards, measurements, goals, and feedback loops. Then you can make a plausible argument that if the company actually carried out your customer-pleasing ideas, it would have good odds of decent margins and returns on investment.

Do It Without Asking

In one seminar I led, a group of executives from diverse industries agreed on one suggestion to middle managers: "If you're prepared to demonstrate that it's good for the customer and good for the company, then do it without asking." I've already discussed the "good for the customer" piece. Now consider the second half of the executives' suggestion. In my 20-plus years of consulting and researching this issue, I have found repeatedly that the most successful and rewarded middle managers are the ones who say, "If I haven't been explicitly told 'no,' I can do it." So they don't ask.

Think like a businessperson, not as an employee. Don't ask for permission to take action, and stop waiting for someone to give you permission. Working independently, develop big goals that will address some big gaps, and then start with small and meaningful steps toward your goals. Find fellow maniacs, grab the resources you need, and gather supportive data. On your own, you can continue to monitor your progress, using quick feedback to guide your next steps, and carefully building momentum.

Some initiatives might require approval from upstairs, especially if they involve big capital investments. But those are exceptions, and here's the rule: Working on behalf of customers and the company as a whole without explicit assent from on high is the core of leadership. Think about it: You're smart enough not to flagrantly blow up the entire system. If something is deadly wrong with your progress, you'll be stopped; most likely, you'll stop yourself. But why abort the entire process by asking for permission beforehand, when you know that there are always people in a bureaucracy who view their jobs as thwarting meaningful change? If you continually ask for formal blessing before making your move, you'll become enmeshed in a quagmire of politics and bureaucratic delay. Or worse, you'll perpetually have to deal with scared naysayers and uptight nitpickers.

Don't Let the Career Skeptics Get You Down

Don't even think of wasting your energy on career skeptics on staff who view you with horror or disdain. If you're ever challenged, explain your actions on sound business principles and then continue to act without asking for permission. Put the burden on someone else to explicitly order you to stop. More likely than not, you won't ever see those orders. Michael Abrashoff, who had a brilliant Navy career and captained what was called "the best damn ship in the Navy," told a group of us that one can respect a hierarchy without fearing it. How did he get away with all his "crazy" actions that boosted morale and battle readiness but went right against the grain of conventional military protocol? Often he just did it. Sometimes he would fire off a message to his superiors that read: "Unless otherwise directed, here is what I will be doing...." He told us he never got stopped, second-guessed, or even questioned.

Don't Give Up Even If They Want You To

If you do get orders to stop, don't automatically roll over and play dead. If you feel strongly about your cause, stay true to it. A few years ago, I caught up with Ken Olevson, whom I had written about in a prior book. He had moved on and was the head of a small division in a large, rigidly hierarchical corporation. Olevson calculated that a third of the division's customers were draining more resources than the income they provided. After a lot of discussion and analysis, Ken and his team concluded that the best course of action was to fire those customers, take the short-term hit on revenues, concentrate on providing better service to the remaining customers to avoid further price cuts, and build the business with augmented pricing and new customers whose values and goals "fit" with the division's.

Corporate went ballistic over this decision, and Olevson was told to cease and desist immediately. Instead, he flew to headquarters and fought his superiors with strategic logic, hard data, and sensible financial projections. In his view, the folks at corporate were simply wrong, and he was prepared to go to the mat on this issue. He won. So did his credibility and reputation within the company, especially when he turned out to be right.

Yes, you must prudently pick your battles, and, yes, there are times when you would be wise to beat a (temporary) retreat, but too many managers back down too fast. Don't wait for top management to get religion. Fight for your cause, and teach them the religion with results.

Bob Busch, a senior executive at power and energy company PSEG, told me the best management lesson he ever learned early in his career was about the importance of breaking out of his self-imposed straightjacket: "When I was a young manager," he recounted, "I was cautious. I always waited for my boss's directives. One day he came to me and said, 'What have I specifically told you that you *can't* do?' 'Uh, nothing,' I stammered. 'Exactly,' he responded. 'I hired you because I wanted your brains. Instead, you've built your own box around yourself. Climb out of it.'"

As middle managers, most of our fears of punishment and retribution are self-imposed. However, if you're in an organization that persistently smothers your efforts to initiate positive changes, if you're in an organization where your job and career are really and truly threatened if you make conscientious efforts to create new value for customers and shareholders, then you should admit that you're on a sinking ship and start polishing your resume. You're worth a lot more than that, and a lot of progressive, break-from-the-pack companies will appreciate you if your current one doesn't.

It is risky to break from the pack, especially if you're not the CEO. But as we've seen, the risk of standing still is greater—for your company and for you. I've seen too many well-meaning, risk-averse, conforming managers passed over for advancement, or even downsized, because the decision-makers didn't see what special value they were contributing. Such employees have trouble finding work elsewhere because their resumes don't suggest much other than that they took orders well.

Step 12: Know When to Hold, Know When to Fold

Leading the pack requires immense time, energy, commitment, and devotion. It's not for the faint of heart. Rather than being the boxer who stays in the ring too long, one of the most important and honorable attributes of a great leader is to know when to stay and when to exit. You might want to leap from your pack into another pack, an entirely new business, and then work to break out from that one. Or, you might want to exit the race altogether. But as a leader, you make the decision. Don't let events or others do it for you.

To a use a poker metaphor, when should you hold, when should you fold? Peter Standish at Warner Records is eloquent on this point. "When you lose the passion and love for what you do, it's time to find another career," he says. "You've got to have a passion. It can be a project, an endpoint, a personal vision, but it's got to inspire you and drive you past those distractions which load up every organization, like bureaucratic b.s., political battles, and unfair policies. My passion is the music and the artists and the Warner colleagues I work with, and the great CDs and DVDs and promotions we can create together. I work my butt off, but without the passion, I would be consumed by all the frustrations in my company and all the difficulties in my industry. Passion and love get you through all that crap. It's like a marriage. When you lose the passion and love, it's time to leave."

Paul Orfalea, for instance, left. I worked with the Kinko's founder in the 1990s, when he was beginning to express stress and unhappiness because he felt that "the company owned me, I didn't own it." Orfalea stepped down as CEO/chairman in 2000, engineering the sale of the company to private equity firm Clayton Dubilier and Rice, which ultimately sold it to FedEx.

On the other hand, Ken Olevson, like countless other talented maniacs, worked with passion and integrity, got amply rewarded, and ultimately concluded that the fit with his employer wasn't great for the long haul. He found an even better position in another company. In 1999, Bernard Rapoport retired from his leadership position at American Income Life Insurance, and wrote me that "at 82 years old, I will be starting a new company. I don't know exactly when because I haven't made the selection, but there is no use wasting time. If I am not building, I am not happy." When I talked to his assistant, Barbara Chonko, in late 2005, she told me that she can barely keep up with him; he's involved in several boards and is an active partner in the management of three small niche companies in the specialty glass industry. When I caught up with the man (88 years old!) himself, he described each of his companies with enthusiasm and told me that he's having a ball. He's still holding.

Knowing when to hold and when to fold is an act of reality and integrity. That distinction brings us, finally, to Robert Winquist and Sherry Backman, who head VSi, that contrarian children's sticker company I described at the beginning of this book. If you remember, VSi lost its pack-leading edge when its competitors began to imitate its products and processes. I wish I could tell you inspiring stories about how VSi once again broke from the pack, but the reality is a little more complex.

As Sherry Backman told me, "In the beginning of VSi 10 years ago, I sometimes worked up to 120 hours a week. I sometimes slept in the office. The business succeeded beyond my expectations, but I burnt myself out. Over the past couple years, when we became one of many suppliers and we didn't stand out any more, and the industry stopped growing, I had to question whether I had the energy to continue. Robert and I began to have conversations about closing down or selling out."

Backman said that once the company got pulled back into the pack by imitators, VSi survived with a little profit because it figured out ways to cut more costs and get to market with new products a little faster. But Sherry Backman and Robert Winquist knew that such steps were too small and incremental to have a sustained impact. The company stayed mired in the pack. The in-house energy and excitement dipped. Backman and Winquist's frustration and pessimism grew—until one day the big "aha!" moment came when they realized that they didn't have to limit their output to the flat flat-vending industry. Their further investigations showed that VSi could maintain its current business as a cash cow and exploit a new, potentially huge opportunity by bypassing the vending machines altogether and going right to the customer. While they are still staying in the flat vending business, they are also switching to another set of sticker markets that offer untapped break-from-the-pack possibilities.

Winquist and Backman are drawing plans to partner with distributors to place their stickers and tattoos right on retail store shelves. They are also targeting new direct customers, like doctors and dentists, who might want to receive regular state-of-the-art customized stickers to give out to young patients. Most radically, they are developing and manufacturing a toy sticker- and tattoo–printing machine, to be sold in retail stores, that will let kids make their own stickers. They also intend to capitalize on their *www.stickers.com* website to make it more of an interactive community of kids, an initiative that will further extend the VSi brand and allow kids to pay online to create their own stickers and order them directly from the Web. They also want to emulate HP, which reaps a profit bonanza from its inkjet cartridge aftermarket products for printers. "Imagine—we can create our own cartridges to supply our machines that kids will use to make their own stickers and tattoos," exults Sherry Backman. "We can become the industry standard."

Will all these ambitious plans allow VSi to break from the pack again? Quite possibly, though there's no guarantee for anyone. Most promising is the fact that Winquist and Backman now have a "fire in the belly" again because they can once again see exciting growth opportunities. They also finally understand the concept of unleashing other people's talent, so they won't be working 120-hour weeks anymore. But they'll be working. They're not ready to fold 'em yet. They're holding. I wish them luck.

As I wish you luck. Breaking from the pack in the relentless Copycat Economy is no small feat. But it's a doable accomplishment, and, dare I say, a noble one. This book has provided you with the tools and blueprints to achieve it yourself. You, too, have the capability to help your organization break into the lead and provide yourself and your customers, employees, and investors the joy and reward that come with being on the leading edge. I wish that fate for your organization, and I hope that, regardless of your job title, you will choose to make yourself one of the leaders in that effort.

EPILOGUE

It's a March morning in 2006 and I'm having breakfast with Robert Winquist. I show him a preliminary draft of this book, noting that he and his children's sticker company, VSi, in effect, started and ended the book. I direct his attention to Figure 1, the conceptual framework introduced in the Prologue. As I explain the components of the model, he begins to chuckle. "This describes everything we've gone through," he says.

He points to the "The Pack" Bubble in the diagram and recounts the ravages of the imitation and commoditization that he and his rivals have faced over the past few years. He concludes his tale of woe this way: "We (the vending supply companies) were demoralized. We used to phone each other and lament how bad it was. Look at our name: Vending Supply, Inc. We supplied product to companies that operated vending machines. The entire industry had consolidated and those big vending machine companies kept driving our prices down. Collectively, they had hundreds of thousands of machines and were demanding that we sell to them virtually at cost. They showed us no sense of partnership or loyalty. We thought we were weak. We didn't own or even operate our own machines. Everyone, including us, thought we were trapped. We were stuck in the bubble along with everyone else, at the mercy of a commoditized market. Our margins were impossibly thin. It wasn't worth doing anymore. There was no optimism about the amount of money left to be made."

So what changed? Winquist points to the six "Curious, Cool and Crazy/Calculated Reinvention" launch pads and laughs: "What changed was that we said, wait a minute, we're the ones that are creating all the great stuff that the vending machine operators need to stay in business. It was the 'cream of all jest' when we realized that there was nothing to stop us from bypassing the whole system and selling all our great art and ideas directly to the kids themselves in a ten dollar vending machine toy."

Winquist goes to his car and brings back a brightly colored 11 × 13 × 3 inch durable cardboard box with four see-through display columns—two displaying pull-out rolls of stickers and two displaying pull-out rolls of temporary tattoos—and a functioning coin slot. The box is called "The Original Sticker Machine" and on the back of the box it says: "Hey kids, the great stickers and tattoos once sold only in vending machines are here for you now!"

"What could be more deviant than a vending supply company selling the entire equipment and product line directly to the end user as a toy?" he asks. "That's happened only once before in our industry. The guy who invented and patented the giant spiral gumball machine made ten times as much money by selling the toy version to the toy retail chains than he ever did selling the real thing to the vending companies. We can sell an entire sticker machine for less than ten bucks with a full line of our best products from the last ten years. We'll continue selling to 3,000 vending machine operators for the time being, but our new business is going to have 40 million kid-distributors! It's so radically out of the box that it even scared us. But now we're getting big fourth quarter orders from retailers like Wal-Mart and Bed, Bath and Beyond based on a prototype. They love it."

He has an immediate reaction to the strategy choice of Dominate or Leave : "Who wants to dominate when there's no profit? For the time being, we're still in the old business for the cash flow, but our attention is on the new profit opportunities. As the old business commoditized, we realized that even if we grew our market share by slashing prices or buying other companies, there was nothing left that's worth dominating. When there's no profit margin, being bigger is an empty and meaningless achievement. We've now figured out what we can dominate. It'll be a whole new market. We created it and we'll be the only ones there…at least for a year or so. We'll take advantage of that lead time to figure out how to stay ahead."

He ponders the notion of the Higher Cause, and nods. "You know what inspires us? The idea of giving power directly to the kids. Bypass the whole distribution system and let the kids have it all. And let them make money on it too if they want; there's a coin slot in the sticker box, we figured they can triple their own investment if they sell the stickers to their friends. Empower the kids—that's what we're about."

Winquist really lights up when he starts talking about the injunction to Build a Defiant Pipeline. "This is my favorite. Now that we've put on a new set of glasses, we're just burning with new ideas for products, like different kinds and sizes of sticker boxes, new 20-foot rolls of product to put in the boxes, belt dispensers of stickers that look like whistles, create-a-scene sticker games, sticker jackets that themselves are stickers…. Now that we're not just supplying stickers that fit into a vending machine, every day brings new ideas that run counter to how we used to do things."

He doesn't even let me finish describing the path to Take Your Customer to an Impossible Place. For him, it's obvious. "We showed the sticker box to the same focus groups of kids we've always used to give us feedback.. They were stunned. They think it's the coolest thing they've ever seen. They get an entire sticker machine stuffed with 20-foot rolls of their favorite products—for ten bucks. They never imagined they could get anything like that."

It takes Winquist a little longer to absorb the idea that to Take Innovation Underground is much more than simply keeping costs down. Then he says, "Of course, now I get it: We've done some amazingly creative things to miniaturize the entire production system and we can now cut the per-sticker cost to a fraction of what it used to be. But the really big savings come with our new business model. The big problem before was all the layers of middlemen which had marked up the printing cost ten times before it reached the kids. Now, there's only one middleman—the retail store—or no middleman if they go right to our stickers.com website. By cutting out all those layers, we can lower our price per sticker and still get a much fatter margin."

I tell Winquist that to Consolidate for Cool may not be relevant to VSi because he has no immediate acquisition plans. But he looks at this concept from the perspective of the other players in the industry, who are consolidating, but *not* for cool: "Everyone in the industry is thinking about acquisitions or doing it. They're consolidating for size, volume, and efficiencies—but the whole industry is still sagging. We didn't want to go that route. We're directing our energy to a whole new venue, and we're traveling with a new partner, TMI (Tattoo Manufacturing, Inc.). We're going to do wonderful things."

Winquist leans back and reflects, "When you're stuck in the pack, you realize what you're missing. It's not just the money. It's the excitement of doing something really well that you're really good at and being recognized by the marketplace for it. It's a sense of purpose. It's your groove of excellence. Without these things, it's just a job, and who wants that? Now, I'm feeling so excited that my plans for retirement are suddenly on hold."

He looks at me seriously: "The joy is back," he says.

INDEX

opening doors and windows, revving up
your base, 265-266
optimism, 260
Orfalea, Paul, 279
Organization Bob, 177-180
Ornish, Dean, 33
Ortho-McNeil Neurologics (OMN), 123
Osborne, Jackie, 269
Osher, John, 243
outsourcing, 146-147, 215-218
underground, 215
overpaying, reasons for M&A failure, 233

P

Page, Larry, 153
Palmisano, Sam, 15, 65-66, 146
PalmPilot, 156
parameters defining appropriate and
inappropriate behaviors, 261
PARC, 160
Pardi, Jaimie, 112
partners
be a magnet for crazy partners, 169-171
leadership, outside partnering, 273-274
passion, 89-91, 142, 279
disciplined lunacy, 98-100
Pastor, Rafael, 197
PayPal, 245-246
PDAs, 156
Pearsall, Jeff, 90, 93
Pepsi, alliances, 248
Perdue, Jonathon, 112
Perez, Antonio, 83
Peters, Tom, 4, 142, 263
Pfizer versus Genetech, 117-118
PFM (Public Financial Management), 90
building a dominating culture, 129
dominance, 112-114, 128
SwapViewer, 166
taking customers to an impossible place,
182-183
pharmaceutical industry
growth, 47
Jet Genetech and Pfizer, 117-118
OMN (Ortho-McNeil Neurologics), 123
Phat Fashions, 171

Phillips, Kevin, 182
pipelines, 155
defiance, 158-160
be a magnet for crazy customers, 166
*be a magnet for crazy employees,
167-169*
*be a magnet for crazy partners,
169-171*
be like a NASCAR racer, 164-165
become a pipeline for design, 171
cannibalization, 160-161
customer anthropology, 162-164
dominate or leave, 175-176
targeting new terrain, 171-173
*thinking broadly, acting narrowly,
174-175*
power of, 156-158
Pixar Studios, 3
versus Disney, 119-120
PlayStation, 166
Polycom, 243
Postrel, Virginia, 94
Pottruck, David, 111
Powell, Colin, 56, 86, 107
leadership, 268, 270-271
PowerBar, 188-189
Prahalad, C.K., 206
prices, lowering prices for customers, 212
priorities, leadership, 270-272
Privett, Stephen, 259
Proctor & Gamble
customer anthropology, 163
higher causes, 139
talent, 243
profit, 211
Progressive Insurance, 53
projections, reasons for M&A failure,
232-233
Public Financial Management. *See* PFM
Puma AG, 157
Purcell, Philip, 231

R

R&D (research and development), 159
radio, 52

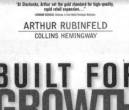
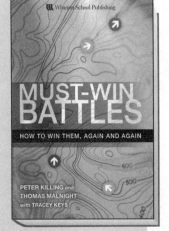